MINORITY REPORTS

MINORITY REPORTS

Voicing Neglected Biblical Texts

Mark Klitsie
Foreword by Bill Baltz

WIPF & STOCK · Eugene, Oregon

MINORITY REPORTS
Voicing Neglected Biblical Texts

Copyright © 2016 Mark Klitsie. All rights reserved. Except for brief quotations in critical publications or reviews, no part of this book may be reproduced in any manner without prior written permission from the publisher. Write: Permissions, Wipf and Stock Publishers, 199 W. 8th Ave., Suite 3, Eugene, OR 97401.

Wipf & Stock
An Imprint of Wipf and Stock Publishers
199 W. 8th Ave., Suite 3
Eugene, OR 97401

www.wipfandstock.com

PAPERBACK ISBN: 978-1-4982-3596-9
HARDCOVER ISBN: 978-1-4982-3598-3
EBOOK ISBN: 978-1-4982-3597-6

Manufactured in the U.S.A.

All Scripture quotations, unless indicated otherwise, are from the Revised Standard Version of the Bible, copyright 1952 [2nd edition, 1971] by the Division of Christian Education of the National Council of the Churches of Christ in the United States of America. Used by permission. All rights reserved.

Scripture quotations marked NIV are taken from the Holy Bible, New International Version®, NIV®. Copyright © 1973, 1978, 1984, 2011 by Biblica, Inc.™ Used by permission of Zondervan. All rights reserved worldwide. www.zondervan.com

Scripture quotations marked NRSV are taken from the New Revised Standard Version Bible, copyright 1989, Division of Christian Education of the National Council of the Churches of Christ in the United States of America. Used by permission. All rights reserved.

Scripture quotations marked NASB are taken from the NEW AMERICAN STANDARD BIBLE®, Copyright © 1960, 1962, 1963, 1968, 1971, 1972, 1973, 1975, 1977, 1995 by The Lockman Foundation. Used by permission.

Scripture quotations marked KJV are taken from the King James Version. Public Domain.

"Merciful God" reprinted from *Paper Bridges: Selected Poems of Kadya Molodowsky* translated by Kathryn Hellerstein. Copyright © 1999 Wayne State University Press, with the permission of Wayne State University Press.

This book is dedicated to our kids, Ezra and Louisa.

Thanks to editor Susan Carlson Wood and to Bill Baltz for his criticisms and encouragement. Thanks to Lauralee Farrer for editing the earlier PhD dissertation rendition of this book.

*Enlarge the place of your tent,
stretch your tent curtains wide,
do not hold back;
lengthen your cords,
strengthen your stakes.*

ISAIAH 54:2 (NIV)

CONTENTS

Foreword | vii
Glossary | xiii

Introduction | 1
1. God in a Straitjacket, Supplied by Well-Meaning Christians | 16
2. How "Omni-God" Arose in History | 37
3. Towards a Mature Faith: Commonsense and Multifaceted Theology | 60
4. The Pathos of YHWH, Yeshua, and the Holy Spirit | 75
5. Applying Multifaceted Theology | 105

Conclusion | 160

Appendix A: Preincarnate Son in the Older Testament? | 165
Appendix B: More Competing Scriptures in the Bible | 176
Appendix C: The Practical Theology of Hasidism and Abraham Heschel | 183
Bibliography | 193

FOREWORD

MARK KLITSIE'S INTENT IN writing is to present and bring to the forefront overlooked, ignored, and not openly studied Scriptures for our consideration—to challenge our learning so as to stimulate new growth. *Minority Reports* calls us to study all of God's Word and to grapple with parts of Scripture that are not typically taught or preached in churches today.

Mark's appendix "More Competing Scriptures in the Bible" initially disturbed and unsettled me, but then challenged me to a further "tension of trust" (as I call it)—to spend time in God's Word, with the guidance and counsel of the Holy Spirit. He dared me to expand my awareness and vision of all that our God is and wants us to know about him.

Remember Paul's words to Timothy?

> All scripture is inspired by God and profitable for teaching, for reproof, for correction, and for training in righteousness, that the man of God may be complete, equipped for every good work. (2 Tim 3:16-17)

Take a deep breath. Inhale the Holy Spirit's guidance as you study less familiar words of God.

Mark's beliefs and writings are not now completely my own beliefs; nor should they be. Mark is not my source of truth. But he has been a great stimulator towards a fuller and a more complete end. My conscience is captive to the Word of God. Only God is Lord of it. Only God's Word reveals the truth. Only God's Word and the inspiration of his Spirit have the right to bind my beliefs and truths. It is not surprising that Presbyterians use "God alone is Lord of the conscience" as one of their key beliefs.

I personally like how Mark holds back his own thoughts and biases and just presents the thoughts and considerations of many to challenge and enhance our thinking and our beliefs. Mark's desire is to open our eyes to consider others' thoughts.

Just as we need each other, we need other viewpoints

- to stir us to greater thinking,
- to expand our view, enlarge our awareness,
- to open our minds to a greater view of the God of us all,
- yet always to have a theology of one who has a personal relationship with our personal God.

Let Mark lead you to confront, to know better, deeper, and more personally "a God who has a personality." Learn that he is "gritty, willful, relational, loving, and engaging."

As Abraham Heschel offers, "It's an engagement of the whole life . . . with all of one's being. Every action and gesture is done to consecrate our life, including eating, working, and resting . . . to be in love with God . . . and what God created. Once you are in love you are a different being." If you've been married for any length of time as I have (46 years), you can see how you have been shaped by your relationship: How much more so with a God who is very personal?

Mark reveals more of our God—one who is not distant or hidden like the Wizard of Oz, does not give like Santa Claus, nor rescue like Superman. The God we should see is a God of love, compassion, caring, and helping, one who calls us to a beautiful relationship with him and yet is angered by the world and destroys it in Noah's time, dunks Jonah in the ocean, obliterates Sodom and Gomorrah, and permits his favorite, chosen people to be overcome by evil Babylonians.

In getting to know Mark personally, I've learned I do not always have to "connect the dots," as he would say. I am reminded that our Lord said such words as "My ways are not your ways" and "It's not for you to know the times and the seasons." Having questions not always resolved completely draws me closer to our Lord. This has led me to discover my personal "tension of trust."

You might ask me, "What was my first reaction as I began to read this book?" I stalled in accepting it. Stirred, challenged, and ready to quit, I felt the Scriptures Mark offered must be wrong. I stepped back from thoughts of God being "crooked to the crooked," being angry, that there was "wiggle room" (room to negotiate with him). But then I realized that not everything needed to be fully understood, buttoned up, but should be left dangling in my tension of trust.

Mark offered this to me, "It's the Hebraic approach. 'I despair, yet I am full of hope; I am perplexed, but I have abundant assurance; I am sad, but I have unshakable joy; I am angry, but I have unsurpassed peace.'"

My personal belief is that all Scripture is to be "inspired" to each of us individually, personally, and specifically to meet our personal need and understanding as inspired by the Spirit of God. Appreciate the challenge of a positive tension, suspended in faith, while held by God's Spirit.

Stay with the book; and you'll be blessed by journeying the path of study. Just as I read *Minority Reports*—and tripped, stumbled, but persisted in walking ahead of you, allow yourself to know God more fully. Let it stir in you a "tension of trust."

May God's richest blessings be upon you, my brothers and sisters.

Rev. Bill Baltz
Pastor, Presbyterian Church (USA)
MDiv, Fuller Theological Seminary
Gardnerville, Nevada
November 2015

GLOSSARY

anthropomorphism. Using human words and categories to describe God.

Arminianism. The stream of theology named after theologian Jacobus Arminius (1560–1609), emphasizing that humans have free will, developed to counter extremes in *Calvinism and *predestination. *See* free-willism.

Calvinism. *See* Reformed theology.

determinism. The doctrine that all events, including human action, are ultimately determined by external causes: Human free will is an illusion. Different kinds of determinism include psychological, sociological, genetic, and theological (hyper-Calvinism).

epistemology. The branch of philosophy that asks, what is knowledge? How is it acquired? How reliable is it?

evangelical. Conservative Christians who take the Bible seriously, including some Catholics. The more strict evangelicals can be called fundamentalists (*see* fundamentalism).

evolutionism. To be distinguished from evolution (e.g., the science of biological evolution). Evolution*ism* is the *philosophy (ideology)* of evolution, which commonly conflicts with the Bible. For example, Hitler used evolution*ism* (Social Darwinism) in justifying the killing of the weak, after the dictum "survival of the fittest."

free-willism (*Arminianism). Emphasizing the role of free will, supported by certain Scriptures, e.g., "choose whom you will serve" (Josh 24:15). John Wesley (1703–1791), who founded the Methodist church, held this view. In contrast is *Calvinism, which says, "God chooses us"—also supported by Scripture.

fundamentalism. A form of Christianity that developed in the 1930s in reaction to theological liberalism. The "Fundamentals" it promoted were biblical inerrancy, virgin birth, atoning death, resurrection, and second coming of Jesus.

immutability. God cannot and does not change or change his mind.

impassibility. God cannot and does not suffer. Only Jesus' human side suffers.

kenosis. The self-humbling of God. For example, Jesus emptied himself of all power and prestige (Phil 2:7).

natural theology. The understanding of God that derives from reason and ordinary experience of nature. God is good, all-powerful, and all-knowing. For example, Einstein acknowledged there is a God (like 95 percent of people on earth), but not the *personal* God of the Bible, who concerns himself with humans and their behavior. This is the easy default position.

omni-attributes. All of the below omni-descriptions.

omni-God. God is all of the below omni-descriptions.

omnipotent. God is all-powerful.

omnipresent. God is everywhere.

omniscient. God is all-knowing.

Open theism (Openness theology or Presentism). This newer approach to theology is somewhere between *Arminianism (*free-willism) and *Process theology. It considers things to be more open-ended. God sets general parameters, but humans have room to wiggle. Humans have a give-and-take relationship with God, contributing to God's project here on earth.

postmodernism. The paradigm that replaces modernism. We transitioned from modernism to postmodernism somewhere in the 1980s. It says there is no meta-story or absolute truth. It focuses on the unrepeatable, the marginalized, the obscure, and particulars.

predestination. All events and those chosen are predetermined. An idea found in the Bible and highlighted by *Calvinists. For example, God predestines specific events of Joseph's life. Joseph had a dream that his brothers would bow down to him and serve him. This all came true, to a tee.

Presentism. *See* Open theism.

Process theology. An approach that regards God more as a verb than a noun: God is evolving with us in an evolutionary manner. God creates the world, but the world is also creating God. Openness theologians say God can change, but they do not push the idea as far as Process theology. Pierre Teilhard de Chardin typifies Process theology.

progressive Christian. A new label for the liberal Christian who emphasizes love and care for the poor and the environment. They support LGBT rights and stress "social justice."

reductionism. The continual temptation of scientists, theologians, thinkers, and people in general to reduce complex issues into simplistic explanations—which are claimed to be sufficient explanations. Even Job was guilty of it. God accuses Job of reductionism by pointing out things he did not incorporate into his analysis of the world's working (Job 37:14-22).

Reformed theology. A vibrant, growing, intellectually aggressive theology based on John Calvin's teachings (1509–1564), backed by Scripture. The acronym TULIP stands for Total Depravity, Unconditioned election, Limited atonement, Irresistible grace, and Perseverance of the saints.

theodicy. The philosophical or theological inquiry of why a good God allows evil. Volumes of books have been written on this dilemma over millennia.

Trinity. The Christian conception of God as three Persons in one: Father, Son, and Holy Spirit. The word is not found in the Bible, but its truth becomes evident from reading the Bible (especially the New Testament).

INTRODUCTION

THERE'S BREAD AND THERE'S wine. If bread is the gospel, then wine is analogous to the "minority reports" showing YHWH's vulnerability, suffering, and anger—just the right amount induces well-being. But too much makes one ill. However, this is no reason to shy away from these "minority reports." Frankly, most Christians find them annoying. I do too. Voicing them makes things untidy and often leads to paradox, tension, and a little ambiguity.

Since studying at Fuller Theological Seminary, Pasadena, California, for decades (MA, ThM), and studying under some exceptional rabbis in Jerusalem, I found the courage to challenge some prevailing church theology. I have become less intimidated by inherited theology and prefer to go with *raw Scripture*. I have concluded that the Bible is inescapably complex and messy, as is life. Now I voice minority Scriptures when need be. They can show YHWH as vulnerable and, at times, voluntarily withholding his all-powerfulness-all-knowingness-and-all-presence. Consistent with this, God-on-earth, Jesus, reflected the same:

- Vulnerability: "Jesus wept." (John 11:35)
- Sometimes, Jesus's power was limited and contingent on human anticipation: "And He did not do many miracles there because of their unbelief." (Matt 13:58 NASB)
- And, in Philippians 2:5–8, Jesus "empties" himself (in theology called *kenosis*): "Have this mind among yourselves, which is yours in Christ Jesus, who, though he was in the form of God, did not count equality with God a thing to be grasped, but emptied himself, taking the form of a servant, being born in the likeness of men. And being found in human form he humbled himself and became obedient unto death, even death on a cross."

Indeed, YHWH's power, knowledge, and presence are self-restrained in order to allow humans space to act; otherwise we would be mere puppets. Orthodox Jewish theology holds to God's *tsimtsum* (withholding). Without this "withholding" creation would not have been possible. It is considered God's greatest act of *gevorrah* (strength) that he, at times, withholds his omni-attributes (omni-presence, omni-power, and omni-knowledge from the human environment).[1] Of course, by definition, YHWH, the author and creator of *everything*, is all-powerful, all-present, and all-knowing in the abstract, but in the biblical narratives, he sometimes, voluntarily, chooses to withhold his omni-attributes. (To contrast, the Qur'an depicts Allah as *always*-potent.) Back to YHWH: He empowers humans—to a degree—to make their own history, as well as influence history. All at a risk. An old Jewish saying quips: "God has one hand tied."

Muhammad, the founder of Islam, was aware of this Jewish idiom, as it is disparagingly mentioned in the Qur'an: "cursed be they who say God has one hand tied." Robert Reilly, writing about Islam, says Allah, unlike the Judeo-Christian God, is pure will and power; he is not constrained by anything; he is unequivocally omni-potent.[2] Allah's omnipotence is safeguarded by Islam's principle of *shirk*. *Shirk* means comparing anything to Allah. Allah is omnipotent in such a way that no other person or thing can even be potent. One commits *shirk* by diluting Allah's omnipotence, in any manner. For instance, considering anything divine in the human, such as the biblical notion of "the image of God" would be considered a *shirk*.[3]

The Bible: How Do We Read It?

Let it speak for itself. Allow the different voices of the Bible to coexist with each other. Awkwardly place them side-by-side. Let the Bible's poetry dialogue with its prose, and let its proverbs debate its few anti-proverbs. Consequently, YHWH surfaces as predominantly present, engaged, active,

---

1. Through conversation with Doron Ben Avraham, a friend of mine, while he visited the United States from Israel in 2001, as learned from Rabbi David Aaron, Israel Center, Jerusalem.

2. I heard Reilly interviewed on the radio about his book *The Closing of the Muslim Mind*. He documents how Islam committed "intellectual suicide" in the ninth century when it adopted this radical approach to Allah's omnipotence and the principle of *shirk*. He says modern science could not have arisen in Islam as *everything* is an act of Allah. An apple falling off a tree is an act of Allah. To suggest that there are independent laws of nature would be a *shirk* challenging Allah's all-supreme control.

3. This emphasis is acute in Ashari theology, founded by the theologian Abu al-Hasan al-Ash'ari (d. 936 AD). The disciples of the school are known as Ash'arites.

personal, merciful, and powerful; and yet, on rare occasion, as absent, silent, angry, "impersonal," "punitive," and "powerless." My approach is emboldened by the postmodern spirit of today—no, postmodernism is not all bad—which is rightfully suspicious of grand schemes and *over*confidence in reason and certitudes. Yes, certitude is found in the Word of God, but the interpretation of Scripture gives rise to debatable theologies. Most things in the Bible are *settled* and some matters are *contingent*. For example, Jesus's atoning death *settles* forgiveness of sins, healing, and deliverance—for those who want it. Conversely, *contingent* matters appear in all the verses that are structured so: "*If* humans do X, *then* I (YHWH) will do Y." The latter works on the micro-level for individuals (John 3:16) and the macro-level for nations (2 Chron 7:14, "*If* my people humble themselves and pray, . . . *then* I will heal their land").

Like life, the Bible is not orderly. It is a dialogue of dissonant and unresolved voices. Judaic scholar David Blumenthal likens it to a "backstitch" where one progresses forward by circling backward, and thereby, coincidentally, creating the strongest method for connecting parts of a garment. "Ideas appear and reappear; motifs surface in different contexts, with different emphasis; the fabric as a whole actually becomes clearer that way."[4] Going with the situatedness and concreteness of the Bible, one forfeits the satisfaction of neat and tidy theology. My hard look at the Holy One shows him fiercely loving, gritty, and willful. He is not what one would consider today as a "saint." He is holy, mysterious, terrible, and irresistibly magnetic. The holy frightens and compels. (This is similar to Shackleton's advertisement, needing men to join his venture to the South Pole in 1902. The advertisement warned of extreme danger, isolation, inhospitable location, bad food, low pay, and sacrifice. To his surprise, he received thousands of applicants.)

In the 1970s I was a new Christian at the University of Port Elizabeth, South Africa. When confronted by somebody saying the Bible had paradoxes or even "contradictions," I assumed that person had a hidden agenda to undermine its authority as liberal theologians were apt in doing. I did not realize at the time that paradox in the Bible is no big deal—to the Hebrew mind. Later at a Jewish seminary in Jerusalem (Ash HaTorah Yeshiva), I learned that paradox is part of Talmudic tradition and the Bible. Paradox is only a problem if one is wedded to a rationalistic-modernist mindset where "contradictions" are not allowed. There has been a turnaround, even in science, where paradox is needed to explain the behavior of subatomic particles and the dual nature of light.[5] Unknowingly, church people already employ

---

4. Blumenthal, *Facing the Abusing God*, xxii.
5. Mathematically the different possible outcomes of a subatomic particle can be

such apparent contradictions. For instance, we should *not* give food to those unwilling to work (2 Thess 3:10); yet we need to give to those who ask for food (Matt 25:42). Biblical instructions can pull in opposite directions.

We live life in series, one moment at a time. We cannot experience everything at once, and so the theology we write reflects our individual walks with the Holy One. My conclusions about YHWH's terrible side in no way diminish my experience of him as good.

Words Can Be Prostituted

Words can be prostituted and change meaning over time. So I avoid using the generic word "God" because it evokes an image of him that is more general, abstract, distant, and impersonal. When I say "Omni-God" I am referring to the God-of-the-philosophers promoted by some pastors and theologians. I opt for using "YHWH," "the Holy One" or "Hashem," denoting the particular God-of-the-Jews. Our English Bibles normally say "the Lord" instead of YHWH. The correct spelling of the Tetragrammaton YHWH is unknown; since written Hebrew does not show the vowels of words, any vowels can be inserted between the consonants, Y, H, W, H. It could be written as Jehovah or Yahweh or even something else—we do not know exactly. I have thought of *not* using YHWH because it is so sacred to some Jewish people and may cause offense. Hashem, on the other hand, is a name for God commonly used among orthodox Jews. Hashem simply means "the Name." Although these names may be jarring to the reader, I prefer to use them—to tweak new content into the word "God," emphasizing that he is thoroughly personal, unique, sometimes gritty, and absolutely relational.

Furthermore, I favor addressing YHWH as "he" even though Genesis states that he is both male and female (1:27). I believe there is wisdom behind why the Bible defaults in calling YHWH a "he" or why YHWH primarily presents himself as a he. Jewish commentator Dennis Prager justifies the Bible's use of the male pronoun this way: Look at the prisons of today and yesteryear, they are largely filled with men (about 90 percent) and so living in such a world, which the Bible describes as "fallen" (my word), the male image of YHWH apparently needs to predominate to counter this situation.

In addition, I prefer to use the original Hebrew name of "Yeshua" instead of the Greek equivalent, Jesus. To uphold the continuum of the Old

---

calculated exactly. However, which outcome happens cannot be predicted. At the subatomic level, as strange as it sounds, the universe is "indeterminate." In the dual nature of light, sometimes it behaves as a particle, and sometimes as a wave.

and New Testaments, I prefer to use "Older Testament" for the Old Testament, as "Old Testament" has a denigrating ring to it and gives the impression that we can neglect its contents. Using "Older Testament" indicates an ongoing importance. So too, to encourage seeing the continuum, I usually use "Newer Testament." Obviously, there is a difference between the Older Testament and Newer Testament, but I push for more continuity.[6]

You will also notice that throughout the book I avoid saying a theology is wrong or right. Rather, I press for a different balance or emphasis. At times I may criticize an author and then turn around to use the same author to support a different idea (e.g., accomplice to murder[7] John Calvin, anti-Semite[8] Martin Luther, J. I. Packer, Bruce Ware, John Piper, Thomas Weinandy, and Wayne Grudem). I seek to evaluate any author or theology for both truth and error in my quest for better balance. I assume that I too could be wrong in some matters. My fallback position is Scripture.

Our Indebtedness to the Jews

The Holocaust has affected both Jewish and Christian theology, raising terrifying questions about YHWH's presence or absence, human faith and anguish, human weakness and deliberate evil.[9] Scholar of Judaism David

6. Certainly there is a discontinuity between the "Old" and "New" Testaments, but not as large, as many contemporary Christians declare. Daniel Fuller demonstrates the damage done by dividing the Bible into "Old"/"New" Testaments or *dispensations*, with typical dispensations being the Mosaic Law (or Israel), the current dispensation of grace (the present church), and the future millennium (book of Revelation). When overplaying these demarcations, people tend to roll all of God into the Jesus of the New Testament (who is perceived as merciful, loving, and forgiving) and downplay—if not ignore—YHWH of the Original Testament (who is seen as angry, revengeful, and unforgiving). To this, James Barr says, Scriptures are not allowed to speak for themselves, but are subjected to *our* control and *our* analysis. And, because we tend to be slaves to our "modern European categories," we are unaware of the "paradoxical Hebraic" nature of the Bible and miss its underlying continuum. Fuller, *Gospel and Law*, 18–46. My study will reveal an unbroken line of YHWH's engagement and concern for humanity from the OT to Yeshua in the NT and may show the reverse of the prevailing church consensus: the God of the OT is compassionate while Jesus of the NT intensifies judgment. Kindness and severity of judgment is intensified with Yeshua (Rom 11:17–22).

7. John Calvin was involved with the burning at the stake of Michael Servetus for not believing that Jesus was the eternal Son of God, not believing in the Trinity, and declaring that infant baptism was invalid. Calvin insisted that he must die, but he pled mercy that Servetus should not die by burning but by the sword. Nevertheless, in 1553 he was burned in Geneva.

8. See Luther's *On the Jews and Their Lies*.

9. The wording and juxtaposing of this sentence has been influenced by Abraham Heschel.

Blumenthal tackles the Holocaust straight on, challenging both religious Jew and committed Christian. Is God still present in history?

> If you are religious, what do you think? Are you among the pious avoiders? Among those who say that God could not have been involved because God gave humankind free will, an act which relieves God of all responsibility? Are you among those who believe that God is too good to be responsible? That God was absent? Or, are you among the heretical avoiders? Among those who deal with this question by denying God? You must take a stand, if God is integral to who you are . . . . [I say] God is, indeed, present and responsible even in moments of great evil. God is, indeed, partly responsible for the *shoah* [Holocaust]. In a certain sense, God is capable of tolerating, or even causing great evil. Still, God is also capable of great good, of deep blessing. God's presence is part of our ongoing lives, as . . . God's people. This leaves us with a God who is not perfect, not even always good, but is still our God and the God of our ancestors.[10]

My virtual rabbi, Abraham Heschel (who escaped going to Nazi death camps twice and who lost most of his family and Hasidic community in the Holocaust), described the dilemma of his life this way: "To live both in awe and consternation, in fervor and horror, with my conscience on mercy and my eyes on Auschwitz, wavering between exaltation and dismay."[11] After the horrors of the Holocaust, he dedicated *The Prophets* (1962) "to the martyrs of 1940–45." Not afraid to implicate Hashem in this tragedy, he included the epigraph, "Why dost Thou hide Thy face?" (Ps 44:24). To contrast, many Jewish thinkers understandably avoid explaining the Holocaust. Elie Wiesel, for one, was asked if he had a theological explanation for the Holocaust, to which he replied, "I hope not."[12] Heschel, in true Hasidic manner, engaged life full on, often repeating the Hasidic saying on mourning, "He who stands on a normal rung weeps; he who stands higher is silent; but he who stands on the topmost rung converts his sorrow into song."[13] Incidentally, the book of Psalms follows a similar pattern of processing pain: the early Psalms are full of protest, sorrow, and weeping, whereas Psalms 146 to 150 are solely dedicated to praise.

After the destruction of the World Trade Center on September 11, 2001, Jews and Christians have been grouped together by the enemies of

---

10. Blumenthal, "Despair and Hope in Post-*Shoah* Jewish Life," 122–23.
11. A. Heschel, *A Passion for Truth*, xiv.
12. Merkle, *Abraham J. Heschel*, 62.
13. *A Passion for Truth*, 283.

Western civilization, Islamic militants. Dennis Prager, a Jew, says Jews are beginning to realize that the friends of Israel are not found in American universities, the UN, or the media (they tend to be lopsided against Israel), but in evangelical churches where support for Israel is firm.[14] Nevertheless, Jews are understandably wary of this support as Christians have turned against them in the past, for example, in the Crusades, the Inquisition, and Nazi Germany. Even Martin Luther, our great Reformation leader, initially was friendly to the Jews but later turned against them when they resisted the gospel. In Luther's anti-Semitic treatise written in 1543, *On the Jews and Their Lies*, he describes Jews as a "base, whoring people," who are "full of the devil's feces . . . which they wallow in like swine," and their synagogue as a "habitual whore and an evil slut." He encouraged people to burn Jewish Talmuds, synagogues, and schools. Houses owned by Jews were to be razed, and the owners made to live in agricultural outbuildings. Rabbis were to be forbidden to preach, and to be executed if they did. Jews were to be put to work as agricultural slave labor.[15] And so, regrettably, Hitler could have drawn all his verbal ammunition from Luther alone, to defame and kill the Jews.

Some Jews today are suspicious of Christian affection towards them, as they wonder if they are viewed as mere pawns in the Christian expectation of the Second Coming of Jesus (i.e., a concept known as "instrumentalism" to skeptical Jews). I do not believe, as some Christians may, that YHWH has ceased to care for the Jews and only uses them as "instruments" for his purposes in the final acts of history. Sadly, popular British theologian N. T. Wright states that the Older Testament promises relating to the restoration of "Zion" (Jerusalem, the Land of Israel, the Jews, and the temple) no longer apply and are transferred to Jesus and his people, that is, the church.[16] This is called "replacement theology" and is pervasive in our churches. In effect, the Jews are no longer YHWH's chosen. Christians need to consider that if YHWH might abandon so many unconditional promises to Israel, is he also capable of forsaking Newer Testament promises to Christians? Christians, similar to the Older Testament Hebrews, have been equally "stiff-necked" (to use the biblical word employed by the prophets to describe rebellious Israel). The accusation of "stiff-necked" can also be leveled at recent evangelical Christians around the world. Steven Keillor attests that most

---

14. Dennis Prager, Jewish thinker and radio talk-show host, deduces this from interviews around the United States and from the media. *Dennis Prager Show* AM 870, November 9, 2002.

15. Luther, *On the Jews and Their Lies*, in *Luther's Works* 47:268–71 (cited in http://en.wikipedia.org/wiki/On_the_Jews_and_Their_Lies).

16. Wright, *Jesus and the Victory of God*, 363.

evangelical Christians before the Civil War in America were *not* against slavery.[17] Similarly, when I was living in South Africa in the 1950s through the 1980s, most evangelical Christians were not against the oppressive sin of Apartheid. Moreover, during Nazism, some Christian theologians in Germany, not wanting to give credit to Jews for Christianity, purged their theology of all Jewish roots. To be specific, they emphasized the idea that Jesus was Aramaic, even Aryan, and not Hebrew.[18] (This is similar to people calling Jesus a "Palestinian" and not a Jew, for example, Palestinian Authority President Mahmoud Abbas; Jeremiah Wright, President Obama's former pastor, or Palestinian Christian author Naim Ateek[19]). If some Christians are so sure that YHWH has abandoned the Jewish people as unworthy—in spite of his repeated unconditional covenant with them,[20] then they ought to be concerned that, maybe, Jesus will come back to earth with a "Third Testament," in response to the less-than-stellar Christian performance. Incidentally, Muhammad carried the biblical "stiff-necked" description of the Jews into the Qur'an, explaining why Allah has shifted from the "people of the book" (the Jews plus Christians) to favor Muhammad and his message. He also said the blessing of Allah is not on Isaac (Israel) but on Ishmael (the ancestor of the Arabs).

Here is another scandal for the world to stomach—the enduring chosenness of the Jews. This affront was my experience studying in Ashrams in India and exposure to Muslims in Jordon, Syria, and Egypt. Romans chapter 11 indicates that Jews have a vital task in the full redemption of the world, identifying "now" as the "time of the Gentiles" after which the Jews will be reinstated. Who will be saved? Paul states that everybody will be judged according to what they know (e.g., by relationship with Yeshua, knowledge of the Law, or by one's conscience). For the Christian, the coming of the Messiah will be the Second Coming. For the Jew, it will be the "first" coming, and thereafter, judgment. When living in Jerusalem in the early eighties, Robert Lindsay of Baptist House Church said the book of Revelation gives further insight into the role of the Jews: The woman (Israel) gives birth to the male child (Yeshua and the church). The dragon (Satan) chases the woman, who flees into the wilderness to a place prepared by YHWH. Revelation bears testimony to the Diaspora (dispersion) of the Jews and to the

17. Keillor, *God's Judgments*, 139.

18. S. Heschel, *The Aryan Jesus*.

19. Cohen, "Jesus the Palestinian?"; Richardson, "Jeremiah Wright"; Showers, "Jesus the 'Palestinian.'"

20. Gen 15:18–21. Also, Ezek 36:22–32 stresses that YHWH acts on behalf of the Jews for *his name's sake* and not because the Jews are necessarily righteous. Making it abundantly clear, Ezekiel repeats it three times in succession (20:9, 14, 22).

idea of YHWH looking over them in exile after which they return to be the witnesses for him. Revelation 12 illuminates:

> And a great portent appeared in heaven, a woman clothed with the sun, with the moon under her feet, and on her head a crown of twelve stars; she was with child and she cried out in her pangs of birth, in anguish for delivery. And another portent appeared in heaven; behold, a great red dragon, with seven heads and ten horns, and seven diadems upon his heads. His tail swept down a third of the stars of heaven, and cast them to the earth. And the dragon stood before the woman who was about to bear a child, that he might devour her child when she brought it forth; she brought forth a male child, one who is to rule all the nations with a rod of iron, but her child was caught up to God and to his throne, and the woman fled into the wilderness, where she has a place prepared by God, in which to be nourished for one thousand two hundred and sixty days . . . But the woman was given the two wings of the great eagle that she might fly from the serpent into the wilderness, to the place where she is to be nourished for a time, and times, and half a time. The serpent poured water like a river out of his mouth after the woman, to sweep her away with the flood. But the earth came to the help of the woman, and the earth opened its mouth and swallowed the river which the dragon had poured from his mouth. Then the dragon was angry with the woman, and went off to make war on the rest of her offspring, on those who keep the commandments of God and bear testimony to Jesus. (Rev 12:1–6, 14–17)

The soul-force of Judaism is of particular resonance to the Christian as it is the same sap, the Holy Spirit, if you will, that nourishes the trees of both faiths. This is not the God of Islam. The main principle of Islam is *submission*. Allah wields unqualified omnipotence; everything is determined by him. Allah's will is absolute and not dependent on anything humans do.[21] Allah has no associates; he has no son; and he "is not referred to as Father in the Koran—he is too high for that."[22] Christine Darg says Arabs still carry "feelings of disinheritance and injustice," dating back to the origin of the Arabs, when Abraham cast out Hagar and her son Ishmael. Today's Arab religion, Islam, still "memorializes and perpetuates Ishmael's rejection, since one of its 'mantras' is that God has no son and therefore cannot be a father."[23] All-powerful Allah, though infinitely merciful, dictates over

---

21. A. Heschel, *The Prophets*, 2:21–22.
22. Ibid., 2:21.
23. Darg, "It's Complicated."

humanity and speaks in monologues. I do not mean this as a criticism of Islam but a mere description of it. (Islam can create many righteous Muslims who can be exemplary citizens and outshine many Christians.) By comparison, in Judeo-Christianity, YHWH dialogues, makes covenants, seeks to partner and "wrestle"[24] with humankind so as to establish his kingdom here on earth. He takes delight in delegating authority and responsibilities to created beings, like angels and humans, and at times refers to human followers as "sons," "daughters," and "friends" (John 15:15). Diagrammatically Islam is a circle (humanity is the circle) with Allah at its center; Judeo-Christianity is an ellipse with two centers: one humanity, the other YHWH. Though this "kingdom" means different things to Jew and Christian, it is the domain of the same God—the God of Abraham, Isaac, and Jacob. We are called to voluntarily partner with YHWH in his "project to repair the world." The Newer Testament calls this the "kingdom of God or Heaven," already here and not yet come.[25] In Judaism, similarly, the goal is to repair the world, known as *tikkun olam*. Thus, we puny humans play a role, to restore YHWH's omnipotence.

Among other things, I believe rejuvenation will come to the church by returning to its Hebraic roots and embracing "Hebrew block logic" (discussed below). Church people fail to articulate the competing ideas in the Bible: YHWH is naturally loving and merciful, yet demanding; he is perpetually awesome, yet on occasion his behavior is awful; he is intimately related to us, but once in a while he is to be feared, because he is totally other. Not acknowledging these competing ideas, one is stuck only asserting the safe and comfortable truths about God (mercy, compassion, sovereignty, and "Otherness"). The terrible and dangerous matters about YHWH go unvoiced. Healthy fear that engenders YHWH's "steadfast love" (Ps 103:11) is a lost demeanor in our culture. Rightfully, many books have been written to distance the idea of a punishing God, because many people have been wounded by such images of God.[26] Psychologists can attest that many people are paralyzed by guilt feelings and excessive fear of a punishing

---

24. Jacob's name was changed to Israel because he wrestled with the Angel of the Lord.

25. Yeshua sometimes indicates that the kingdom of God is present now (Matt 12:28: "But if it is by the Spirit of God that I cast out demons, then the kingdom of God has come upon you"), whereas in other instances he indicates that the kingdom of God is *in the future* (Mark 14:25: "Truly, I say to you, I shall not drink again of the fruit of the vine until that day when I drink it new in the kingdom of God"). An in-between text, Col 1:13, says in the Greek, "For [the Father] is *rescuing* us from the dominion of darkness and transporting us into the kingdom of the Son he loves." The Father "rescued," "is recuing," and "continues to rescue us."

26. Aaron, *Love Is My Religion*, 15.

God. This is all true, but on the other hand, many people could have avoided ruin in their lives if only they had more fear of YHWH. Unfaithfulness, lying, adultery, greed, promiscuity, divorce, substance abuse, rape, and even murder could have been averted.

Postmodernism Isn't All Bad

Christians, in general, view postmodernism (the philosophical mindset that comes after modernism) as a threat to their faith. Postmodernism is difficult to define. Ashley and Walker say postmodernism gives priority to emotions, intuition, personal experience, the particular, and mystical experience.[27] Hiebert says postmodernism focuses on the self and the now, with little sense to be made of history, which is not homogeneous or evolutionary or purposeful, but rather a meaningless jumble of particulars. Postmodernism, he adds, stresses "the unique rather than the general; the unrepeatable rather than the recurring; . . . diversity rather than unity. It is interested in the eccentric, the marginal, the disqualified, and the subjugated."[28] (You will notice that I use the last point to advance my cause—to voice the "marginalized," "disqualified" texts of the Bible. I call these awkward, neglected texts the "minority reports" of the Bible.)

The following paragraph is for philosophic thinkers (skip if this does not interest you): Judeo-Christian thinkers may be threatened by the chaos and intricacy of postmodern philosophy. Philosophy—essentially the study of everything—is necessarily as complex as life. Where to begin a critique? Postmodern logic may be sound, its concepts and arguments may be convincing; however, one needs to go to the foundational pillar[29] on which all of philosophy rests, that is, *epistemology*. Epistemology is the study of how we know, or how we can be certain that we know. Epistemology deals with the assumptions and presuppositions of the thinker. If the foundation of a philosophy is demonstrated to be incomplete, then convincing arguments based upon it will crumble. Postmodernists make a gross assumption that there is no *meta-story* (or absolute truth); however, they fall into a trap of self-refutation because they depend on a meta-story themselves! That is, *there is no meta-story!* Essentially, their starting point is nothing more than an article of faith. Peter Kreeft calls this prevailing mindset "the tyranny of tolerance"; Pope Benedict XVI calls it "the dictatorship of relativism";

---

27. Ashly and Walker, "Speaking the Language of Exile," 259–68.

28. *Missiological Implications of Epistemological Shifts*, 53.

29. For example: C. S. Lewis and Francis Schaeffer used this strategy in their apologetics, which proved to be effective.

de Tocqueville calls it "soft totalitarianism";[30] and Allan Bloom, critiquing the American university scene, calls it "the closing of the American mind." What seems an opening of the mind is in fact a closing of the mind: if all ideas are equal, there are no masterpieces in art—all are equal—no value judgments can be made as there are no absolute standards to measure anything. In effect, people are so open minded that their brains fall out. The result, Bloom concludes, is that people are like "spineless jellyfish" merely drifting with the flow of culture as it presents itself. They are like mirrors only reflecting back what is given to them. Critical thinking is lost.[31]

The Scandal of Exclusivity Versus Comfortable Universals

Michael Wyschogrod explains the scandal of Judaism.[32] Why does God proceed by election rather than being the impartial father of all peoples?[33] Behind the question lurks the pain of exclusion. If God elects one individual or group, the someone else whom he does not elect is left to suffer exclusion. With such exclusion comes envy of the elected, and anger—perhaps even hatred—of the one who has done the excluding. (Much of anti-Semitism through the ages can be attributed to the chosen people idea.[34]) David's love for YHWH reaches great heights because he is so deeply grateful for his election, but the postmodern reader finds it difficult not to have some sympathy for David's enemies whose downfall is certain because they have not been chosen and have dared to conspire against the elect of YHWH. Would it not have been better for God *not* to have favored Israel, so as not to hurt the other peoples of the world?[35] Islam does better in this way, Allah does not choose a people or a tribe, rather, all humans approach Allah on

---

30. Refer to "Goodness, Beauty and Truth," podcast, www.peterkreeft.com, at approx. 17 minutes (accessed December 2009).

31. Bloom, *Closing of the American Mind*, 25–43.

32. Wyschogrod, *Body of Faith*, 60.

33. God speaks to a small select group of people in order to speak to all people. A contemporary example of how well communicating to the larger society through a particular subculture works, consider the movie: *My Big Fat Greek Wedding*. Against all movie expert expectations, the movie did exceptionally well in the larger society. The experts projected no interest in the movie except for Greek immigrant populations; however, they were wrong, as each subculture, whether Hasidic Jew, fundamentalist Christian, or Mexican immigrant saw itself portrayed in this particular story.

34. Prager and Telushkin, *Why the Jews*, 40–45.

35. Wyschogrod, *Body of Faith*, 60.

the same footing. This seems more fair. Humans merely come to Allah and "submit."[36]

The Hebraic worldview is scandalously exclusive. YHWH chooses a particular tribe, Israel. He is biased towards the land of Israel with its capital, Jerusalem, and makes salvation come through their particular Messiah. To a philosopher—who is always trying to find universals—these particulars seem silly. (Philosophy is a hierarchical enterprise where the more universal concept takes precedence over the specific; in this manner God, the biggest "idea" of all, rules over all other ideas.) Philosophers have little difficulty asserting God's being omni-this and omni-that, as they are safe, respectable universals. However, the philosopher usually concludes that God is impersonal, as the impersonal is more universal than the personal. Philosopher George Vick concurs that modern philosophy, since Descartes, leaves the impression that God is an abstract *non-Person*. To contrast, the earlier philosophies of the Scholastics (circa 1100–1500, e.g., Thomas Aquinas) saw the Lord as a Person—*the ultimate source and perfect template of personhood*.[37]

To go in the direction of the general, the all-inclusive, and the universal is easy. For example, it was easy for Einstein to assert a "Universal God," but he made it clear that he did not believe in a personal God who was concerned about humans doing good or evil. Universals are difficult to counteract: Who can fault the assertion that God is the "Absolute," "the Unconditioned," or "Wholly Other"?[38] I am sure YHWH is flattered by people who bring attention to these universals, but they are overplayed. It is YHWH's nature to "empty" himself, to hyphenate his name with humans, to incarnate into our carnal world, and to share power and prestige with humans and angels.[39] To assert that YHWH, the God of the universe, *also* has the particulars of quasi-locality, quasi-timeliness, personhood, or pathos is awkward—repulsing the sophisticated thinker.

---

36. The main tenet of Islam.

37. Philosopher George Vick at California State Los Angeles, through personal conversation.

38. Eloquent Catholic theologian Thomas Weinandy likes to go in this direction, *Does God Suffer?* 69–82. It is difficult to critique the high conceptual language of Weinandy, who draws from the patristics and Thomas Aquinas. These notions about God derived from philosophy and Scripture are logically and conceptually sound. However, the contradictory *kenosis* Scriptures are superseded or ignored.

39. Again, in theology this is called *kenosis*.

All Theology Is Anthropomorphic, Even the Sophisticated Intellectual Stuff

We will never be able to prove the existence of YHWH absolutely. I believe he wants it that way, so only those who want him find him. Do I have doubts about taking the Bible so literally, about the situatedness of YHWH, about his sharing the same frame of reference as humans, talking to humans, pursuing relationships with humans, and having feelings of frustration when that intention is thwarted? Am I making the Protagonist of the Bible too concrete? Again, it is a matter of choosing one's metaphors. There is no escape; we are all trapped in the same reality, that is, everybody has to choose their metaphors *or lack thereof* about God. To put it another way, as *anthros* (humans), any assertion about God is anthropomorphic. If readers disagree with my assertions, in the end, it only means the readers are asserting their anthropomorphisms over mine, even if they are more sophisticated, rationalistic, articulate, or even mystical (popular new age writer Deepak Chopra falls into this category)—they are, in the final analysis—still anthropomorphic.

A "systematic" theologian may look at my messy theology and say it is merely a hodge-podge assemblage of theology. My response: Inherited mainstream systematic theology is also a hodge-podge assemblage of theology. To simplify, all our inherited theology originally came from Jerusalem, it was filtered or bottlenecked through Europe then bottlenecked to us in America (if you live here). With each step in transmission things were lost, regained, twisted, reformed, and reconstituted. This includes our inherited church mannerisms, church décor, piety, demeanor in prayer, and God-talk. All are bits and pieces—filtered to us, from Jerusalem. I agree with Clark Pinnock that theology is a human construction, even when based in divine revelation. Consequently, our interpretations are provisional and makeshift. Full comprehension is reserved for the end of time.[40] Or to paraphrase Paul, "Now we know in part; then we will know fully" (1 Cor 13:12).

The Bible is as complex as life. Popular categories of theology do not always mesh well with the texts. In approaching and interpreting the Bible I do not pretend to have a foolproof way of understanding the Bible that is all encompassing. Knowing YHWH is analogous to knowing another human being—it is an organic and irreducibly complex process. Being a postmodernist (i.e., someone who is self-conscious about the limitations of objectivity), I recognize the hindrances to a complete understanding of the Bible. Trying to get a clearer picture of YHWH is an ongoing process, not a

---

40. Pinnock, *Most Moved Mover*, ix.

one-time event. We make constant revisions throughout our lives as we take into account distortions and previously unrealized data from Scripture. I agree with Blumenthal that no completely objective theology can be written—it is impossible. Only local theologies can be articulated.[41] Theology is intertwined with our personalities; thus my book is autobiographical—even though I have tried to be objective with rigorous study and reflection. Put another way, to say one's theology is one hundred percent "objective" is analogous to a person saying he or she does not speak with an accent; all other people speak with an accent.

Questions

1. Is it helpful to consider some parts of the Bible as "wine" and others as "bread"?
2. Klitsie says postmodernism isn't all bad—what do you think?
3. Do you feel indebted to the Jews?
4. Do you agree with Klitsie that a *complete* theology is not possible?

---

41. *Facing the Abusing God*, 14.

1

GOD IN A STRAITJACKET, SUPPLIED BY WELL-MEANING CHRISTIANS

"Spiritual Tourists"

Yes, the Holy Spirit has been given so we can know all the truth about our salvation. Yet a bit of the Bible remains buried. Christians, especially Gentile Christians, are unaware that they are "spiritual tourists" when reading the Bible. It reminds me of the time I visited the pyramids and the Sphinx in Egypt—I could scantly penetrate the full meaning of what happened there with the pharaohs, his people, and their religious craft. Similarly in our Bible exploration, our tour guides—Bible translators and commentators—are limited and far removed from its historical stories. We are like "spiritual tourists." Commonly in Bible study, if a text is unclear or uncomfortable, we leave it out. However, in the last few decades, following the Holocaust, both Jewish and Christian scholars have published an excess of books re-examining the neglected and jarring references about YHWH's unpopular behavior.[1] The "shadow" side of YHWH with his disturbing "ambiguity,"

---

1. A fellow PhD student at Fuller Theological Seminary, Athena Evelyn Gorospe, in her unpublished paper, "Shifts in the Portrayal of God in Theology of the Hebrew Scriptures," traces this shift over the last 30 years:

Works in the pre-'80s presented a transcendent, coherent, and "Wholly Other" God, as reflected in the works of W. Eichrodt, *Theology of the Old Testament* (German, 1933–39; English, 1961, 1967); T. C. Vriezen, *An Outline of Old Testament Theology* (Dutch 1st ed., 1949; English, 2nd ed., 1970); Gerhard von Rad, *Old Testament Theology* (German, 1957–60; English, 1962–65).

In the '80s the "shadow" side of God was reclaimed: God is seen as a dramatic "oppression," and "savagery" are admitted. YHWH as a dramatic character, suffering, revealing, and sometimes hiding himself, is accepted. And, at times, the female metaphors for YHWH are acknowledged.

For example, YHWH "creates" evil (Isa 45:7). He seems responsible for several "evils": He sent an evil spirit (Judg 9:23; 1 Sam 16:14; 1 Kgs 22:19-22); he turned the Egyptians against Israel (Ps 105:25); Samson's evil desire was "from the Lord" (Judg 14:1-4); YHWH's judgment caused people to eat their children (Jer 19:9); he "misled" people (2 Sam 17:14; 1 Kgs 22:22-23; John 12:39), and raised nations against nations (1 Chron 5:26; 2 Chron 21:16; Isa 10:6). Also, it seems, YHWH "allowed" himself to be "allured" by Satan (Job's prologue). He "repents and regrets" (Gen 6:6; Jonah 3:10). He could not predict if Israel would return to him (Jer 3:7, 19, 20). Furthermore, YHWH can be irritable (Exod 4:14; Num 22:28), persuadable (Exod 32:11-14), jealous (Exod 20:5; 34:14), impatient (Hos 4), angry (Exod 32:10), and frustrated (Hos 11:2). Yeshua in the Newer Testament seems to reflect the same. Between the lines of the Gospels one can detect Yeshua's frustration, sadness, persuadability, and even surprise (as with the centurion's show of faith). Yeshua's power appears to be limited, at times, as he could not do great miracles in Nazareth: It was contingent on human participation.

Holy, the Ultimate; Good, the Penultimate

A challenge to a mature faith is what to do with these sometimes awkward, mismatched data in the Bible about YHWH and his relationship to the world. At seminary, I never got a sufficient answer from my theology

---

character by Dale Patrick, *The Rendering of God in the Old Testament* (1981); the female metaphors for God are resurrected by Phyllis Trible, *God and the Rhetoric of Sexuality* (1978), and Sallie McFague, *Metaphorical Theology* (1982), *Models of God* (1987); the suffering and hiddenness of God are emphasized by Terence Fretheim, *The Suffering of God* (1984), and Samuel Balentine, *The Hidden God: The Hiding of the Face of God in the Old Testament* (1983). Disturbing portrayals of God's ambiguity, oppression, and savagery are shown through Phyllis Trible, *Texts of Terror* (1984), James Crenshaw, *A Whirlpool of Torment* (1984), and W. Lee Humphreys, *The Tragic Vision and the Hebrew Tradition* (1985).

In the '90s there was a shift from the coherent God to the abusive, ambiguous, and negative God, exemplified in the following works: Walter Brueggemann, *Theology of the Old Testament* (1997); David Clines, "Images of Yahweh: God in the Pentateuch" (1992); Cheryl Exum, *Tragedy and Biblical Narrative* (1992); David Penchansky, *What Rough Beast* (1998); Tod Linafelt and Timothy Beal, eds., *God in the Fray* (1998); David Penchansky and Paul Redditt, *Shall Not the Judge of All the Earth Do What Is Right?* (2000); David Blumenthal, *Facing the Abusing God* (1993); Jack Miles, *God: A Biography* (1995).

professors on Isaiah 45:7, "I form light and create darkness, I make weal and create woe," or Lamentations 3:38, "Is it not from the mouth of the Most High that good and bad come?" The modernist theologian, working with the determining concept of the goodness of God, ignores these obscure references in which YHWH creates darkness, evil, or the bad. The postmodern Christian can say, "yes, YHWH is good—the Bible overwhelmingly shows this—but we need to incorporate these rare 'harsh' traits into his character."

I explain YHWH's authorship of "bad" in a fragmentary, postmodern way: He is not responsible for every calamity in the world; yet he does take credit for events often interpreted as evil: incidents such as the utter destruction of the Amalekites (1 Sam 15:18), Uzzah being killed for touching the ark (2 Sam 6:7), and the Israelites' siege and captivity by the Babylonians (2 Kgs 24:10). All are "bad" things instigated by YHWH. Lamentations records the horrific suffering and exile of disobedient Israel, even though they were forewarned. Deuteronomy 28:53 warns that parents will eat the flesh of their children: this comes true in Lamentations (2:20; 4:10). Deuteronomy 28:30 says wives will be raped: this comes to pass in Lamentations 5:11. By the way, the sweetest Scripture used in church culture is found in the midst of this bitterness, notably: "The steadfast love of the Lord never ceases" (Lam 3:22).

Typically and understandably Christians use the tame word "ordained" (John Piper and Wayne Grudem).[2] That is, God "ordained" evil; however, the biblical references sometimes imply a stronger willfulness on the part of YHWH: "I am shaping evil against you and devising a plan against you," "I am bringing upon this city . . . all the evil I pronounced," and "I will punish . . . with the sword, with famine, and with pestilence" (Jer 18:11; 19:15; 27:8; Lev 26:16–46).[3] In these instances, YHWH "wills" it, showing deliberate, direct action. Many would discount these references as merely "symbolic," but the question still remains: What do they symbolize anyway? Two brief clarifications are in order:

1. Usually the evil we experience in the world is just part of living in a fallen universe; however, on odd occasions, we could attribute evil to YHWH directly. For example, Abraham Lincoln attributed the savage Civil War as judgment for the sin of slavery in his Second Inaugural Address. (The war cost 620,000 lives and $20 billion—about 10 times

---

2. Piper and Taylor, *Suffering and the Sovereignty of God*. I also heard this from Wayne Grudem's excellent podcast "Systematic Theology."

3. 2 Kings 19:7 shows YHWH directly involved in creating a lie and the subsequent killing of the king of Assyria.

the value of all the slaves in 1860).[4] As Lincoln was delivering this message, the African Americans present were heard saying "praise be to the Lord" again and again.

2. Direct judgment from YHWH is always coupled with the word "so." Consider Jeremiah 32:42, "For thus says the Lord: Just as I have brought all this great evil upon this people, *so* I will bring upon them all the good that I promise them." The Lord's ultimate intention for humanity is health, abundance, prosperity, and security (Jer 33:6); the believer's response is invariably: "the Lord is good, for his steadfast love endures for ever!" (Jer 33:11)

YHWH—determined to engage with humans—is *"damned if he does and damned if he doesn't"* intervene in human affairs. President Clinton found out this truism. He would be damned if he got involved with Rwanda—possibly losing many American soldiers—to stem the rise of violence before the genocide of 1994. (He did not do this, because America had just been defeated by Somalian rogues in Mogadishu; see the movie *Black Hawk Down*). Equally, he would be damned if he did not get involved. Relief worker Dr. James Orbinski estimates that Clinton could have saved one million Rwandan lives if America had gotten involved.[5] In a similar vein, historian Paul Johnson points out the "humbug" surrounding Mahatma Gandhi's nonviolence mystic. Yes, Gandhi was a great man, but he was not a saint. Indeed, Johnson tells, he led hundreds of thousands to death by stirring up civil unrest in India, all the while maintaining a pretense of nonviolence.[6]

Heschel shows the error of making *goodness* the ultimate characteristic of God. Educated at the height of German intellectualism in Berlin in the 1930s, Heschel records this assessment:

> I realized that my teachers were prisoners of a Greek-German way of thinking [modernism]. They were fettered in categories which presupposed certain metaphysical assumptions which could never be proved.... They spoke of God from the point of view of man.... The problem to my professors was how to be good. In my ears the question rang: How to be holy.... To the philosophers the idea of the good was the most exalted idea, the ultimate idea. To Judaism the idea of the good was penultimate.

---

4. Keillor, *God's Judgments*, 121.

5. See the documentary *Triage: Dr James Orbinski's Humanitarian Dilemma* (2007). Nobel prize winner James Orbinski, from "Doctors Without Borders," reports this truism about the genocide in Rwanda.

6. Carney, "Why America Will Stay on Top."

> It cannot exist without the holy. The good is the base, the holy the summit.[7]

> The holy is the essence, the good is its expression. Things created in six days He considered *good*, the seventh day He made *holy*.[8]

YHWH has been restrained in a straitjacket of "good" as defined by human standards or Greek philosophy; the higher concept of "holy" permits a more visceral depiction of YHWH. Well-intentioned pastors and theologians who insist on the "noble" attributes of God have manicured YHWH instead of vitalizing him. Under the guidance of the goodness principle we miss his "gritty" characteristics. For example, in Genesis, YHWH is embittered by humankind's wickedness and decides to destroy all humans and living things (6:5–8).[9] Similarly Yeshua, in the Newer Testament, was not always "nice"—contrary to common perceptions. He was harsh to the good, rich, young ruler; he lashed out at the Pharisees, calling them "vipers"; and in the book of Revelation, he is portrayed as judging, vengeful, and frightful. *Maranatha!* ("Come, Lord Jesus!") urges a happy *but terrifying day*. This is reminiscent of Psalm 99:1, "The Lord reigns; let the peoples *tremble!* He sits enthroned upon the cherubim; let the earth quake!"

For humans, good is easier to embrace than holy. It is erroneously assumed that holy is synonymous with good. Rabbi David Stern says "holy" means set apart and does not necessarily mean "good."[10] From the contexts in the Bible surrounding the use of "holy," one can augment the definition: separate, pure, terrible, merciful, vengeful, and awesome. The three eternal ideas in Greek philosophy were goodness, beauty, and truth—very noble ideas to attach to God. But sometimes "good" does not mesh with YHWH's activities. Consider these Scriptures: YHWH orders and is intimately involved in the Canaanite genocide (Deut 7:1–2; 20:16–17); YHWH is depicted as terrible (Deut 7:21), jealous (Exod 34:14), angry (Num 25:3–4, 11), wrathful (2 Kgs 23:26), and someone to be feared (Exod 14:31). These unusual references make it difficult to see YHWH as absolutely "good" in the way humans imagine. Thus the higher term *holy* needs to be employed. "Good" places God in a box where he is chained to only do good as we define it. The Greek philosophers and theologians, noble in their intentions, attached the highest good to God. *Good* is a nice word to philosophize about; it fits so beautifully into rational constructs about God. But *good* does

---

7. A. Heschel, *Moral Grandeur and Spiritual Audacity*, 129.
8. A. Heschel, *God in Search of Man*, 17.
9. For more details about YHWH's "grittyness," see Miles, *God: A Biography*, 3–7.
10. Dickson, *The Gospel according to Moses*, 45.

not always fit with the "willful," "just," and "loving" Protagonist of the Bible, entangled in our messy world.

Marcion's Heresy Today

In the year 144, Marcion was expelled from the church for his heretical belief that the Older Testament should be discarded because it contained unflattering revelations of God as angry, ignorant, cruel, punishing, mutable, even delighting in war and sometimes creating evil. Marcion encouraged moving to a new, enlightened view of God, supported mainly with Paul's letters. Marcion said the "New Testament God" is good, graceful, mild, placid, incapable of anger, entirely a-pathetic, and free from all affections.[11] Effectively, many Christians today fall into the Marcionite mold: Jesus is nice, malleable, and accommodating, and the Older-Testament God is wrathful and demanding. Thus, Barbara Rossing, a graduate of Harvard and Yale, an ordained minister in the Evangelical Lutheran Church, lopsides the book of Revelation. Avoiding an acknowledgement that Yeshua has a warrior side, instead she prefers a nonviolent "Lamb theology." Yeshua is "lambkin," "lamby," and even "fluffy."[12] These seemingly abstract theological understandings have consequences for human behavior—even swaying our eternal destiny. Studies show that people who believe in a loving, compassionate God are more likely to cheat than those who believe in an angry, demanding God. A study titled "Mean Gods Make Good People: Different Views of God Predict Cheating Behavior," published in the *International Journal for the Psychology of Religion*, reinforces many previous studies: There is no difference between the ethical behavior of believers (whose God is nice) and nonbelievers.[13] In other words, "God fearing" people are less likely to sin.

Campbell Dismisses "the Warlike, Territorial, Masculine YHWH"

Christians have opted for a more feminine, less demanding God. Notably, evangelical pastor Rob Bell, author of *Love Wins: A Book about Heaven, Hell, and the Fate of Every Person Who Ever Lived*, likes to emphasize God's

---

11. A. Heschel, *The Prophets*, 2:80.

12. Rossing, *The Rapture Exposed*, viii, 109–13. She says the "lion-like wrath of the Lamb" is not biblical (p. 2).

13. Morris, "Study Links Willingness to Cheat, Viewpoint on God."

love in an "unconditional" "feminine" way. To Bell, in the end, it seems everybody goes to heaven: "an untold number of serious disciples of Jesus across hundreds of years have assumed, affirmed, and trusted that no one can resist God's pursuit forever, because God's love will eventually melt even the hardest of hearts."[14]

Popular PBS-TV spiritual/myth spokesperson Joseph Campbell believes we have passed the Age of Pisces (zodiacal sign of the Fish), which had a masculine energy, symbolized by exploitation, dominance, and the rational mind. At the current time, he believes that the Age of Aquarius (the sign of the Water Bearer) ushers in a feminine energy characterized by compassion, intuition, and oneness with nature. It is arguable that our society has now banished "male energy" in favor of a "feminine," postmodern energy.[15] Campbell's spirituality largely influenced George Lucas's epic *Star Wars* movies. Further, Campbell suggests that our understanding of God is evolving and ready for a new stage. The God/gods of old were experienced as warlike and domineering. YHWH, the God of the Older Testament, was bloodthirsty and cruel (Deut 7:1–6; 10; 20:10–18; 6:10–12). In Campbell's words:

> War gods of this kind, always tribal in their ranges both of mercy and of power, have abounded over the earth as the fomenting agents of world history. Indra of the Vedic Aryans, Zeus and Ares of the Homeric Greeks, were deities of this class, contemporary with Yahweh; and in the period (sixteenth to twentieth centuries AD) of the Spanish, Portuguese, French, and Anglo-Saxon struggles for hegemony over the peoples of the planet, even Christ, his saints, and the Virgin Mary were converted into the tutelaries of pillaging armies.[16]

Campbell says the old gods are dead or dying, and people everywhere ask, "What is the proper, enlightened image of God that will promote a unified, harmonious earth?"[17] He adds, voicing a typical postmodern sentiment:

> [in] the new mythology, which is to be of the whole human race, the old Near Eastern desacralization of nature by way of a doctrine of the Fall will have been rejected; so that any such limiting sentiment as that expressed in 2 Kings 5:15, "there is no

---

14. Bell, *Love Wins*, 108.
15. Campbell, *The Inner Reaches of Outer Space*, 16.
16. Ibid., 15.
17. Ibid., 17.

God in all the earth but in Israel," will be (to use a biblical term) an abomination.[18]

Campbell's sentiments need to be felt because they represent a postmodern platitude. (I will counter Campbell, arguing for the "primitive," "territorial" YHWH of the Bible.) Today, Western culture avoids the loving *but demanding* YHWH of the Bible by embracing a spirituality without religion: it chooses to be spiritual without God. The Dalai Lama's recent books have topped bestseller lists because they tie in with the current ethos of tolerance and peace without religion. This form of popular Buddhism appeals with its offer of high experience and low commitment. Philip Goldberg says it's the future dominant religion. This kind of non-theistic spirituality brings apparent harmony among peoples since no one has to deal with the messy implications of a demanding, merciful, holy, willful YHWH.[19]

George Orwell mistakenly prophesied that the threat looming over the Western world was totalitarianism, as depicted in his novel *1984*. What we have today is not "Big Brother" of *1984* controlling what we do and think, but the exact opposite. Os Guinness explains:

> Far from having Big Brother watching over us . . . we have . . . Big Mother-goddess Liberty who is casual to the point of carelessness about what we think or do. Our Western nightmare turns out to be, not totalitarianism and manipulation, but triviality and meaninglessness, masked often by a feverishness mistaken for vitality.[20]

Of course, what is called for is a balance of both male *and* female in the world, as this represents YHWH's correct image. Also, YHWH is merciful *and* demanding.

Disallowing Paradox

Christians who are nervous about biblical paradox are forced to take sides. A contemporary example is the rift between Classic theists and Openness theists. Both sides have scriptural support. Sadly, evangelicals break fellowship with one another over this. Wayne Grudem and Bruce Ware (Classic theists), who affirm that God has *complete* knowledge about the future, led the rally to oust Clark Pinnock, John Sanders, and Greg Boyd (Openness

---

18. Ibid., 18.
19. Veenker, "Spirituality without Religion," 34. Also see the article "Making Space for Sane Spirituality" by Philip Goldberg, who sees it as the religion of the future.
20. Guinness, *The American Hour*, 383.

theists) from the Evangelical Theological Society (ETS) because they say God can "change his mind" and does "not completely know" the future decisions of humans. Both sides take the Bible seriously and both have Scripture backing their positions.[21] Regrettably *sola scriptura* (Scripture alone) takes a back seat as inherited concepts about God are pushed. The "Omni-God" of Classic theists is not permitted to behave as some minority Scriptures indicate (Gen 6:6–7; Exod 32:11–14; Judg 2:18; 1 Sam 15:11, 23; 2 Sam 24:15; 1 Chron 21:15; Ps 91:15; 106:45; Isa 63:9; Hos 9:10; 11:1; 13:6–8; Jer 2:2; 3:19; 8:18; 18:8–10; 31:20; Amos 7:3, 6; Jonah 3:10, 4:2; Rom 8:23, 26; Eph 4:30). The principle of paradox is the missing element in this impasse. Theologians who defend the classical view of God use the rule of *analogia fidei*, "the analogy of faith." This rule dictates that the less clear or atypical Scripture concerning any topic is to be subordinated to the preponderance of clear Scriptures on the same topic (Num 23:19; 1 Sam 15:29; Ps 110:4; Jer 4:28; Zech 8:14–15; Mal 3:6; Jas 1:17). For example, Christians who oppose Openness theology state that if a few Scriptures record that God "repented," these need to be ignored because the consistent whole of Scripture denies that God can change his mind.[22]

Bruce Ware, an opponent of Openness theology, chooses to emphasize Scriptures that show YHWH's otherness rather than YHWH's condescension to the human. I think it is easier to promote the total-otherness-of-God Scriptures. How can you go wrong elevating God too much? But what is lost is YHWH's *self-imposed* humiliation. Ware's book *God's Lesser Glory: The Diminished God of Open Theism* takes on the task of rightfully proof-texting God's sovereignty and power:

> All the peoples of the earth are regarded as nothing.
> He does as he pleases
> with the powers of heaven
> and the peoples of the earth.
> No one can hold back his hand
> or say to him: "What have you done?"
> Daniel 4:35 (NIV)
> Our God is in the heavens;
> he does whatever he pleases.
> Psalm 115:3

Employing "the analogy of faith," Ware, with these "Omni-God" Scriptures, attempts to trump and thereby nullify any other Scriptures

---

21. Neff, "Closed to Openness," 21.
22. Huffman and Johnson, *God under Fire*, 69.

that indicate YHWH's self-imposed limitations,[23] such as YHWH's taking advice, changing his mind, and taking a novel line of action suggested by a human. The interchanges of Abraham and Moses with YHWH vividly illustrate such behavior. In both the Older and Newer Testaments, YHWH and Yeshua show surprise, disappointment, and sometimes, oddly, exhibit limited knowledge on a subject.[24] In Genesis 22:10–12, YHWH does not know if Abraham will sacrifice his son Isaac (YHWH says afterwards, "now I know you fear God, since you have not withheld your son, your only son, from me").[25] Sometimes YHWH cannot predict how people will act; he uses fuzzy words like "maybe" or "perhaps" (Exod 4:8; 13:17; Jer 26:3; Ezek 12:3). In the story about decadent Sodom and Gomorrah, YHWH is "unaware" of the extent of their sin (Gen 18:20–21).

Having a postmodern orientation helps resolve the conflict because it "accepts diversity, the unrepeatable, the jumble of particulars and heterogeneous information." The believer's locus of truth is a *Person* (YHWH/Yeshua), not a system of theology or an inherited yet-needed church doctrine. Let's face it: it is difficult to quantify, categorize, and systemize the Protagonist of the Bible—or for that matter, any typical human being. I suggest incorporating *all* the varied Scriptures about YHWH's interactions with humans: most are absolute; some are transitory, timely, or local. This can be done without relativizing the truth away (a danger of postmodernism). We hold Classic theists to be right while simultaneously asserting the references to YHWH's occasional limitations ("powerlessness," "frustration," "indecision," and "need"). Marvin Wilson advises using "Hebrew block logic" to incorporate these varied Scriptures:

> The Greeks often used tightly contained step logic whereby one would argue from premises to a conclusion, each step linked tightly to the next in coherent, rational, logical fashion. The conclusion, however, was usually limited to one point of view—the

---

23. Ware, *God's Lesser Glory*, 229.

24. For example: Jer 19:5: "building the high places of Baal to burn their children in the fire as burnt offerings to Baal, which I did not command or decree, *nor did it enter my mind*" (italics added). Other "entering-God's-mind" texts are Jer 7:31; 32:5. Or see Jer 3:6–7: "The Lord said to me in the days of King Josiah: Have you seen what she did, that faithless one, Israel, how she went up on every high hill and under every green tree, and played the whore there? And I thought, 'After she has done all this she will return to me'; but she did not return, and her false sister Judah saw it"; also see verses 19–20. Yeshua was surprised about the centurion's faith. Yeshua does not know when the end of the world will happen. Yeshua is only able to heal a few people in Nazareth because "their faith" limited his healing power. Between the lines of the Gospel stories one can easily detect the disappointment, anger, and frustration of Yeshua with humans.

25. Brueggemann, *Genesis*, 187.

human being's perception of reality. By contrast, the Hebrews often made use of block logic. That is, concepts were expressed in self-contained units or blocks of thought. These blocks did not necessarily fit tightly together in any obviously rational or harmonious pattern, particularly when one block represented the human perspective on truth and the other represented the divine. This way of thinking created a propensity for paradox, antinomy, or apparent contradiction, as one block stood in tension—and often-illogical relation—to the other. Hence, polarity of thought or dialectic often characterized block logic.[26]

Another example of "Hebrew block logic" is found in the conundrum of Pharaoh hardening his heart but then having his heart hardened by God (compare Exod 8:15 with 7:3). The sharp edges of Scripture need not be filed down but left in tension. In this regard, Christianity can learn from Judaism, which is at ease with paradox. Heschel writes:

> A polarity lies at the very heart of Judaism, the polarity of ideas and events, of regularity and spontaneity, of uniformity and individuality . . . of law and inwardness, of love and fear, of understanding and obedience, of joy and discipline, of good and evil drive, of time and eternity, of this world and the world to come, of revelation and response . . . of empathy and self-expression, creed and faith, of the word and that which is beyond words, of man's quest for God and God in search of man. Even God's relation to the world is characterized by the polarity of justice and mercy, providence and concealment, the promise of reward and to serve Him for His sake. *Taken abstractly, all these terms seem to be mutually exclusive, yet in actual living they involve each other.*[27]

A way Christians can implement "Hebrew block logic" is to format Christian biblical commentaries like the Jewish Talmud. Place the Scripture in the middle of the page, to the left have a straightforward commentary from a scholar of old, to the right have a contemporary author give a contrasting explanation and then at the bottom of the page give an exposition from a poet or devotional author. Let there be *conversation*; our faith is in YHWH, not in our crude "maps" about the Bible. To visualize the issue, think of describing YHWH as similar to seeing a three-dimensional building in space—we can only see a maximum of two sides of the building at one time. Raw Scripture is rife with anthropomorphisms. They must be

---

26. Wilson, *Our Father Abraham*, 150.
27. A. Heschel, *Moral Grandeur and Spiritual Audacity*, 384.

given equal status with propositional assertions about God whether we are capable of merging them neatly together or not.

YHWH's transcendence is not the trump card subsuming references to his immanence. Isaiah neatly places YHWH's immanence and transcendence together in one phrase, "for great in your midst is the Holy One of Israel" (12:6b). To generalize, the more educated one becomes, the more the humanness of YHWH is disparaged; anthropomorphisms are replaced with more sophisticated labels and concepts. This is a forlorn pursuit as all and any descriptions of YHWH are at heart anthropomorphic—because all human communication (even the most refined), is anthropomorphic. We are inescapably *anthros*. However, being "YHWH image bearers" gives us license to regard our projections about YHWH as fairly accurate (loving, engaged, jealous for loyalty, concerned for justice, and relational).

Everything Has to Be Buttoned Up

Athol Dickson, a Christian who immersed himself in a synagogue Bible study for a time, contrasts church and temple culture:

> Unfortunately, most theological conversations I have had in church have been the self-reinforcing kind: a group of people sitting around telling each other what everyone already believes. If some brave soul interjects a radical new idea or questions one of the group's firmly held views, it is usually an unpleasant experience. We shift in our seats uncomfortably until someone rises to the bait. The discussion remains civil, but it seems that any challenge to the group's theology must be corrected, so all comments are solidly aimed at that goal: arriving at a preconceived answer.[28]

Dickson notes the difference in the synagogue: It's a more open environment. "Nothing seems to be out of bounds, no subject too sacred for doubt and challenge . . . they dare ask if God might be limited, or 'in a learning process,' or fickle, or mean spirited." Here questioning is not doubting but trusting. "It takes more faith to ask than it takes to fear the asking."[29] This kind of *chutzpah*, or talking back to Hashem, was exemplified by Abraham: "Far be it from You to do such a thing, to slay the righteous with the wicked, so that the righteous and the wicked are treated alike. Far be it from You! Shall not the Judge of all the earth deal justly?" (Gen 18:25 NASB).

---

28. Dickson, *The Gospel according to Moses*, 64.
29. Ibid., 17, 19.

Abraham's cheekiness, running the danger of making Hashem angry (Exod 4:14), is a stance of engagement and respect rather than detachment.

The Flat Land of Modernism

Modernism misshaped theology. Christianity immersed in the predominant culture of modernism primarily valued analysis and criticism of the Bible. This came to my attention while studying at Fuller Theological Seminary in Pasadena for two decades. Good came from this movement—enriching our understanding of the Scriptures—but also distraction and damage. The worship of science influenced biblical interpretation. Science reigned as the most objective way to find truth—a confidence originating with the Enlightenment. Science or "scientific positivism" enjoyed a reputation of indisputable objectivity and was considered the most reliable way of quantifying truth.[30] This "certainty" of science prevailed for two hundred years, fixing itself in our Western culture. This exaggerated "objectivism" fueled the historical-critical method in theology.

"Objectivism" tainted both Christianity and Judaism. Recently the Reform movement—the largest Jewish denomination, "founded in the 19th century and steeped in the rationalism of the Enlightenment"—shifted away from minimalistic rationalism (a process of reducing the rich stories, poetry, and wisdom of the Bible to mere historical, cultural, linguistic, and superstitious factors) to explore a fuller range of religious heritage.[31] The certitude of modernity's scientific method was undermined by people like Michael Polanyi, a professor of physical chemistry and philosopher of science, who observed that scientific knowledge is *not entirely objective*. True objectivity, he argued, does not exist because the scientist (a subject) inevitably influences the outcome of scientific experiments, which are based on experiments done by subjective others. Hence, pure objectivity is impossible.[32]

Positivism, Scientism, or Naive Realism is characterized by overconfidence in the scientific method believed to be reliable, objective, and devoid of any subjectivism, and therefore an unbiased view of reality. Abuse is evident today: for instance, the media can misuse the word "scientific" to clinch arguments when, in fact, at times, the science can be *agenda driven*. I witnessed this on *Nightline*, when Ted Koppel interviewed a scientist,

---

30. Brueggemann, *Texts under Negotiation*, 1–2.

31. This shift was undertaken at the Central Conference of American Rabbis in Pittsburgh in May 1999. Stammer, "Rabbis Vote to Revive Observance of Traditions," A3.

32. Polanyi, *Personal Knowledge*.

Hamer, who discovered the Q28 "gay gene." The unsettling part was that Koppel portrayed gayness as 100 percent genetic—like eye or hair color. End of issue. What was not discussed was that genes—especially behavioral genes—are plastic and elastic, they interact with each other, and they do not necessarily manifest their information. In fact, at times the environment may turn them on or off. To be specific, if a person has the diabetes gene, it may lay dormant for a lifetime, but it could be switched on by extended stress, bad eating habits, and lack of sleep. In this exposé by Koppel, a slice of the discussion was based on solid science, but the extrapolation (gayness is 100 percent biologically determined) was agenda driven. Koppel regressed into black-and-white thinking. The nuance of the interplaying factors of human volition and environment were not cited.[33]

Richard Rorty defines objectivity as that which is agreed on by "everyone in the room."[34] Until recently, Western ideals of objectivity relied primarily on white males agreeing on and labeling truth—a monopoly that only changed when others, such as women or non-Western people, forced their way into the room. A flagrant example of the failure of scientific objectivity is when the early anthropologists of England postulated that the skull of the Caucasian man was more advanced than other races. Later, this conclusion was disproved when non-Western people became anthropologists and claimed the equally spurious conclusion that Caucasians are the more primitive race because they are known to have more body hair. Moreover, recently, African American theologians have been let into the room, like James Cone, who makes us aware that Jesus was not white, and YHWH is preoccupied with the oppressed, the poor, and the disenfranchised.[35]

With the help of Paul Hiebert, I detect four weaknesses in modernist theology:[36]

1. *Idea-olatry* (as in idolatry). This is an overconfidence in the capabilities of the human mind. Educated people are especially prone to this defect. The finiteness of the human mind is ignored as the mind is *idolized*. Frequently people do not sufficiently differentiate between divine revelation recorded in Scripture and human theology that endeavors to interpret that revelation. Sometimes final authority is given to theology. In the process, unclear or paradoxical Scripture is routinely ignored—or no place is left for mystery or tension. For instance, I have noticed that the knee-jerk reaction

---

33. Satinover, author of *Homosexuality and the Politics of Truth*, helped me clarify this paragraph. It needs to be noted that human psychology is always based on three factors: biology, environment, and will. Like a three-legged stool, all three play a role.

34. Rorty, *Philosophy and the Mirror of Nature*.

35. Cone, *A Black Theology of Liberation*, 53–74.

36. Hiebert, *Missiological Implications of Epistemological Shifts*, 20–22.

against the notion that "YHWH is impacted by humans" stems first from accepted theological concepts (e.g., the omni-attributes or "Omni-God") and only second is it checked by Scripture.

2. *Eternal static ideas override a dynamic YHWH.* In its search for unchanging truth, modernity ignores the Bible's claim that the locus of truth is in a dynamic Person—YHWH. The Bible stories showing YHWH's dynamic exchanges with humans are replaced with substitute concepts and ideas. The substitute concept is considered closer to the truth. This can be attributed to Greek influence that considered *ideas* to be unchanging and eternal, and events to be temporal or even unreal. T. F. Torrance elaborates:

> Thought operated with a radical dichotomy between a realm of ideas and a realm of events, and it took its stand within the realm of ideas as the realm of the ultimate real. From this perspective it could only regard the Christian doctrines of God at work in history, of the coming Son of God into human and creaturely existence, of the Eternal entering the world of space and time, as unreal, or at best as a "mythological" way of expressing certain timeless truths.[37]

3. *Feeling is of little or no use.* Many theologians rightfully show the folly of following emotions. When studying at Francis Schaeffer's place, L'Abri, Switzerland, I was reminded plenty how off-track Christians can get with emotionalism in the church, especially the Pentecostal and charismatic types. But Schaeffer failed to show the damage done by intellectual*ism*, the kind that created "Omni-God," the God-of-the-philosophers. By emphasizing objective knowledge, modern theology elevates the mind to the exclusion of feeling. It assumes that once people have the right knowledge, they will live according to it and go to heaven.

4. *An underdeveloped sense of the depth of things or simple arrogance.* Modernism brings into theology the strong individualism that characterizes modernity. Disagreements about theology often lead to confrontation and conflict. Because each of us assumes that we are reading the biblical text honestly and without bias, we judge others as mistaken. Recognizing that the Bible is sometimes unfathomable helps. Under the yoke of modernism, Christian apologists countered the rival ideologies of their time *tit for tat*. If modern scientists spoke in arrogant absolutes, evangelical apologists countered in kind. A case in point has been the debate over evolution where scientific absolutism has been matched with idealistic, biblical literalism. Hiebert shows the folly of idealist, biblical literalism:

---

37. Torrance, *Theological Science*, 17.

Idealist theologies preserve the certainty of objective truth and absolutes. They reject the relativism that leads us to nihilism, but the price of this certainty is high. To claim that what is in the human mind is objective reality is to deny the ultimate reality of God and his deeds in history. It is to locate truth in the self and to deify the human mind. And, as many Third World theologians point out, it can lead to Western theological colonialism and a failure to take them seriously.[38]

YHWH Lost His Name

David Clines says a tragic thing happened between the fifth and second centuries BC: God lost his name. In particular, the Jews stopped using God's personal name YHWH, replacing the intimate with the generic words "God," the "Lord," the "Name" (Hashem), the "Holy One," the "Presence," and even the "Place."[39] What does abandoning a personal name signify? If the YHWH associated with specific acts in the Older Testament is replaced by a more scholasticized, manicured "God," much is lost. Generally, the word "God" tends toward philosophical abstraction, leaving the personal obscured. As Clines points out, the word "God" is found in the dictionary and defined in abstract terminology, whereas the word "YHWH"—not in the dictionary—is found in an encyclopedia where YHWH is associated with Israel in historical interactions. Both Christians and Jews have shied away from the seemingly quaint "YHWH" as representing a Person who is willful, loving, emotional, and engaging.[40] Unlike "Omni-God," sometimes he is unpredictable, as when YHWH killed Uzzah for touching the Ark. There, David was "afraid" of YHWH (2 Sam 6:6–9). Two early Christians, Ananias and his wife, Sapphira, were struck dead for lying to the Holy Spirit (Acts 5:1–5). But then, on occasion, it's okay to bend the rules a bit as in 2 Chronicles 30:17–19, where YHWH overlooks the violation of sanctification rules. These depictions of YHWH have been embarrassing to both Jews and Christians. Clines says that in the second century BC, Septuagint translators removed many of the anthropomorphisms of the Hebrew Bible,[41] explaining them away as primitive or metaphorical.[42]

---

38. Hiebert, *Missiological Implications of Epistemological Shifts*, 59.
39. Clines, *On the Way to the Postmodern*, 498.
40. I think that Judaic scholar Michael Wyschogrod would back me up here.
41. *On the Way to the Postmodern*, 500.
42. Cross, *Oxford Dictionary of the Christian Church*, 61.

Judaism and Christianity primarily hinge on having a relationship with Hashem/YHWH/Yeshua—*the Ultimate Person of the universe*. One cannot have a relationship with an abstraction. So serious is the problem of a depersonalized God in Judaism that Michael Wyschogrod believes it to be life-threatening: How can a human have a personal relationship with an "Unmoved Mover"? (The Greek philosopher Aristotle applied this concept to God.) This charge applies equally to Christians. The great Jewish thinker Maimonides (a rabbi of the Middle Ages)—whose influence is still felt in today's Judaism—reduced the God of the Bible to Aristotle's ideas: God is totally different from humans and is not impacted by them. The default position for many nominal Jews and nominal Christians is this: God is impersonal and remote and does not concern himself with the mundane affairs of humans. Wyschogrod emphasizes that Judaism needs to recognize that "the God who appears in the Bible is a very *specific Person* with certain definite character traits."[43] Hashem is a Person, apprehended usually in *local*, *timely* and *particular* events in our world. Accordingly, he cannot be encapsulated within a concept. We can only make sketches of him subject to constant revision. No doubt his character is constant, but his personality is multifaceted. YHWH is revealed *and* concealed in the Bible. Proverbs 25:2 indicates that it is the glory of God to conceal things. At the giving of the Ten Commandments the Lord appears from the "darkness," or within the "fire" and "clouds" (Deut 5:22). With the coming of Yeshua, the Lord is again revealed *and* concealed. On the Mount of Transfiguration, Peter, James, and John witness Jesus's glory; yet, an "overshadowing cloud" blocks their experience and terrifies them (Luke 9:34). The Lord is knowable and unknowable; even the seraphim cover their faces; prophets collapse crying "Woe is me!" (Isa 6:5). Humans cannot see him and live, yet he is continually revealing himself to us.[44]

Tidy "Omni-God" versus YHWH

YHWH's dealings with humanity cannot be neatly systematized or generalized because YHWH is not a Law, a Principle, or a System—*he is a Person*. His ways of relating vary: He appears. He demands. He forgives.

---

43. *Body of Faith*, xiv.

44. I do not concern myself with trying to explain the consciousness of the biblical writer or prophet, but only try to understand the conscious thoughts and feelings communicated. I assume that when a prophet speaks he is not only speaking the divine view but inevitably brings a personal view too. Thus inspiration is both a divine situation and a human situation.

He momentarily withdraws. He grieves. He speaks. He heals. He pursues. Theologian William Dyrness makes an interesting observation: Although a well-studied theologian can have the satisfaction of having a more *tidy and clear* theology, on the downside, he/she is more removed from concrete reality. Because reality is so *messy* and varied, YHWH's dealings with humans are likewise—it's not a simple, clean affair.[45] YHWH's stance towards us (though informed by his Word) can, on occasion, be transitory, timely, particular, local, and personal. As a result, competing truths arise:

- "I [YHWH] kill[46] and I make alive; I wound[47] and I heal" (Deut 32:39).
- Yeshua is the *lion* and the *lamb*. He brings the *sword* and *peace* (Matt 10:34; Rev 5:5; John 1:36).
- YHWH shares no human form (Deut 4:12), yet he shares the likeness of human form (Ezek 1:26).
- No one has ever seen YHWH (Deut 4:12; John 1:18), yet we may see him (Isa 6:5; John 14:9).
- He is everywhere (Ps 139:8), yet oddly, he can be present in one place (Gen 18:1, 2; Exod 25:8; Ps 135:21).
- He is overwhelmingly *awesome* (Exod 15:1), and yet, on odd occasions he can be *awful* (Ps 89:7 says "greatly terrible";[48] Exod 34:10; Deut 10:17; Judg 13:6; 1 Chron 17:21; Neh 1:5; 4:14; 9:32; Job 37:22).
- The Lord shows kindness to the meek (Matt 5, the beatitudes), and yet he shows kindness to anyone he wants (Exod 33:19).
- He does not change (Ps 102:25–27; Heb 6:13–20), yet he changes—sometimes (Gen 6:6; Jonah 3:10).
- He lacks nothing and does not need humans to serve him (Acts 17:25), yet we are partner workers (1 Cor 1:9), and he desires our friendship (Isa 41:8).

---

45. Personal conversation with William Dyrness, Fuller Theological Seminary, Pasadena, CA.

46. 2 Samuel 24:16: "But when the angel stretched out his hand toward Jerusalem to destroy it, the Lord relented concerning the evil, and said to the angel who was bringing destruction among the people, 'It is enough; now stay your hand.' The angel of the Lord was then by the threshing floor of Araunah the Jebusite."

47. 1 Samuel 5:6: "The hand of the Lord was heavy upon the people of Ashdod, and he terrified and struck them with tumors, both in Ashdod and in its territory."

48. Psalm 89:7: "A God feared in the council of the holy ones, *greatly terrible* above all that are around him" (italics=Septuagint and Syriac Versions).

- He is beyond human counsel (1 Sam 15:29; Isa 40:13–14), yet Moses and Amos successfully changed his mind (Exod 32:11–14; Amos 7:2–3).
- He is *always* close (Heb 13:5), yet he may momentarily withdraw to test what is in our heart (2 Chron 32:31).
- He chooses us (John 6:44), yet we choose him (Deut 30:19).
- He lives in the light (Rev 22:5; Ps 27:1; Isa 2:5), yet, oddly sometimes, he dwells in deep darkness.[49] (It is helpful to note that he may be in the darkness but he is not the darkness.)
- All things work for good (Rom 8:28), yet we can *irretrievably* loose people, things, and/or opportunities. (King David lost his kingdom and son after his affair with Bathsheba; repentance did not retrieve those concrete loses.)
- You are dead to sin (Rom 6:11), but still, you have to fight against it, as if you are alive to it (Heb 12:4).
- Do not judge each other (Matt 7:1); yet judge each other (1 Cor 6:1–5).
- Scripture is God's Word, *not* from humans (Exod 34:27; Jer 30:1–4; 1 Thess 2:13; 2 Pet 1:20, 21; Rev 2:1, 8), yet humans give some input too (Luke 1:3; John 20:31; 2 Cor 2:3–4, 9; 13:10; Jude 3, Ecclesiastes, Song of Solomon).[50]

For a more exhaustive list, see Appendix B.

Granted, some of the paradoxes above can be reconciled because they employ a metaphor or use the language differently; but others not. Biblical paradoxes—such as being saved by *faith* or *works*—are contradictory in the abstract. But in real life they involve each other. The Newer Testament declares that we are saved by *faith,* yet even Luther knew that there was a contradictory minority Scripture found in James ("faith without works is dead"), which annoyed him to great length. In the preface to the German

---

49. 1 Kings 8:12: "Then Solomon said, 'The Lord has set the sun in the heavens, but has said that he would dwell in thick darkness.'" Cf. Deut 5:22; 2 Sam 22:12; Ps 18:11, "shrouded in thick darkness."

50. "All scripture is given by inspiration of God, and is profitable for doctrine, for reproof, for correction, for instruction in righteousness" (2 Tim 3:16). Obviously, the Bible is primarily brought about by God, but with modest human contribution. Plain examples of words from humans in the Bible include Exod 4:1; 1 Kgs 19:14; Isa 6:5, and Ecclesiastes. Paul even includes words from a pagan source, *The Hymn of Zeus*, in his sermon at Athens (Acts 17:28, "your poets say we are offspring from God"). In this way, the Bible is a divine and human book; it is a co-revelation that reveals both the nature of YHWH and humans.

Bible he translated, he called James an "Epistle of straw," not worth reading. And so he got rid of that nuisance. So much for his guiding principle *sola scriptura* (Scripture alone) and respecting the canon of Scripture. Despite all this, each side of the paradox needs to be voiced; one asserted without the other becomes a distortion of the truth, even if the paradoxical Scripture is a minority. The Hebrew word for truth, *emet*, is composed of the first, the middle, and the last letter of the alphabet, signifying that it embraces all—so we include all. Consequently, paradoxes are closer to the truth than any straightforward, substitute compromise statement. Terence Fretheim reminds us that "God cannot be captured in any text or language or image or system; God will always be a 'problem' in one way or another."[51]

Why these paradoxes? I believe, partly, because the Holy One wants to confound us, to challenge us—intimacy with him isn't easy. Being "perplexed" continues with Paul and the disciples in the Newer Testament (2 Cor 4:7 and Luke 24:4). In a way the Holy One is saying "don't prepackage me"; "struggle with me, do not be afraid, *I am right there with you*." Anthol Dickson raises this question: "What if it is the struggle he desires as much as the truth itself?"[52] Abraham, the father of our faith, lived in unpleasant paradox: On the one hand, Hashem commanded him to sacrifice his son, on the other hand, it was forbidden to murder. Abraham resists the impulse to focus on one truth at the exclusion of the other. To find a solution he acknowledges both truths but looks to the Truth (Hashem) to get him through the struggle. So, Hashem is not a mechanical System we can predict with precision. Rather, we need to abide in him to see us through life's perplexities. In this manner, the name of God given to Moses—*Ehyeh Asher Ehyeh* (or *Ehyeh* for short), meaning "I will be what I will be" or "I am what I am"— I believe, was not necessarily given to add new meaning to God's name but primarily to confound Pharaoh *and* the Hebrews.

When acknowledging paradox, one has no need to tidy things up, to harmonize or reconcile scriptural differences. Theologians have an eagerness to iron out paradoxes. For example, Thomas Weinandy says, "there needs to be an interpretative or hermeneutical tool for bringing consistency to [paradoxes]."[53] As is often the case, when paradoxical Scriptures are "reconciled," the different ideas represented are conflated into a single umbrella idea, lessening the jaggedness of Scripture. Often in the process, the Holy One's distinctive character is sanitized. To be specific, if YHWH's kindness is emphasized without his judgment, our image becomes lopsided. The

---

51. Fretheim and Froehlich, *The Bible as Word of God*, 106.
52. *The Gospel according to Moses*, 70.
53. *Does God Suffer?* 60.

Bible does not speak with a single voice: Paul, representing the major thrust of the Newer Testament, says we are saved by *faith alone*; James, a minority voice, adds that *works* are needed to prove the faith valid. It helps to listen to the Bible's authors as if they were in a conversation about the complex YHWH-human relationship. The ethos of our time, postmodernism, has it hazards, but it helps us allow such competing theologies to remain in tension without urging synthesis.

In short, allow the sharp angular Scriptures to stand on their own, don't "reconcile" them. Suspend closure if the Scriptures don't fit; this is part of living by faith. And don't underestimate common people's tolerance for tension; in real life we live with plenty of it. By the way, a reputable and mature scientist would exhibit the same qualities: respect the data, don't fudge the data. If the data doesn't fit into your grand scheme, stay with the data, not your pet scheme. Suspend closure if discrepancies exist, and live with delayed gratification. In science, the greatness of the scientist, the excellence of the university, or the number of scientists agreeing on any given topic—can mean little. In the end, the data wins, even if a "nobody" scientist, from an insignificant university brings it forward.[54] Always, eventually, the data is the victor. It is the trump card because it represents reality. I believe the same applies to Scripture.

Questions

1. Which is the more encompassing word for YHWH: holy or good? How do you understand Scripture's use of these words?

2. Klitsie says we should use paradox, even contradiction, in our theology. Do you agree?

3. The Marcionite heresy says the warlike, judgmental God of the Older Testament is out, and the Newer Testament God of love and peace is in. What do you think?

4. In science, data trumps consensus. Should that be the case with our understanding of the Bible? Can, and should, Scripture trump our inherited doctrines, theology, and traditions?

---

54. For example: In 1912, scientist, Alfred Wegener, put forward the theory of "Continental Drift." Namely, the primitive earth only had one single land mass, after which the land mass broke apart and drifted into their present continents. Most scientists considered him a fool, and only decades later (1950s) acknowledged his theory.

2

HOW "OMNI-GOD" AROSE IN HISTORY

THE OMNI-GOD-OF-THE-PHILOSOPHERS STARTED INFILTRATING Christianity already in the first century. Aristotle said God is the "Unmoved Mover." God is perfect. He acts purely (*actus purus*). He is not impacted by humans. He does not react. He has no needs and cannot suffer. He does not change and he does not need to change. And so the "Omni-God"[1] gained prominence, putting God in a straitjacket. Consequently, the YHWH of the Bible was not permitted to be angry, capable of disjunctive responses, frustrated, or needy. "Omni-God" was spurred along by the following factors:

1. Downgrading anthropomorphisms
2. Influence of Greek philosophy
3. Rationalism and modernism
4. Compartmentalization
5. False dichotomies of body and soul (or *eros* and *agape*)
6. Natural theology, the default position
7. Emotional need for "Omni-God"
8. Ethnocentrism
9. Fear of the unfamiliar
10. Separation between the Older and Newer Testaments
11. Flawed ways of knowing

1. Walter Brueggemann uses "Omni-God" or "God who is 'omni.'" *Great Prayers of the Old Testament*, 132–33.

1. Downgrading Anthropomorphisms

As *anthros* (humans) we make up labels to attach to the word *God*; we fill the word with content. Essentially any description of God is anthropomorphic. Many educated people have a knack for favoring the abstract, universal, words like omnipresent, omniscient, and omnipotent (from well-meaning theologians), "Ground of Being" (from theologian Paul Tillich), "Collective Unconsciousness" (Carl Jung), and even elusive words such as "Ineffable" or "Unknowable." *All are anthropomorphisms*. Even the most exquisite insights of a Zen master about the ultimate grounds of reality are, in the final analysis, anthropomorphic. Similarly, the clever deconstructionist language of Robert Wright's *The Evolution of God*—is anthropomorphic. Wright's God, celebrated on PBS-TV—the "Moral Axis of the Universe"—is agreeable. But does this language get us closer to the essence of YHWH? Why choose the impersonal words "moral" or "axis"? Likewise, Hollywood's "God" as depicted in James Cameron's movie *Avatar*—a Universal-Tree-Thing—is similarly anthropomorphic. Though this "God" is said to be above good and evil, Cameron cheats a bit as the story unfolds. The "Tree-God-Thing," which is supposed to "not take sides," does, and fights on the side of good, bringing the story to a happy ending. With this quandary in view, I argue for taking the *given* anthropomorphisms of the Bible seriously, but with common sense (e.g., God is not a "rock," 2 Sam 22:32). It has been the custom of classical theists, embarrassed by biblical anthropomorphisms, to deliteralize the Bible. For example, if the Bible states that the Holy One regretted the creation of humanity (Gen 6:6), they claim he could not possibly have "been sorry." If the Bible presents YHWH as suffering with his people or as a jealous lover, they are certain it does not mean us to take it literally.

Intellectuals commonly downgrade anthropomorphisms as mere "primitive" forms of depicting God. This attitude can be traced as far back as the first century, when Philo—a Jewish philosopher—tried to harmonize Judaism and Greek philosophy (20 BC–AD 50). He insisted that anthropomorphisms only benefited those whose "natural wit is dense and dull, whose childhood training has been mismanaged."[2] His assumption was that references to the personal YHWH are unsophisticated, bringing the divine too much down to the human level. The same happens today: biblical images of a responsive, vulnerable YHWH are neglected, while stereotypical images of God's omnipotence are allowed to dominate current theology, causing a lopsided view of YHWH.[3]

---

2. Clines, "Yahweh and the God of Christian Theology," 324.

3. One can have fun discussions about these "omni-attributes." Omnipotence, for instance: "Could an omnipotent being create a stone so heavy that even that being

How then, are we to interpret the "embarrassing" Scriptures revealing YHWH's irritability (Exod 4:14; Num 22:28), persuadability (Exod 32:11–14), jealousy (Exod 20:5; 34:14), repentance (Gen 6:6; Jonah 3:10), impatience (Hos 4), anger (Exod 32:10), and frustration (Hos 11:2)? Traditional theologians often, and strangely, suggest that in such references God is only pretending to experience human emotion, calling into question the traditionalist's dogma of God's truthfulness and integrity. These Scriptures are dismissed as human ideas projected onto God. If this is so, it begs the question, "What are these anthropomorphisms used to communicate anyway?"

The working assumption of prevailing theology is that God is bigger, more transcendent, and loftier than we can imagine. Thus, anthropomorphisms are rejected and replaced with more acceptable rational constructs. Robert Banks illustrates how, in the process, a personal YHWH is lost, and powerful given metaphors of the Bible are "peeled away so that their conceptual core can be discerned."[4] The rationalist, according to Banks, believes that "until a metaphor ceases to be a metaphor it cannot possess truth. One should as quickly as possible extract the metaphor's conceptual juice and then throw it away."[5] An example of putting away childish perceptions of God is found in Paul Tillich's idea of the "Ground of Being." However, Banks convincingly shows that Tillich does not fully escape using images himself. "They merely exchange one kind of imagery for another. Talk of God as 'the Ground of Being,' for example, only draws on the material ('ground') and ontological ('being') categories and favors the imagery of 'depth' rather than 'height.'"[6] Heschel reverberates a similar challenge to Tillich: "Ground of Being" is meaningless, is God above the ground, too?[7] In this game of dueling images, Tillich favors the more abstract and less personal imagery, leaving a severely diminished view of God. Sadly, traditional theology sought to "de-imagize" the Bible; it substituted the given biblical images with abstract, philosophical words.[8]

It is arguable that all or any description of YHWH is *inescapably* anthropomorphic, as Reade observes, "When fear of anthropomorphism induces men to reject the idea of a personal God, and substitute for it some

---

could not lift it?" If so, then it seems that the being could cease to be omnipotent; if not, it seems that the being was not omnipotent to begin with.

4. Banks, *God the Worker*, 9.

5. Ibid., 13.

6. Ibid., 393–94.

7. A. Heschel, *Moral Grandeur and Spiritual Audacity*, 408.

8. *God the Worker*, 13. Again, theology of the past—traditional theology—has tended to be rationalistic due to the influence of Greek philosophy, the Enlightenment, and modernism.

product of abstract thinking, they simply delude themselves. What they propose, is just as anthropomorphic as what they reject."[9] Herman Bavink is more succinct: "All scripture is anthropomorphic."[10] All alternative labels for God such as Wholly Other, *Actus Purus*,[11] Omnipotent, "Moral Axis of the Universe,"[12] the Unconditioned, the Absolute, and Being[13] are anthropomorphisms in that they are human words applied to God, or deified abstractions created by very clever people. John Calvin says, "God cannot reveal himself to us in any other way than by a comparison with things we know," and more specifically—because we are image bearers of God—*self-knowledge is necessary to understand God*.[14] Jewish thinker Francis Landy says that "man is a metaphor for God."[15] In Hasidic tradition, humans are like the "Holy Scrolls": the mere presence and existence of humans remind us of Hashem—even more than does the Bible Itself.

Both Christian and Jewish[16] theologians are guilty of emasculating Hashem through rationalism. The Christian thinkers include Anselm, Aquinas, Calvin, Hodge, and Carl Henry.[17] Although some of the names mentioned here might not have had a comprehensive theology on God's immutability (God cannot change his mind) or impassibility (he does not experience feelings), they nevertheless failed to assert a strong coherent theology on the pathos and changeability of God.[18] Classic theists show inconsistency when they deny anthropomorphisms of YHWH's less desirable emotions (hurt, anger, vengeance, and jealousy) but accept YHWH's love, joy, will, thought, and action, which can also be construed as merely anthropomorphic. To be pure in obliterating all anthropomorphisms, one

9. Reade, *Christian Challenge to Philosophy*, 67.

10. Bavink, *Doctrine of God*, 86, 92.

11. God is a "pure actor." He does not react; he acts. He does not change; he does not need to change.

12. Wright, *The Evolution of God*.

13. John Sanders explains the weakness of Tillich's "Being" concept in *The God Who Risks*, 31.

14. Lecture by professor Ray Anderson, Fuller Theological Seminary, Pasadena, California.

15. Landy, "The Name of God and the Image of God and Man: A Response to David Clines," 167.

16. For greater detail on Judaism's over-indulgence in rationalism, see Heschel's struggle with the issue: Kaplan and Dresner, *Abraham Joshua Heschel*, 101–5. Also see Luzzatto, *The Way of God*, 31, 33, 145.

17. For more detail, see Ware, "An Evangelical Reexamination of the Doctrine of the Immutability of God." PhD dissertation, Fuller Theological Seminary, Pasadena, CA, 1984. 16–186.

18. Ibid.

would end up a mystic in total silence, with no description of God. To be intellectually honest, we would then have to acknowledge that we have no common world of thought or action and no common frame of reference with YHWH. Hence, all prayer, worship, and engagement with YHWH are suspect and should be viewed as irrational.

Question: If we accept anthropomorphisms, how far should we go in their application? If we accept that YHWH is literally sorry and grieved (Gen 6:6), or that his heart undergoes change (Hos 11:8),[19] should we then accept metaphors literally, for example, he is an eagle (Deut 32:11) or Jesus is a door? Here common sense is required in discerning when a phrase is poetic and meant to be taken symbolically, and when poetic language is meant to be received as "literal" revelation of YHWH's character.

For Judaism, Michael Wyschogrod says, "the Bible does not, of course, specifically say that Hashem has a body, but then again neither does it say that he does not . . . . There is very little description of his physical appearance in the Bible in general."[20] The Bible does little elaboration on descriptions of physical appearances, its only intent is to tell the story. Consider the idea that Hashem descends and walks in the Garden of Eden. At times Hashem limits himself to a local place and time, but often not—he is usually invisible,[21] at least partly because he is too holy for us to bear. Solomon's dedication prayer of the temple illustrates paradox: YHWH was to live in the temple even though he cannot make his abode on earth (1 Kgs 8:27). Anthropomorphic imagery is used only very sparingly in descriptions of actual appearances or visions of YHWH (theophanies). Moses only mentions his back but not his face (Exod 33:23). Exodus 34:5-6 says he "came down," "stood there with Moses," and "passed in front of Moses." Isaiah sees YHWH, but only ventures to describe his robe (Isa 6:1). Ezekiel sees the "likeness" of a human form—no more (1:26-28).

To clinch the argument, the incarnation of the Son of God is the consummate anthropomorphism: the Logos became flesh and blood and tabernacled among us (John 1:14). Yeshua is the exact representation of the divine nature (Heb 1:3), and he who has seen the Son has seen the Father (John

---

19. God also changes his mind and attitude, consider Gen 6:6-7; Exod 32:11-14; Judg 2:18; 1 Sam 15:11, 23; 2 Sam 24:16; 1 Chron 21:15; Ps 106:45; Jer 18:8, 10; 26:3, 13, 19; 42:10; Amos 7:3, 6; Joel 2:13; Jonah 3:10; 4:2.

20. *The Body of Faith*, 99.

21. Exodus 33:20.

14:9). Yeshua revealed God as weeping,[22] susceptible to suggestion,[23] and subject to frustration and disappointment,[24] insult,[25] grief,[26] and anger.[27]

2. Influence of Greek Philosophy

For Plato God is "good" and lives in perfect sufficiency and is never in need of anything. The Greeks always maintained that the gods were immortal, without cares and perfectly happy, indifferent to the world and in no need of human worship.[28] Moreover, at Olympus, the everlasting home of the gods, "no winds beat roughly, and neither rain nor snow can fall; but it abides in everlasting sunshine and in great peacefulness of light, wherein the blessed gods are illumined for ever and ever."[29] By the way, the supreme being of Hinduism, Brahma, is similar:

> Brahma is not a jealous God. On the contrary, he permits and takes benign delight in all the differing illusions that beset the beclouded mind of *Homo sapiens*. He welcomes and comprehends every kind of faith and creed. Though he is himself perfect love and inclined to all of his devotees, no matter what their plane of understanding, he is also and at the same time supremely indifferent, absolutely unconcerned.[30]

Aristotle's God was the "Unmoved Mover," eternal, immutable, immovable, wholly actual, self-sufficient, totally removed, and wholly other.[31] Plato believed that matter, being evil and changeable, continually hinders unchanging, eternal Ideas (or Forms or God) from being accurately expressed in this world. He viewed the material world as a world of shadows, and concluded that absolute, unchanging truth can only be perceived by the contemplation of the Ideal World. (Modernist theology emphasizes the

---

22. John 11:35.

23. Matthew 8:5–13; John 2. Jesus says no to Mary, but then turns the water into wine at the wedding in Cana.

24. Matthew 23. I don't give a particular verse; frustration, anger, and disappointment appear between the lines.

25. The Holy Spirit can be "insulted and outraged" (Heb 10:29, *The Living Bible*, Catholic Edition).

26. Luke 19:41. Also, the Holy Spirit grieves (Rom 8:26; Eph 4:30).

27. Matthew 21:12.

28. *The Prophets*, 2:12, 13.

29. Ibid., 2:13.

30. Ibid., 14.

31. Ibid.

same—abstract, conceptual ideas about God.) As a result of this perspective, an ontological dualism arose according to which the material world is evil and the spiritual world is good. Prevailing church culture, at times, gives the same impression: Evil and suffering is contained within and confined to the realm of earthlings but cannot reverberate back into the uncreated order where God, who is "absolutely other," lives in heaven. Jesus momentarily came to earth, suffered, then went back to peaceful heaven. This tendency is the polar opposite of the heated agitation of the prophets: YHWH is utterly impacted and involved with rebellious humans.

Greek thinking has infiltrated both Judaism[32] and Christianity. Heschel says the Hellenization of Jewish theology goes back to Philo. Greek intellectual sophistication successfully portrayed the God of the Bible as an "Absolute Notion" or "Idea" who was beyond emotions and feelings. The passionate YHWH of the Older Testament and the Newer Testament was replaced by the immutable, impassible God of Greek philosophers. Greek philosophy portrayed God as an abstract and uninvolved Deity who lived in changeless perfection outside of time. Reflexively, under the direction of Greek philosophy, theologians understood the phrase "image of God" in spiritual terms because of the denigration of the physical world, including and especially the human body. Wyschogrod says,

> For the Greeks, the material order is lower or unreal and there was consequently little difficulty in defining man without reference to his body. The Bible does not know of this disassociation and speaks of man as being created in the image and likeness of God without expecting that this will be taken automatically to refer to the non-visual [non-physical] likeness of an endowment, such as reason.[33]

Thus, the "likeness" we share with YHWH was constricted to reason (the Greeks' favorite occupation). In time, the YHWH of the prophets—who was engaged, concerned, and passionate about humans—was replaced by the God-of-the-philosophers. To the Greeks, emotions were unfit for deities. God was beyond temporary earthly emotions, which were considered transitory and punitive. Assuming ideas to be eternal, God's nature was gradually distorted by theologians: a YHWH with pathos was transformed into the God-of-the-philosophers (Plato, Aristotle, Parmenides, and the Stoics). Only describing God through "eternal Ideas" and reason made him unchanging, immutable, and static.[34] According to Warren McWilliams, the

32. A. Heschel, *Moral Grandeur and Spiritual Audacity*, 155.
33. *Body of Faith*, 4.
34. McWilliams, *The Passion of God*, 10–11.

Greek penchant for the "Otherness of God" filtered through the theologies of Clement, Origen, and Augustine, who emphasized God as impassible.[35] Anselm agreed with those who preceded him, but left open the idea that God appears to be compassionate:

> But again, how art thou at once compassionate and impassible? For if thou art impassible, thou canst not suffer with others, and if thou canst suffer with others, thy heart is not wretched out of sympathy for the wretched—but this is what being compassionate means. Yet if thou are not compassionate, whence does such great consolation come to the wretched?[36]

Protestant Reformers held to the concept of God's impassibility (God does not feel), though Luther reasoned that if Christ suffered, God suffers.[37] Today there is a growing awareness of the pathos of YHWH, especially through the works of Abraham Heschel and Jürgen Moltmann. Ironically, it is liberal theologians who appeal to Scripture for a personal and changeable YHWH. In reaction, conservatives counter, giving precedence to the philosophical concept of God's immutability rather than submitting to Scripture, showing a YHWH impacted by humans. More Catholic[38] and evangelical theologians are warming up to the idea of YHWH's malleability. Evangelicals Emil Brunner, Karl Barth, and Jürgen Moltmann all insist that God is capable of change.[39] However, evangelicals such as J. I. Packer and Carl Henry affirm the classical doctrine of immutability—that God is changeless, without qualification.[40]

Currently, Openness theology has taken the changeability of YHWH further to include that he takes risks and does not exhaustively know the future. (YHWH knows the past and present perfectly, but does not know the future completely—humans will contribute to this somewhat open-ended future.)

---

35. Ibid., 12–13.

36. Fairweather, *A Scholastic Miscellany*, 77.

37. Althaus, *Theology of Martin Luther*, 197. Althaus argues that Luther holds to deipassionism rather than patripassionism; that is, God rather than the Father suffered.

38. See for example, Stokes, "Freedom as Perfection"; Clarke, "A New Look at the Immutability of God"; Hill, "Does the World Make a Difference to God?"; and Schoonenberg, "God as Relating and (Be)coming."

39. It is not my intention to go into much detail here. For a more complete overview of the major theologians on the topic, see Ware, "An Evangelical Reexamination of the Doctrine of the Immutability of God," 229–35.

40. Packer discusses this in *Knowing God*, 67–72. Also see Carl Henry, *God, Revelation and Authority*, 5:286–94.

3. Rationalism and Modernism

Modernism, rationalism, and scientific positivism gave theology a false sense of objectivity through the form-critical method. Although this approach offered many new insights into the Bible, it stripped the flesh—in the form of YHWH's responsiveness and vulnerability—from the Bible, leaving mere bones: God the "Unmoved Mover." In the process, YHWH was de-personalized, accentuating his "Otherness." Rationalism still has appeal today. It is difficult to counter thinkers who make God "Wholly Other," immutable, and impassible. For example, Catholic thinker Thomas Weinandy convincingly shows God as "Wholly Other," supported by great Christian thinkers of the past: Justin Martyr (103–165), Irenaeus (130–202), Clement of Alexandria (150–215), Origen (185–254), Tertullian (160–220), Lactantius (240–320), and Aquinas (1225–1274). Weinandy's comprehensive and complex study on the matter is impressive; however, he elevates his rational/philosophical conclusions over any Scripture that indicates YHWH's malleability. His logic and reasoning are sound, and the conclusions he draws from these great thinkers convince the reader that YHWH is immutable and impassible.[41]

Weinandy's study is exhaustive and exhausting, with a thread running through his study defined by negation. A simplified version of his arguments might assert that God is *not* small, he is *not* located in one place, and he is *not* limited in power. Therefore, God is very, very, big, living in total blessedness and happiness, without problems or frustrations. (The Monty Python filmmakers made fun of this Totally Other God: "O God, You are so Very, Very, Big, Huge . . ."). Central to those who oppose the idea of the pathos (feeling) of YHWH, like Weinandy, is Aquinas's use of *actus purus*: God acts purely—never reactively, affected by no one and nothing. Conceptually, Weinandy wins the discussion, with support from the Scholastics, and "proves" that God is absolutely and completely "Wholly Other." With this kind of one-sided conclusion, Scriptures referring to YHWH's changeability "must" be interpreted anthropomorphically.

In a similar vein, classical theologians who argue that God can't change his mind or be impacted by humans use the philosophical notions of God's omnipotence and omniscience as trump cards. The intentions behind such convictions are noble, ascribing to God the highest power. However, we need to describe YHWH as he appears in the Bible and not prescribe him according to any preconceived notions (God can't be persuaded or suffer or be influenced by humans). John Sanders echoes, "It is *not* up to

---

41. Weinandy's study on God's immutability and impassibility is the most proficient I have found to date. *Does God Suffer?* 83–112, 120–46.

human beings to dictate the sort of providence God must exercise. Instead, we should try to discern the sort of sovereignty God has freely chosen to practice."[42]

4. Compartmentalization

A typical compartmentalization argument debunking the idea that God suffers goes like this: "The christological tradition, inherited from the Fathers and Scholastics, held that the Son of God did suffer, but *as man and not as God*."[43] The guiding principle holds that God cannot suffer, therefore, the divine nature of Jesus did not suffer, while the human nature of Jesus did. Jung Lee says this is an artificial separation created by the early church[44] to address otherwise unanswerable questions. Personally, I don't understand how the Council of Chalcedon in the year 451 spoke with such precision about splitting Jesus's natures, Scripture says nothing about these "two natures." The Bible has little concern for these philosophical distinctions; it rather focuses on the essentials of the divine-human relationship.

The biblical revelation does not concern itself with demarcating the two categories theologians have differentiated—the transcendence and immanence of God. Weinandy further splits these two realities of God's character, giving higher order of importance to the transcendence, which takes "ontological precedence" over immanence. He argues that God's immanence is dependent upon his transcendence.[45] It might be perceived as noble to enshrine YHWH's "Wholly Otherness" and to make his love totally other. Who dares to counter this? I do. Weinandy says (get ready for this poetic mouthful!), "God's love is immutably and perfectly actualized in his total otherness, God's wholly-other love is present to and active within the created order in all its wholly otherness without losing its wholly fully actualized otherness in so doing."[46] These fawning words, however, detract from raw biblical revelation. Terence Fretheim opposes the splitting of "Wholly Otherness" from the immanence of YHWH: "this God is present—not some emanation of God, nor some bits and pieces of God, but God in all of God's Godness is present."[47] The biblical reference, "In your midst is the Holy One" (Isa 12:6; Hos 11:9), shows the indivisibility of YHWH's

---

42. Sanders, *The God Who Risks*, 11.
43. Weinandy, *Does God Suffer?* 15, 173.
44. Lee, *God Suffers for Us*, 36–37.
45. Weinandy, *Does God Suffer?* 42.
46. Ibid., 168.
47. Fretheim, *The Suffering of God*, 70–71.

transcendence and immanence. Bifurcation is unnecessary as humans are not ontologically different to YHWH.[48] We are only different in a matter of degree—Yeshua affirms: we are "gods" (John 10:34; Ps 82:6). We are similar to YHWH (Gen 1:27); yet obviously humans are created, fallen, and limited. The emphasis of YHWH's Wholly-Otherness is excessive, distancing, and unnecessary. YHWH is immanent, voluntarily engaging in our world, operating wholly within our frame of reference, while simultaneously being wholly transcendent.

5. False Dichotomies of Body and Soul (Or Eros and Agape)

God's *agape* love for us has been characteristically understood as spiritual, a love that is unconditional, impartial, and expecting nothing in return. Humans are consigned to the "weaker," physical, or sensual love, *eros*, which is capable of jealousy. C. S. Lewis popularized the different kinds of love in his book *The Four Loves*. However, to be biblical, we should reject the popular distinction between *eros* and *agape* as it reflects a false dichotomy between body and soul not found in the Bible. Interestingly, the Eastern Orthodox Church has not made as marked a body-soul distinction. As a result, they bypassed the entire transubstantiation-of-the-Eucharist debate of the Catholic and Protestant churches. To them it was a non-issue, as the material-spiritual elements of humanity are unified. Catholics and Protestants were animated by Augustine's body-soul dichotomy, which originated with Plato's material-spirit split. The biblical view is that the body and soul are *aspects* of the human person. The biblical dichotomy does not refer to a division within humans, but to a divide between "of the world" or "of God." Weinandy explains:

> In both the Old and New Testament the word "flesh" (*basar* in Hebrew and translated as *sarx* in Greek) designates the whole human being in its creatureliness with an emphasis on its frailty, weakness and sinfulness. Equally, the Hebrew word *nepes* (translated as *psyche* in Greek) designates not the "soul" as such but the complete human being as "living," and that one is only "alive" in relation to God.[49]

---

48. Weinandy disagrees, *Does God Suffer?* 53.
49. See ibid., 148 footnotes.

William Dyrness correctly indicates we *are* a soul rather than we *have* a soul.[50] Judaic scholar Wyschogrod says: "Human love, correspondingly, must not be bifurcated into the *agape-eros* mold or similar scheme."[51] The Bible shows that Hashem loves us in a human way. For example, in the Older Testament he chooses friends Abraham, Isaac, and Jacob, and in the Newer Testament he chooses Peter, James, and John. Consequently, YHWH has chosen not to love in the undifferentiating way assumed to be "godly"—he has favorites, as do humans. "Godly" love would be impartial, remote, abstract, universally applied, and devoid of passion. Accordingly, Martin Buber would characterize a relationship with this dispassionate love as an I-It relationship.[52] Instead, in the Bible, Hashem meets people in a Person-to-person manner, devoting himself completely to the individual, listening with all his being to the person. At the same time the outcome of the encounter is not controlled and no certainty of result is preordained. Compare the dialogues of Hashem with Moses or Yeshua with Peter. In Buber's terminology these would be characterized as I-Thou relationships. Wyschogrod emphasizes the reciprocity in Hashem's love:

> The love with which God has chosen to love man is a love understandable to man. It is therefore a love very much aware of human response. God has thereby made himself vulnerable: he asks for man's response and is hurt when it is not forthcoming.[53]

Wyschogrod argues that human beings as image bearers evidence a mixture of *eros* and *agape*.[54] As depicted in the Bible, God's love is not indifferent (the way *agape* is defined). Response is always sought, needed, and hoped for: So YHWH has chosen to love in a mixture of *eros* and *agape*, too. The type of love evident in humans and in God, whether *agape* or *eros*, varies from situation to situation; the mixture of the two constantly changes in differing human-God encounters. Whether God's *agape* love for humanity or the human type of love, the weaker *eros* love, predominates is a question so complex as to be unknowable, and therefore inherently unfruitful

---

50. Per lecture, Fuller Theological Seminary, Pasadena.

51. *Body of Faith*, 61.

52. Heschel criticized his friend Buber's spirituality, particularly Buber's popular book *I and Thou* as a "vague encounter" with God, and Buber unhelpfully substituted a "symbol" for the transcendent Subject. Heschel labeled Buber a humanistic existentialist, while Buber considered Heschel a subjective existentialist because of Heschel's notion of divine pathos and the prophet's experience of God's feelings. See Kaplan and Dresner, *Abraham Joshua Heschel*, 223–25, 228.

53. Wyschogrod, *Body of Faith*, 63.

54. Ibid.

for consideration. Later I will show that the Bible only uses one word to describe love, whether its object is food, YHWH, sex, money, or a spouse.

As an example of the more "carnal" love (*eros*), consider this, why did Hashem chose Abraham? The biblical text does not give any reasons why Abraham was singled out. Rabbis have contrived reasons, the most popular being that Abraham was a natural philosopher and saw through the foolishness of idol worship and reasoned his way to the one God.[55] Allowing that Hashem loves in a human way, this would imply that he simply "fell in love" with Abraham for unexplained reasons.[56] The Genesis narrative leads us to believe that Abraham was not searching for Hashem—he showed up unbidden. Likewise, Hashem shows up uninvited to Jacob. Jacob had an inglorious past; he cheated his brother and tricked his father. Moses did nothing to initiate the burning bush encounter and seems reluctant to take on Hashem's task. James Kugel, an expert on ancient texts, argues that ancient writers did not deem it proper that Hashem should choose just anyone, therefore pious biographies were written to justify his actions, say with Abraham or Ezra.[57] Though YHWH shows no partiality in his love (Matt 22:16), paradox is evident as he seems to love some more than others, for example, Yeshua chooses only Peter, James, and John to meet Moses and Elijah on the Mount of Transfiguration.[58] Why were the other apostles left out?

With this unified perspective on love applying both to Creator and creature, the anthropomorphisms depicting YHWH's emotions and willfulness gain legitimacy: YHWH has condescended to our world, has give-and-take relations with humans, makes covenants with humans, and even allows his name to be hyphenated with human names (YHWH-of-Abraham-Isaac-and-Jacob; Yeshua-of-the-church). Risk is involved, as inevitably YHWH's name is defamed. The reciprocal relationship often results in human disloyalty—both the Jews and the church have failed, while YHWH has been faithful and has been let down by the people he loves.

---

55. *Jubilees* 12.17–22 describes Abraham as a pious man who seeks God, seeks righteousness, and looks to God for direction (should he leave his homeland?). According to James Kugel, the *Book of Jubilees* was probably written by a Jew 200 years before Christ. It is a rewrite of *Genesis*; that is the way they made commentaries of the Bible then. Kugel, *The God of Old*, 39–40.

56. Kugel, *The God of Old*, 65–66.

57. Examples include the *Testament of Levi*, Apocalypse of Esdras, and Apocalypse of Baruch. See Kugel, *The God of Old*, 42–46.

58. Matt 17:2 and Mark 9:2.

6. Natural Theology, the Default Position

Natural theology,[59] popular to moderns, has maintained its appeal now to egalitarian postmoderns: God is totally impartial; he has no favorites; the dispensation of his love and chosenness is carefully meted out to those who are deserving. God does not need one nation (e.g., Israel) to work through, any more than he requires a particular savior (i.e., Yeshua). Rather, God is the father of all nations equally. The concept of nation is not allowed to intrude into the relationship between God and the individual person. Although this God seems more just, he is also more remote and mechanical (i.e., impartiality implies a certain remoteness).

David Clines identifies the damage done by natural theology in the way many Christians see God as essentially "loving, supportive, and safe." The anthropomorphisms of the Older Testament showing YHWH's abrasive but loving relatedness are ignored, and "the supreme expressions of universality" of the Newer Testament are overemphasized. Consequently, God is in danger of evaporating into "spirit," "light," and "love." These tenderly cherished tenets of natural theology are an elegant flight from the reality of YHWH.[60] Clines warns: "One result of the absence of YHWH from Christian consciousness has been the tendency to focus on the person of Christ as the exclusive manifestation of deity."[61] Clines continues:

> A Christian theology—perhaps any theology—does not care for these fragmented glimpses of the divine reality [loving and abrasive relatedness of YHWH]. Nothing must be discrepant, no act of God may sound willful, everything must be shown to be purposive. All of the abrasive aspects of the divine personality must in the end be subsumed under the rubric "love." But the more that note is insisted upon, the more the reality of such negative encounters with God that the Old Testament witnesses to is set aside. And the more it is insisted that God is ever-loving, ever-patient, ever "positive" in his relationships with humans, the more religion becomes a cradle or a cocoon, and the less true it is to the reality of human experience of God.[62]

---

59. "Natural theology" was a favorite philosophy in the eighteenth and nineteenth centuries, returning to knowledge of God drawn from nature as distinct from knowledge of God derived from special revelation (the Bible).

60. Miskotte, *When the Gods Are Silent*, 177–78.

61. Clines, *On the Way to the Postmodern*, 2:505.

62. Ibid., 504.

Natural theology, then, tends to mute the intentionality and responsiveness of YHWH, replacing anthropomorphisms with neutral, colorless assertions about God.

7. Emotional Need for "Omni-God"

Traditionally, religious consciousness demands an omnipotent, omniscient God commanding adoration and obedience. Voicing the minority Scriptures showing YHWH as persuadable, vulnerable, passionate, or needing response does not mesh well with prevailing religious sensibilities. People want a risk-free God—a God that is in total control of all contingencies in our precarious world—so they may feel secure. Indeed, Mozley points out, theologians disparage these anthropomorphic depictions of YHWH (persuadable, vulnerable, passionate, or needing response) because there is less intellectual satisfaction in not being able to predict grand schemes about God, such as those afforded by hyper-Calvinism or hyper-fundamentalism.[63] If God has pathos and can sometimes change according to different human situations, his predictability and transcendence bleed away. When God's impassibility and immutability remain intact, things remain tidy.

Bruce Ware, a defender of God's omni-attributes, argues that God's "success rate" is tarnished if we accept that God can make "mistakes."[64] A very noble undertaking by Ware, but how far do we take it? Consequently, he suggests, we cannot ascribe unqualified glory to God.[65] This line of reasoning illustrates an emotional need for an all-powerful and sovereign God to facilitate worship, an approach that cannot acknowledge any "failures" of God. These "failures," of course, should be appropriately attributed to a complex weave between YHWH engaging fallen humanity and human participation—together driving a *sacred drama*. Furthermore, I say, we should worship YHWH not because of his "success rate," but because he is our Creator and Deliverer.

If God is God, the philosophers reason, he cannot be subject to frustration or suffering as that would imply he is limited in power and resources. Divine suffering would inconveniently entangle God in time, contradicting the idea that God in heaven is unaffected by earthly matters. Even more fundamental, suffering is assumed to be intrinsically evil, philosophically

---

63. Mozley, *The Impassibility of God*, 172.

64. Israel wanted a king like the other nations, YHWH did not want to give them a king. Then YHWH changed his mind and gave them King Saul. Things went bad and YHWH regretted his decision—a mistake.

65. Ware, *God's Lesser Glory*, 224–25.

barring God from subjection to it. Baron Friedrich von Hugel believes this is so, and he asserts, "the life of God is a blessed life, and, as such, happy with the perfection of happiness."[66] Weinandy says the Trinity is incapable of suffering, they never suffer and they never experience inner angst.[67]

As expected, by abandoning "Omni-God," the security of God's having a *perfect* plan for one's life is threatened. This dictum has its basis in Scripture;[68] however, other Scriptures that Openness theologians bring to light show there is "room to wiggle" as far as YHWH's "plans" for our life are concerned.[69] A necessary synergism between the human and the Divine needs to occur to bring these "plans" to fruition. Emotionally, it is difficult to let the assurance of "all things work together for good" (Rom 8:28) to be counterbalanced with other Scriptures showing that opportunities, people, and things can be irretrievably lost.

A book that greatly influenced me when I first became a believer was *Your God Is Too Small*, by J. B. Phillips.[70] Phillips, a theologian and Bible translator, heightened my awareness of how humans are prone to quantify and domesticate YHWH, forcing him into a box of their own construction. Narrow Bible translations and unexamined beliefs about YHWH limit our perception of him. Often we opt for the status quo ("Omni-God"), avoiding Scripture that does not fit into our theology or is not easily explained.

8. Ethnocentrism

Acknowledging our cultural and experiential biases can release us to embrace the greater riches of YHWH. We gravitate toward Scriptures that mesh with our personal life experiences. A prime example of bias is reflected in Martin Luther's preface to the New Testament of 1522. It shows how Luther distorts the importance of the different issues to suit his experiences:

> From all these books, you can, in a flash . . . distinguish which are the best. John's Gospel and St. Paul's epistles, especially the one to the Romans, and St. Peter's first epistle contain the true kernel and marrow among all the books, for in these you do not

---

66. Von Hugel, *Essays and Addresses on the Philosophy of Religion*, 199.

67. Weinandy, *Does God Suffer?* 226. He derives these conclusions first from philosophical argumentation and then from Scripture.

68. Jeremiah 29:11.

69. Again, the concept of paradox applies here. For example, James 4:2b, "You do not have, because you do not ask." We can miss Hashem's plans for us if we do not ask, or if we ask amiss.

70. Phillips, *Your God Is Too Small*.

find Christ's deeds and miracles described very much but you do find emphasized in a most masterful way how faith in Christ overcomes sin, death, and hell, and gives life, justification, and blessing—which is the true nature of the Gospel. If I should have to choose between the deeds or the preaching of Christ, I would prefer to leave the deeds go, for these don't help me, but his words are the words of life . . . .

Therefore John's Gospel is the only Gospel which is delicately sensitive to what is the essence of the Gospel and is to be widely preferred to the other three and placed on a higher level. Likewise, the epistles of St. Paul and St. Peter are to take precedence over the three gospels of Matthew, Mark, and Luke. To sum it all up—St. John's Gospel, and his first epistle, St. Paul's epistles, especially those to the Romans, to the Galatians, and to the Ephesians, and St. Peter's first epistle—these are the books which show you Christ and teach everything which is needful and blessed for you to know, even if you don't see or even hear any other book . . . . Wherefore St. James' epistle is a true epistle of straw compared with them, for it contains nothing of an evangelical nature.[71]

Luther's premise was that if a book speaks more clearly to you, such as the epistles of St. Paul, then they must be more inspired. He was obviously not conscious of his ethnocentrism (the attitude that the world revolves around your particular tribe) as he is attracted to books written for Greek audiences (and subsequently Westerners) and shies away from books that implement Hebraic revelations and understandings about YHWH. Cross-cultural expert Charles Kraft says the lesson to be learned here is that Westerners should not allow their cultural preferences to prejudice them against certain Hebrew portions of Scripture.[72]

To be fair, Luther was fighting a different battle: fighting against salvation-through-works and the selling of indulgences by the Catholic Church. Thus came Luther's emphasis on the salvation-through-faith Scriptures. Here is Luther on the prophets: "[The prophets] have a queer way of talking, like people who, instead of proceeding in an orderly manner, ramble off from one thing to the next, so that you cannot make head or tail of them or see what they are getting at."[73] Luther, a lawyer type of person, was unable to

---

71. Quoted in Reus, *History of the Canon*, 322, 329.
72. Kraft, *Christianity in Culture*, 232.
73. Quoted in von Rad, *The Message of the Prophets*, 15 footnote.

penetrate the Prophets. He was unaware that his personality and limited life experiences disallowed him access.

What is the remedy? By exposure to testimonies of Christians from around the world, we invariably realize that Westerners do not have a monopoly on the truth about the Bible. To be specific, the experiences of Christians in house churches in China or Christians living in Africa or South America supply vital insights into how the Father, Yeshua, and the Holy Spirit work differently than in the American experience.[74] Ethnocentrism can be circumvented when we recognize that there is not just one theology, but many—Jewish, African, Chinese, Indian, as well as feminine and masculine, theologies of the oppressed, the powerful, and the in-between, to identify only a few. Identities are retained. In the end of time, YHWH has chosen to keep tribe and nation distinctions and seems to value different expressions of culture. In heaven we do not return to the Garden of Eden but to a City inhabited by different tribes and nations with rich and diverse cultures (Isa 60:4–11, 17–21; Rev 7).

9. Fear of the Unfamiliar

The notion that YHWH is capable of feeling was labeled the heresy of "patripassionism" by early church fathers who denied that God the Father could suffer. More currently, David Wells, attentive to the corrosive influence of postmodernism on truth, accuses Openness theology (which includes the notion of the pathos of God) of giving in to the pressures of a pluralistic society by creating God in the image of the prevailing culture. Nevertheless, Charles Kraft reveals that people are afraid to explore broader approaches to theology for fear of being branded heretics:

> The scriptural data that we seek to understand may be likened to a great mountain filled with gold ore. To mine that ore a number of mine shafts need to be drilled into the mountain. To date, the theological mine shafts into the mountain of revealed truth have nearly all been drilled in a strictly limited area. This area is defined by Western culture. There are several shafts, representing several varieties of Western cultural perspectives. But most of those shafts have either combined with one another to make a single large tunnel of Western Christian theologizing or they have been abandoned with a HERESY sign posted over the entrances to them. Meanwhile, throughout the world, the members of the other six thousand or more cultures have

---

74. Dyrness, *Invitation to Cross-Cultural Theology*.

largely been given the impression that mining in God's mountain can be done only by entering where Western theologians have drilled, as long as there is no HERESY over the entrance. The rest of the mountain remains largely untouched.[75]

Kraft's perspective also applies to how Euro-American Christians often prefer the Greek portions of the Bible:

> As we study the Scriptures our cultural perspective is like a magnet. It draws to us, as it were, those portions of Scripture in which God's message is presented in ways most meaningful to those of our culture. Those portions written to people within Greek culture, therefore, tend to speak most clearly to us Euro-Americans, since we have been so strongly influenced by Greek thinking.[76]

Kraft, who was a missionary in Nigeria for many years, found that Africans had a greater affinity to the Older Testament and the Hebrew portions of the Newer Testament, as these were the portions that shared commonality with their culture.[77] Africans readily recognize the world of the supernatural with its atoning sacrifices, blessings, and curses that are meant to be taken quite seriously.

The fact is, Western Christian churches need believers from other cultures—including gender cultures—to obtain a well-rounded understanding of Scripture (i.e., "It takes a village" to understand the Bible). Again, the book of Revelation, chapter 7, speaks of such a time in heaven when all the nations and tribes will attest the salvation of our Lord through the personal workings of the Lamb. Each nation, tribe, and people will bring praise to him. Revelation shows that the "something larger" at work in the nations is, in fact, God's Spirit. Revelation reminds us that all our theological proclamations are necessarily understatements. Further, Christ's revelation is not complete: "I have yet many things to say to you, but you cannot bear them now. When the Spirit comes, he will guide you into all the truth" (John 15:12–13). In this light, postmodernism presents an opportunity for marginalized and neglected Scriptures to be considered anew.

---

75. Kraft, *Christianity in Culture*, 3.
76. Ibid., 233.
77. Ibid., 234.

10. Separating the Older and Newer Testaments

Taking the anthropomorphisms of God more seriously helps unite the Older and Newer Testaments. A popular idea in Christian culture is that images of love, mercy, and compassion are narrowly associated with Jesus, while less palatable images of wrath and holiness are associated with the God of the "Old" Testament. Said another way, the God of the "Old" Testament is distant whereas the God of the "New" Testament is close. Charles Spurgeon reflects this idea:

> The dispensation of the old covenant was that of distance. When God appeared even to His servant Moses, He said, "Draw not nigh hither: put off thy shoes from thy feet". . . the thought of distance was always prominent . . . . When the gospel came, we were placed on quite another footing . . . distance gave way to nearness.[78]

Yes and no. Yes, Yeshua calls us friends (John 15:15); however, a gulf remains between YHWH and humans. In Revelation 1:13–17, Yeshua appears in all his grandeur with "eyes like a flame of fire . . . his voice like the sound of many waters . . . his face was like the sun . . . . When I [John] saw him I fell at his feet as if dead." This Newer Testament reference mirrors the picture of Moses on Mt. Sinai that Spurgeon describes. No change here. Furthermore, the common notion that God is less judgmental in the Newer Testament can be turned on its head. One can effectively show that Yeshua spoke more about judgment and hell than any other spokesperson in the Bible. One can make the argument that the Older Testament shows more love, mercy, and compassion (Exod 15:13; 2 Sam 24:14; 2 Kgs 13:23) than the Newer Testament. A line of continuity can be drawn from the Older Testament to the Newer Testament regarding the closeness of YHWH with his approaching an incarnate state.

The incarnation of YHWH into our suffering did not commence with Yeshua and culminate in his crucifixion but is evidenced throughout the Older Testament. God-with-us is particularly evident in the Prophets. Through the prophets we witness the *kind* of God this is: this is not a God who suffers-at-a-distance but YHWH who is intimately-involved-with-humankind. The prophets' suffering mirrors the suffering YHWH. Prophet and YHWH are interwoven and cannot be meaningfully separated without losing perspective on the purpose of the prophets as God's mouthpieces. Fretheim explains:

---

78. Spurgeon, *Morning and Evening*, 15.

in the prophet we see decisive continuities with what occurs in the Christ-event. God's act in Jesus Christ is the culmination of a longstanding relationship of God with the world that is much more widespread in the Older Testament than is commonly recognized.[79]

Said another way by theologian Edmond Jacob: "A line not always straight, but nonetheless continuous, leads from the anthropomorphisms of the earliest pages of the Bible, to the incarnation of God in Jesus Christ."[80] Seeing the pathos of God in the Older Testament helps to maintain the continuity between the Older and Newer Testaments about the same relentless, determined love of YHWH. The cross reflects an already existent suffering God, Jung Young Lee says:

> Divine possibility [suffering] was not the consequence of Incarnation but the Incarnation was the consequence of divine possibility . . . . The Incarnation is certainly not the beginning of divine possibility but the continuation of it with an intensification in time and space.[81]

11. Flawed Ways of Knowing

Hiebert reveals the ways of knowing through the illustration of different umpires at a baseball game:[82] The first umpire is a *naive realist* who believes he has absolute objectivity, and therefore totally trusts his senses and his rational mind. Claiming pure objectivity, he "knows" reality in a literal one-to-one correspondence like a photograph. Thus he says with certitude, "There's balls and there's strikes, and I call 'em like I see 'em." Palestinian Christian Naim Ateek does such. He likes to call Jesus a "Palestinian,"[83] not a Jew, and with his anti-Jewish sentiment, shows bias and plain subjectivism. If he doesn't "like" a text, he dismisses it. This is how he reads the Bible:

> When confronted with a difficult passage in the Bible . . . one needs to ask such simple questions as: Is the way I am hearing

---

79. Fretheim, *Theology of the Old Testament*, 166.
80. Jacob, *Theology of the Old Testament*, 32.
81. Lee, *God Suffers with Us*, 56.
82. Hiebert, *Anthropological Reflections on Missiological Issues*, 23. Hiebert illustrates other epistemological positions, such as Absolute Idealism, Critical Idealism, Naive Idealism/Naive Realism, Instrumentalism, and Determinism. Also see Erickson, *Postmodernizing the Faith*, 105.
83. Ateek, *A Palestinian Christian Cry for Reconciliation*, 11.

this the way I have come to know God in Christ? Does this fit the picture I have of God that Jesus has revealed to me? . . . If it does, then that passage is valid and authoritative. If not, then I cannot accept its validity or authority.[84]

"I call 'em like I see 'em," also happens in science when it is driven by agendas and not the pursuit of truth. This is particularly evident in the "soft" sciences of sociology, psychology, political science, gender studies, and cultural anthropology. Examples abound.[85]

The second umpire is a *radical perspectival realist*. She takes the opposite extreme position that reality only exists in the mind. She doubts whether there is anything "real" beyond her judgments. This umpire says, "There's balls and there's strikes, and they ain't *nothin'* until I call 'em." Existentialists and New Age adherents are represented by this approach, which holds, essentially, that reality is a construct of the human mind. Reality is what you experience, feel, and comprehend as a person: certitude about the external world is avoided. Liberal theologians Rudolf Bultmann or John Shelby Spong fall into this worldview. They assert that Jesus did not physically rise from the dead, but rather rose *in the minds* of early Christians, thus making the resurrection true "as they called it."

---

84. Ibid., 81–82.

85. The "hard" sciences are physics, chemistry, biology, botany, geology, astronomy, mathematics, and usually economics. An example of "soft" science gone wrong is when the "experts" in gender studies say there is no difference between boys and girls; boyness and girlness can be swayed through *mere socialization*. The tragic story of David Reimer illustrates the misguided "science" of expert Dr. Money, well respected during his professional life. "Many years later, however, it was revealed that his most famous case involved fraudulent reporting by Money. . . . [He] reported that he had successfully reassigned [David] Reimer as female after a botched infant circumcision in 1966. In 1997, Milton Diamond reported that the reassignment had failed, that Reimer had never identified as female or behaved in a typically feminine manner. At age 14, Reimer, who had fought against being forced to see Dr. Money since age 7, refused to see him again, threatening suicide if he were made to go. Reimer's parents then decided to tell Reimer the truth about his past and his biological sex. Reimer immediately ended the [female] hormone treatments he had been forced to undergo . . . and began taking hormones to bring about the male puberty prevented by the removal of his testes by Dr. Money. He ceased using the name Brenda, which his parents had chosen for him after he began treatment with Dr. Money, and chose a new name, David." At 15 he had "a mastectomy, testosterone therapy, and a phalloplasty. Later he married a woman who had children from a previous marriage and lived as a man until his suicide at age 38 [shortly after his brother's suicide]. Money continued to publish that his work with Reimer was a 'success' even 30 years later. . . . Reimer's parents have stated that they believe Dr. Money's methodology was responsible for the deaths [suicides] of both their sons." "John Money," Wikipedia, http://en.wikipedia.org/wiki/John_Money (last accessed April 2010). See John Colapinto, *As Nature Made Him: The Boy Who Was Raised as a Girl* (New York: Harper Perennial, 2000. 2006).

The third umpire, a *critical realist*, I suggest is the best way to arrive at the truth. He strikes a balance between the two extremes. Here is an awareness that one can be biased and that knowledge can be distorted by culture, language, and history. Here is a less assuming approach—the individual cannot know truthfully or exhaustively; one needs a community of people to help grasp reality.[86] The critical realist umpire would say: "I call it the way I see it, but there is a real pitch and an objective standard against which I must judge it. I can be shown to be right or wrong." Critical realism (or "critical common-sensism" as Charles Pierce called it), is both "realistic" and "critical." It assumes a reality independent of human opinion.[87] Yeshua was a critical realist; knowing human nature, he knew that divorce would continue, believers in him would backslide, false prophets would arise, and a troubled history lay ahead for humanity. Unlike John Lennon's romantic song "Imagine," humanity is not headed towards a utopia of no war, no greed, no religion, no countries, no poverty,[88] or no private property.[89]

Questions

1. Would you break off fellowship with a Christian if you disagreed with the other's understanding of YHWH, even though he or she has multiple supporting Scriptures?
2. What does Luther's advice on reading the different books of the Bible illustrate?
3. The Greeks believed the gods were totally unaffected by humans. Is YHWH the same?
4. Do you agree with theologian Edmond Jacob? "A line not always straight, but nonetheless continuous, leads from the anthropomorphisms of the earliest pages of the Bible, to the incarnation of God in Jesus Christ."

---

86. James Butler from Fuller Theological Seminary uses the analogy of a few blind people who are commissioned to study an elephant and then asked to collaborate with their findings.

87. *Missiological Implications of Epistemological Shifts*, 69.

88. Yeshua said: "For you always have the poor with you, but you will not always have me" (Matt 26:11).

89. The Ten Commandments are still in play today; private property is to be respected.

3

TOWARDS A MATURE FAITH
Commonsense and Multifaceted Theology

The Harvard Outline versus the Net

When studying at Fuller Theological Seminary, one of the largest interdenominational seminaries in the world, professors allowed and considered different competing ideas, such as predestination versus free-willism. The problem I had was that professors expected us to choose sides—one or the other. I did not fit in because I was a "both-and" person. You were fairly graded whichever side you took, so long as you substantiated your arguments. Your paper was structured to the "Harvard outline": introduction, context, methodology, points, and conclusion. In this way of writing, the biblical material is routinely force-fitted and rearranged into a pyramid: the supporting material provides the base, then the material is argued to a tightly reasoned conclusion—the apex. At the apex, nice clear theological truths are announced. For example, if you were a Presbyterian, you might announce the Calvinist-predestination conclusion, or if you were a Methodist, you might announce the John-Wesley-free-willism conclusion. However, the Bible does not submit easily to these well-organized conclusions, as competing Scriptures are left out.

To contrast a more fitting approach, the net structure better suits the Bible. A net is an interweaving, interlinking, organic whole not easily taken apart. The strength of the Bible's authority does not rest on a base or in one place (the Harvard outline weakness), but is distributed throughout the interlocking net. A net better meshes with life and the complex, messy human-YHWH relationship. The locus of truth, the Newer Testament reminds us, is a living, dynamic Person—Yeshua. It is not some static, tidy system of thought—the Harvard outline inclination.

A challenge to a mature faith is then what to do with the sometimes awkward, mismatched data of the Bible. Astronomer Johannes Kepler (1571–1630) is an example of what to do when data does not fit into the status-quo understanding. In Kepler's time, scientists were biased by the Greek philosophy of perfection: God was perfect; creation was perfect; all the workings of the world could be mathematically expressed in the perfect geometrical forms (the circle, triangle, and square). Kepler, however, discovered evidence that the orbit of Mars did not adhere to a perfect circle as presumed. Incontrovertible data showed that the orbit was off by a few minutes. His peers assumed that the minority data was wrong and ignored it in favor of the established "perfect world" theory. Kepler, against popular opinion, stayed honest with the incompatible data. Having a passion for truth, he struggled with the problem for two years—to finally discover that Mars's orbit actually followed an ellipse and not a circle. In like manner, the reader of the Bible should not ignore Scriptures that do not fit into established theological constructs (such as the cherished "Omni-God" mold).

Common-Sensism, Critical-Realism, and the Concrete

Christians (and religious Jews) believe that YHWH created and placed humans in a *real* world. Genesis 1 establishes this. Hindus, to compare, believe the opposite—the physical universe is *illusion* (*maya*), and the only reality worth pursuing is the spiritual. In their view, human beings are all part of a dream that God (Brahma) is having. I believe critical-realism (or common-sensism) is a reliable tool for the Judeo-Christian thinker to work through the chaos and fragmentation of postmodernity. The Bible illustrates that we can be misled, misinformed, and led astray. We need the standard of Scripture as a light for our feet, and we need a community of faith to unlock the enigma of life. Critical-realism has a built-in humility, as it requires constant accountability to the biblical scholars of today and yesteryear. Critical-realism doesn't claim pure objectivity. It recognizes that we cannot know reality in a literal one-to-one correspondence like a photograph; rather, we have maps or models of reality. In critical-realism, knowledge is the correspondence between our mental maps and the real world: knowledge can be *perspectival*, *approximate*, and/or *absolute*. One can always be corrected when more facts come to the fore or when neglected Scripture is proclaimed. With this model, for example, pastors and theologians can be more apt to keep an open discussion around the understanding of Scripture as there is an assumption of bias through our culture, language, and history. Critical-realism affirms the presence of objective truth but recognizes that it is subjectively apprehended—that the map of reality is only an approximation. With this stance in view, I like to mimic Jewish scholar James Kugel's approach to reading the Bible: Do not be sentimental or weak, but try to penetrate its stories "with sympathy and imagination, no condescension only a relentless desire to enter . . . . [T]he biblical characters can indeed come back to life, and their world, their way of seeing, can let us in to take the measure of things."[1]

Nevertheless, critical-realism poses the danger of relativizing away the truth of the Bible. To prevent this, a distinction must be made between *Scripture*, the final authority, and *theology*, which is an attempt to understand Scripture. The Bible says, "we see through a glass darkly," not because of limits of the divine revelation but because of the limits of human knowledge. Scripture is greater than our understanding of it. Hiebert—who has a missionary background—observes that committed Christians in different cultures will interpret the Scriptures differently because they ask different questions and view reality in different ways. He concludes, "the global church must become an international hermeneutical community . . . to check one another's cultural biases."[2]

The apostle Paul had the approach of a critical-realist, which did not lead to relativizing the Bible. When confronted with the problem that some people were following the different theologies of Peter, Apollos, or himself, Paul did not try to force agreement between their different theologies or to affirm his over theirs. Rather, he affirmed the central tenets of the gospel—namely, the atoning death and resurrection of Yeshua (1 Cor 15; 1 Tim 2:5–16; 2 Tim 2:8). The unity of the church lay in allegiance to the crucified and resurrected Christ. To deny this was not simply another theological point of view, but heresy (Gal 1:6–11). Matthew, Mark, Luke, John, and Paul each cast a different light on Yeshua. Paul recognized theological diversity and saw this variety as an expression of the freedom of the faith and of the many forms the Spirit's work can take (1 Cor 12:4–6; Eph 4:1–7).

---

1. Kugel, *The God of Old*, 3.
2. Hiebert, *Missiological Implications of Epistemological Shifts*, 112–13.

Back to the Hebraic Roots of the Bible

As already mentioned, the early church was infiltrated by the "God-of-the-Greek-philosophers." God was further fossilized by the Enlightenment and modernism. "Omni-God" was fixed by rational and abstract constructs—all done with the good intention to elevate YHWH to the utmost. To counter, the Bible has an aversion for the abstract and ideal. The Hebrews dealt with concreteness, doing, and feeling. To be specific, the Hebrew language is action centered, as signaled by Hebrew sentence structure in which the verb is usually placed before the subject, for example, "He judged, (namely) the king." The reverse is true in English sentence structure, where the noun or subject is placed first, then the verb: "The king judged."[3] Hebrew has few abstract terms, as George Smith points out, "Hebrew may be called primarily a language of the senses. The words originally expressed concrete or material things and movements or actions which struck the senses or startled the emotions. Only secondarily and in metaphor could they be used to denote abstract or metaphysical ideas."[4] Consequently, the Bible shows abstract thoughts or immaterial conceptions through material or physical terminology. Consider the following: "look" is "lift up his eyes" (Gen 22:4); "be angry" is "burn in one's nostrils" (Exod 4:14); "disclose something to another" or "reveal" is "unstop someone's ears" (Ruth 4:4); "have no compassion" is "hard-heartedness" (1 Sam 6:6); "stubborn" is "stiff-necked" (2 Chron 30:8).[5]

Jewish anthropologist Raphael Patai observes that Jews avoid making doctrinal creeds because they favor the concrete over the abstract.[6] In the same vein, Marvin Wilson states that "today's church must not forget that the earliest theology in the New Testament is relational or existential rather than propositional or credal."[7] The Bible's focus is on our relationship with the living YHWH and not on intellectual assent to a creed. The Hebraic worldview can be characterized as primitive, paradoxical, and scandalously exclusive. It is "primitive" or "clunky" because—unlike the sophisticated Greek-Enlightenment-modernist approach—the Hebrews tend to stay with concrete, sensory, and unrefined realities. They have a situatedness and a critical-realism about themselves. The characters and events in the Bible are not described elaboratively as today's novelist would; only pertinent informa-

---

3. Wilson, *Our Father Abraham*, 137.
4. G. Smith, "The Hebrew Genius as Exhibited in the Old Testament," 10.
5. Wilson, *Our Father Abraham*, 137.
6. Patai, *The Jewish Mind*, 67.
7. Wilson, *Our Father Abraham*, 138.

tion is given. The Jews are unapologetic about paradoxes in the relationship between Hashem and humanity.[8] Fortunately, Christians in the past, such as Martin Luther, Jonathan Edwards, and Charles Spurgeon, acknowledged paradox in Scripture. Evangelical theologians appear to support paradox. J. I. Packer, for instance, accepts a principle of "antinomy," but to him it is *not a real* contradiction, but only an apparent one.[9]

Franz Bibfeldt (an imaginary friend of Martin Marty) presents paradox using the following terms: both/and, yes and no, or all-of-the-above thinking.[10] This will not sit well with those who always hold to either/or thinking. However, consider Yeshua's reply to the Pharisees' trick, either/or question about who they should pay taxes to—either God or Caesar (Matt 22:15). Yeshua's reply was both/and: we are to pay taxes to *both* Caesar *and* God. More examples: the kingdom of God is *both* here now *and* in the future; we are *both* part of this world *and* part of the next (John 17:14–18); we are *both* sinners *and* righteous (Rom 7:24; 8:30); and we are obliged to *both* church *and* state authority (Rom 13:1–10).

Here lies the advantage of adopting a Hebrew view. Yes, pastors and theologians acknowledge absolute truth in the Bible, but they can also loosen up to the conversation happening within the Bible with its sometimes-competing ideas: James is chatting with Paul; Psalm 73 is challenging Proverbs; Ecclesiastes is questioning the praises of King David; and Psalm 88 counterbalances the triumphalism of Isaiah or Revelation.

If I may play around a bit: The new science of quantum mechanics of subatomic particles has also come around to a more "primitive," paradoxical, holistic way of describing things, as does the Bible. Subatomic particles—the building blocks of the entire universe—scientists now say, are not indestructible as once thought. Moreover, they behave in a "fuzzy" and even unpredictable way. They are paradoxical as they simultaneously behave as particles and as a wave. They can affect each other's behavior even millions of miles apart (called quantum entanglement). On another note, the prospect of creating artificial intelligence (AI) in computers will require "parallel logic" and "paradox." The normal binary operation of computers (either "on" or "off" / either "1" or "0") cannot simulate nuanced human behavior.

---

8. Examples include Jesus, Paul, and contemporary Jewish authors such as Abraham Heschel, Anson Laytner, and David Blumenthal.

9. Packer, *Evangelism and Sovereignty*, 18–19.

10. Marty and Brauer, *The Unrelieved Paradox*, 196.

Theology as a Crude Map

If our faith is in YHWH over human-made maps about the Bible, we choose a stance of critical-realism that affirms the presence of objective truth that is nevertheless subjectively apprehended. Our map of reality (theology) is only an approximation. Critical-realism does not claim pure objectivity. It recognizes that we cannot know reality in a literal one-to-one correspondence; rather, we have maps or models of reality. Knowledge, in critical-realism, is the correspondence between our mental maps and the real world. Such an approach promotes discussion with fellow believers to continuously check our reality. Knowledge can be *perspectival, approximate, relative,* and/or *absolute.*

Perspectival. When the Bible uses the term "sunrise," to be correct, it should say "earthrise," as the earth does the moving to cause night and day. On another matter, Jesus said the mustard seed is the smallest seed: Yes, for Judea, but not from a global perspective, as the orchid has the smallest seed.

Approximate. Was the story of the Good Samaritan a historical story or a parable? Did the rooster crow once or twice when Peter forsook Christ? Did the Lord chose seventy or seventy two disciples? Did the traitor Judas die by hanging or did he tear open his insides by falling, headfirst? My response to the above discrepancies is a yawn.

Relative. When Yeshua sent out disciples, he gave different instructions about bringing or not bringing sandals, staff, sword, clothing, and purse (Matt 10:10; Luke 22:36)—we can assume these are time sensitive. Also, Yeshua said *only* preach to the Jews (Matt 10:5); yet later this is opened up to the Gentiles.

Absolute. YHWH is present. He is holy. He wants abundant life for all humans. His salvation and judgment is already here and is coming. We need a Messiah. In the next life, the Lord brings complete pleasure and good to his followers.

Common-Sensism Applied to the Creation/Evolution Debate

With a stance of critical-realism (or common-sensism) one can always shift when more facts come to the fore or when neglected Scriptures are proclaimed. With this methodology, biblical thinkers are more apt to keep an open discussion around the understanding of the Bible with an assumption of bias through their particular life experiences, gender, culture, and personality. Christians ought to be the most open-minded in the public marketplace of ideas because our security does not come from dogma, but in a relationship with YHWH, *the integration point of everything*. We have firm beliefs yet we are flexible—we have room to wiggle.

An example where Christians have abysmally failed to leave matters open enough is the evolution/creation debate. Growing up as a Catholic, evolution never was an issue. It was deemed interesting, "I guess that is how God did it" (theistic evolution). Catholics, I guess, learned from history, having fought the wrong battle centuries before. They botched up by opposing Galileo's assertion that the earth revolved around the sun. The Genesis account of creation is so very brief and does not purport to be an exhaustive, scientific description of how things exactly came into being. As Francis Schaeffer used to say, two solid, nonscientific truths are communicated: *God did it* and *humans are special*.[11] Consequently, Christians have tremendous latitude to speculate about the age of the earth, about fossils of primitive "humans," and about dinosaurs. Perhaps God created a pre-Adamic race who lived between verses 1 and 2 of Genesis chapter 1, which he later judged and destroyed.[12]

If we may speculate a bit: Could it be that YHWH used the "mechanism of chance" to create the world over billions of years? According to Proverbs it seems that even the outcome of chance happenings are known to the Lord.[13] Proverbs 16:33 says, "The lot is cast into the lap, but the decision is wholly from the Lord." There is ample precedent in nature for finding solutions by active employment of chance. Chance is used in the human body to fight germs: When a germ penetrates the body, white blood cells divide rapidly using *chance* to create myriads of antibodies with the plan that one of them will "match" the germ. When the correct antibody is found, the *chance* mutation stops, and only the correct antibody is thereafter reproduced until the germ is annihilated. Is it possible that between the lines in the record of YHWH's spoken words of creation, "the mechanism of chance" was similarly employed to assemble the plants, different creatures,

---

11. Francis Schaeffer called these the "limitations" dictated by Genesis (L'Abri, Switzerland, 1981).

12. Genesis 1:2 uses the words *tocu* and *bocu* (formless and void), which are also found in reference to God's destruction of Noah's world, where *tocu* and *bocu* are associated with judgment. This could imply that God created a pre-Adamic world (Gen 1:1) which he judged and destroyed (Gen 1:2). Could it be that God started again and made our world following an attempt that was unacceptable and equally inconsequential to the new, successful story? Bible teacher Derek Prince believes demons are not fallen angels but disembodied spirits that come from this possible pre-Adamic race.

13. The Lord used the casting of lots (chance) to arrange circumstances in order to speak to Zechariah about his coming son, John the Baptist (Luke 1:9).

or even the image of himself (humankind)? Would you break off fellowship with a Christian who speculates this?

Guidelines to Interpret the Bible

In interpreting the Bible I do not pretend to have a foolproof, all-encompassing way to understand the Bible. Here are some guidelines I adhere to in obtaining a more accurate map of the YHWH-human relationship:

1. It takes a village.

No individual (including this author) is able to attain truth about a matter without the help of others. Jewish tradition says, "neither an individual man nor a single generation by its own power can erect the bridge that leads to Truth."[14] The Hebrews treasured the wisdom of their forebears, believing that revelation builds piece by piece with each generation.[15] As the saying goes, "It takes a village to raise a child." Likewise, it takes the whole church plus Israel—men and women, international, present and past—to interpret the Bible. Thus, the reader will notice, throughout this book, I make an effort to collaborate supporting evidence from different sources: biblical scholars, historians, theologians, linguists, Judaic thinkers, and so forth.

2. Right thinking isn't enough, correct attitude is needed.

Often the Bible depicts people falling into falsehood not because they lost intellectual prowess, but because their hearts turned away from the things of the Lord. J. I. Packer's prerequisite for reading and understanding the Bible is submission to the recommendations of Psalm 119,[16] which exhorts us to be awe-struck, humble, teachable, and open-eyed, seeking with our whole heart, learning God's ordinances, thinking, meditating, and asking God for understanding. This Psalm emphasizes that the heart is to be correctly aligned to the Lord of the universe in order to assure correct comprehension.

Likewise, Dutch thinker Herman Dooyeweerd made the human heart the starting point of all inquiry and thought. If the heart's motives and attitudes are misaligned, all subsequent thinking is misguided. Yeshua revealed

---

14. A. Heschel, *Moral Grandeur and Spiritual Audacity*, 9.

15. "And you shall not profane the holy things of the children of Israel, that you die not" (Num 18:32).

16. Packer, *Knowing God*, 22.

the same: "But what comes out of the mouth proceeds from the heart and defiles a man. For out of the human heart come evil thoughts, murder, adultery, fornication, theft, false witness, slander" (Matt 15:18–19). The heart, with its attitudes and motives, influences a person's thinking, seeing, and feeling.[17] Dooyeweerd claims the heart is never neutral—it is either turned against God or turned towards him. Consequently, we are all consciously or unconsciously driven by deep-seated religious presuppositions.[18] Catholic thinker G. K. Chesterton observed that when people cease to believe in God they do not believe in nothing, rather they believe in anything. The theologian, thinker, scientist, or artist can never have absolute neutrality, as all are animated by inner attitudes and motives. Paul further clarifies that when people do not accept the Creator, they replace the Creator with created things (Rom 1:25). Dooyeweerd explains it in a different way: When people cut off orientation to God, they have no other option but to deify something in the created world. Consequently, a substitute philosophy/ideology of material*ism*, environmental*ism*, spiritual*ism*, evolution*ism*, secular*ism*, scient*ism*, or rational*ism* takes the place of YHWH.[19]

Heschel says attitude is crucial when reading the Bible; we may sense the story, the idea, and the concept but miss the pathos and realness of God. "[If we are moved] by intellectual vanity, striving to show our superiority to the text; or as barren souls who go sight-seeing to the words of the prophets, we discover the shells but miss the core.... To sense the presence of God in the Bible, one must learn *to be present* to God in the Bible. Presence is not a concept, but a situation."[20] Thus the Bible is the frontier to apprehending YHWH.

---

17. As an example of how motives can distort thinking, consider the twin studies conducted by scientists Bailey and Prillard (who were animated by a gay agenda). Their much-publicized 1991 study of gay twins was heavily distorted due to the domain of their research being restricted to gay people who read the advertisement for the survey in a gay activist magazine. This was not good scientific research as twins in the larger population were not included. This is an example of an activist-political agenda influencing supposed "objective" science. Similarly, the famous Alfred Kinsey studies (1948) on sexual behavior in America were distorted by a lopsided domain (prisons and brothels). Kinsey said 10 percent of males had a homosexual orientation, when in fact today's estimate is 4 percent (Somashekhar, "Health Survey").

18. Dooyeveerd, *In the Twilight of Western Thought*, 1–60. Kierkegaard also makes this point forcefully in his book *Either/Or*.

19. Dooyeweerd, *Critique of Theoretical Thought*, 12.

20. *God in Search of Man*, 252.

3. Stuff is missing.

I assume our current church culture is incomplete. Christians have been arrogant in the past, distancing themselves from their Jewish roots. As far back as the Newer Testament time, Paul observed the arrogance of Gentile Christians and cautioned, "Consider this: You do not support the root, but the root supports you" (Rom 11:18b). We (Gentile Christians) are the branches artificially grafted into the olive tree (Israel). Our spiritual origin is in the Hebrew patriarch Abraham—we are his seeds (Gal 3:29). And as descendants of Abraham, we are heirs to promised blessings (Acts 2:25; cf. 3:12).[21] Catholics have made progress here: Pope John Paul II—acknowledging indebtedness to the Jews—said they are "our elder brothers" in the faith of Abraham. I take it for granted that our inherited Christianity is impoverished until the full inclusion of the Jews occurs. Only when they find their Messiah will we experience the full "riches" of the gospel (Rom 11:12). In this regard, I suppose that as Gentiles we miss the full import of the Older Testament, which directly bears on a full understanding of the Yeshua in the Newer Testament. Gentiles are often "spiritual tourists," missing the underlying depth of the Older Testament. Yeshua made clear the need for Older Testament knowledge: "Those experts in Jewish law who are now my disciples have double treasures—from the Old Testament as well as from the New!" (Matt 13:52, *The Living Bible*, Catholic Edition). Paul indicates that God's timing in this matter is crucial—now is the time of the Gentiles (Rom 11). I also assume stuff is missing because we do not communicate enough with the international church and the Eastern Church. (The Eastern Church split from the Western Church when the Roman Empire split.)

4. "Know thyself."

Knowing *ourselves* is essential in knowing YHWH. Since we are image bearers of YHWH (Gen 1:26), we learn about the nature of YHWH when we study ourselves (John Calvin made this connection). Human traits such as thinking, self-awareness, love, communication, and feelings are to be found in YHWH. Thus, anthropomorphisms can be taken seriously. Fretheim says, "'the image of God' gives us permission to reverse the process and, by looking at the human, learn what Yahweh is like."[22] So too, to obtain the

---

21. As people of faith we have a familial relationship with "our father Abraham," who is the exemplar of faith (John 8:53; Acts 7:2). Hebrews 11 furthers the idea of Abraham's faithful obedience as a model to Christians.

22. Fretheim, *The Suffering of God*, 11.

full image of YHWH, both male and female persons are needed to give the whole picture, or better yet, the whole community of believers, dead and alive, gives full expression of the "image." Secular people also contribute to revealing the "image," as they are still, inescapably, image bearers.

The Scriptures speak of "knowing" God. In most Semitic languages "to know" signifies sexual union as well as mental and spiritual activity.[23] Therefore, knowledge of God would not only involve abstract ideas about God but would encompass inner appropriation, feeling, and a reception into the soul—of YHWH.[24] Knowing him in this way would include feeling what he feels, at times. This only works when a person has sympathy for YHWH's feelings as exemplified by the prophets. The Newer Testament speaks of this also—Yeshua said the Holy Spirit would communicate the desires, demands, and *yearnings* of the Father (John 16:7–8, 13–14).

5. Avoid reductionism
(making something simple that is irreducibly complex).

In theology, some matters will remain irreducibly complex, namely, the YHWH-human relationship. The secularist, evolutionist, and sometimes the Christian fundamentalist or Christian progressive[25] (yes, you read correctly, Christian progressive) can fall into a misguided stance of equating appearance with reality: This represents an underdeveloped sense of the depth of life.

Abraham Heschel asserts that everything we say about God or the world is an *understatement*—that all our conceptions and verbalizations fall short of fully expressing reality. He says, "any genuine encounter with reality is an encounter with the unknown . . . preconceptual, presymbolic, immediate theory, speculation, generalization, and hypothesis are efforts to clarify

---

23. A. Heschel, *The Prophets*, 1:57.
24. Ibid.
25. For example, progressive Christians have fallen for today's gay propaganda that homosexuality is *merely* the way one is born. Fundamentalist Christians say that homosexuality is *merely* a matter of choice. Both positions are equally reductionistic: Homosexuality is a complex interplay between choice, social environment, and biological predisposition. Talk about black-and-white thinking and not being nuanced about matters! I have found, at times, progressive thinkers to be black-and-white in their thinking: "Low self-esteem creates criminals" (popular mantra in the 80s) or "poverty causes crime." After some research, it was found that prisons are filled with criminals with *high* self-esteem ("Prisoners Have Higher Self-Esteem"). And what about "poverty causes crime"? Well, during the Great Depression violence and crime actually went down (Sullivan, "Experts: Bad Economies Don't Cause Crime Waves").

and to validate the insights which preconceptual experience provides."[26] In other words, preconceptual insights are often lost in our conceptualizations. An idolatry of rationalism goes so far as to suggest that knowledge comes only after a thing is conceptualized, or after the encounter is reflected upon and verbalized. We should always assume that there is a disparity between what we encounter and the words and symbols we use to express them; consequently, whatever we say is an *understatement*.[27] This orientation comes with an awareness of limitation.

Heschel cautions against our lazy reductionist tendencies:

> Religious thinking is in perpetual danger of giving primacy to concepts and dogmas and to forfeit the immediacy of insights . . . concepts must not become screens but windows . . . . The roots of ultimate insights are found . . . not on the level of discursive thinking, but on the level of wonder and radical amazement, in the depth of awe, in our sensitivity to the mystery, in our awareness of the ineffable.[28]

Heschel ends with his favorite word *ineffable*, or mystery. There is a difference between a mystery and a puzzle. A puzzle is something one can figure out, after a time. A mystery remains elusive. In many respects, YHWH is close but elusive.

Postmodernism and Theology

Historian Maxie Burch asks the question: would the Reformation have happened if there wasn't the preceding groundwork of the Renaissance? The Renaissance, definitely, was a threat to the church because of its strident humanism. However, its driving renewing spirit, *ad fontes* (lit. "back to the fountains," i.e., the sources), set the foundation for the Reformation. It gave impetus to reexamine prevailing theology and challenge the backslidden church.[29] Likewise, postmodernism has its hazards, but it can challenge our established, cherished notions about "Omni-God."

Toulmin describes a shift from modernity to postmodernity. Modernity's truth was

- *universal* (something is true only if it is true everywhere);

---

26. A. Heschel, *Between God and Man*, 64.
27. Ibid., 65.
28. Ibid.
29. "Medieval and Reformation Christianity," podcast, at 29 minutes.

- *general* (truth remains true from locale to locale);
- *timeless* (truth does not change with time).

Under modernity's approach it was difficult to piece timely and particular notions of YHWH's wrath, love, vengefulness, mercy, and jealousy into general, universal, and timeless theological concepts. Postmodernism, by comparison, accepts as true that which is particular, local, and timely.[30] Under this paradigm it is easier to voice the paradoxical particulars about YHWH.

Transitory, timely, and particular notions of YHWH (his anger or vengeance) can be kept intact without need for a grand, coherent scheme. When Yeshua was confronted with the question about the way to heaven, he did not direct the hearers to an idea or a grand scheme but to *a Person*—himself: "I am the way, and the truth, and the life; no one comes to the Father, but by me" (John 14:6). The locus of truth is not set in objective, self-subsistent, eternal ideas as the Greeks believed, but wrapped in an eternal *Person* or *Subject*. Abraham Heschel points to the same: "There are no ultimate laws, no eternal ideas. The Lord alone is ultimate and eternal."[31]

Walter Brueggemann compares the postmodern approach to therapy where the therapist is not concerned with the larger scheme of things (though it is important to keep it as a reference); rather, the therapist pursues specific details that hold hidden power over the afflicted. The therapist does not know everything in advance; however, unguarded rumination often produces an insight or illumination that liberates and heals the patient.[32]

David Blumenthal describes a postmodern approach to Jewish theology through the idea of *seriatim*[33] or sailing into the wind. The Bible, like life, is irreducibly complex, filled with variety and nuance, and is not given to easy straightforward acquisition. We walk the path of life in a zigzag fashion, the same way a sailor sails into the wind. To move forward, the sailor sets a goal into the wind but has to tack back and forth across the wind to move. Similarly, the Bible unfolds its contents in a zigzag way, revealing who Hashem is in different historical stories. Commonly Hashem emerges as an absolute, omnipotent Lord, sometimes as a fragile Person. This is how life is—we live life in series, one moment after another, or one event after

---

30. Toulmin, *Cosmopolis*, 186–92.
31. A. Heschel, *The Prophets*, 1:217.
32. Brueggemann, *Texts under Negotiation*, 20–22.
33. *Seriatim* is a medieval Latin word meaning "one after another, one by one in succession."

another. We cannot experience everything at once. Likewise, to a degree, Hashem is different in varying circumstances.[34]

Rabbi Anson Laytner confirms the zigzag way of the Bible, with its use of "the law-court approach"—a distinctly Jewish tradition—where *point* is always met by *counterpoint*. The book of Job specifically uses the law-court pattern. It is implemented as a teaching device to bring forth the full range of details surrounding Job's plight—why is evil happening to him? This question, labeled *theodicy*, is explored by the book of Job, with its characters—including YHWH—using *point* and *counterpoint*. Incidentally, this method is helpful as this vacillation happens naturally when we wrestle with YHWH in times of doubt and suffering.

In the Bible, YHWH is never impersonal. He does not merely apply timeless standards to our lives. His responses are never mechanical, but are mediated by his pathos, causing different outcomes for different individuals or communities according to their actions. For example, Hosea presents a remarkable image of a personal YHWH in love with his people:

> Like grapes in the wilderness,
> I found Israel.
> Like the first fruit on the fig tree,
> in its first season,
> I saw your fathers . . .
> When Israel was a child, I loved him,
> and out of Egypt I called my son
> Hosea 9:10; 11:1
> In some situations, the Lord displays intense anger:
> . . . they forgot me
> So I will be to them like a lion,
> like a leopard I will lurk beside the way.
> I will fall upon them like a bear robbed of her cubs,
> I will tear open their breast,
> and there I will devour them like a lion,
> as a wild beast would rend them.
> Hosea 13:6–8

In a word, with the postmodernist attitude, the difficult attributes of YHWH—his wrath, passion, and vengeance—need not be elevated to primacy but can be affirmed as transitory, particular, timely, and local. The tendency to conceptualize and homogenize different attributes of God into one theological system is decreased, allowing YHWH to be free and personal.

---

34. Blumenthal (*Facing the Abusing God*, 47–52) allows wiggle room and lets the nuances in the Bible remain; however, his methodology, if taken to the extreme, can lead to debilitating fragmentation—which is the ultimate plight of postmodernity.

For example, YHWH can be loving *and* vengeful, mother *and* father, lover *and* warrior (Isa 63:13–16), king *and* sufferer, king *and* servant. He can raise up the poor and give power to a king (1 Sam 2:1–10).

Questions

1. Do you agree with Dooyeveerd that thoughts take second place, that humans are primarily swayed by their heart, which is either orientated towards or against God?

2. Klitsie says the Bible has absolute truth, but parts are perspectival, approximate, and relative. What do you think?

3. Klitsie is going with the more concrete and sensory words of the Bible (like the original Hebrew), and with the *given* anthropomorphisms of the Bible (YHWH can be angry and can be impacted by humans). Theologians through the millennia have replaced these with more sophisticated, abstract, propositional, and conceptual words. Which do you think is closer to the truth?

4

THE PATHOS OF YHWH, YESHUA, AND THE HOLY SPIRIT

HERE IS THE CRUX of my book: YHWH is the "Most Moved Mover" as depicted by the prophets and Yeshua. This is not the detached and remote God-of-the-philosophers—the "Unmoved Mover."

If YHWH is a covenant maker and engaged lover, is he set up for "heartache," as we are, by his choice to commit to humanity so passionately? Is it accurate to say that when the Holy One is betrayed or replaced as a lover, he is "jealous," "angry," and "vengeful," comparable to humans? YHWH's "agape" love is usually regarded as a continuous flow of "unconditional positive regard," never demanding anything in return. People say that he is God, so he doesn't need anything. Right? This love has been compared to the sun: continually radiating out light regardless of response, reliant only on its own resources to emit energy. Does this detached perspective really match biblical evidence? Contrary to popular assumption, the Bible does not split love into *agape* and *eros, divine heavenly love* and *vulgar earthly human love*. To be specific, the Septuagint—the Greek translation of the Older Testament—uses only one word for love, whether its object is food, God, sex, money, or a spouse. Through history people have separated types of love: God's "agape" love and "human love." Plato, the Stoics, Augustine, Luther, Søren Kierkegaard, Catholic theologians, Karl Barth, C. S. Lewis, Jimmy Carter, Bible dictionaries and lexicons, all say this.[1] I argue that

---

1. • In his *Symposium*, Plato made a sharp distinction between noble, heavenly love (*ouranios eros*) and dishonorable, vulgar love (*pandemos eros*). The former seeks after clear, rational knowledge, and the latter is "of the body rather than of the soul." Plato dissociated love from all physical contacts and believed woman had no part in the creation of heavenly love.

human *romantic love* is not a distortion of or qualitatively different from "agape" love but is found on a continuum with "agape" love. Romantic love need not be demeaned as an inferior "earthly" love only consigned to fleshly mortals, but it can be applied to YHWH. Certainly, YHWH's love is grander and everlasting—plenty of Scriptures indicate this. Yet the Bible lets on that this love has romantic overtures for even the most despicable human. Judaic scholar James Kugel says no reasons are given why Hashem "falls in love" with Abraham and Israel. In the Newer Testament why does Yeshua have favorites: Peter, James, and John? Having favorites implies that God's love is not always meted out remotely and abstractly in an impartial manner.

In the biblical narrative we are struck by how the violation of this love between the Holy One and humans elicits a response as passionate and forceful as the bond itself. Wrath and love have an intricate relationship: rather than being mutually exclusive, wrath can prove the intensity of love. The embarrassing monstrous judgment of YHWH *explicit* in the Older Testament and the book of Revelation (*implicit* in the rest of the Newer Testament) is not a denial of his love but evidence of it. Within this paradoxical understanding, even theological difficulties such as the Holocaust and 9/11 must be revisited.

First, some fragmentary glimpses of YHWH's love:

- The Stoics held that "the *passion* of love is a craving from which good men are free." In Greco-Roman culture many philosophers carried forward the view that true love is to be defined as intellectual aspiration. Accordingly, they believed that all emotional expressions of love deserved to be shunned.
- Augustine of Hippo gave Plato's two forms of love a Latin expression by differentiating divine love (*caritas*) from cupid love (*cupiditas*) and by calling the latter the root of all evil. He also believed sex was linked to original sin!
- Luther, trained as an Augustinian monk, proposed that natural human inclinations are antithetical to the realm of divine grace.
- Søren Kierkegaard (a Lutheran) held that *agape* is totally removed from common human affections. He contended that there is not "one single word" in the New Testament commending "earthly love" and "if anyone thinks that a man by falling in love . . . has learned to know the Christian love, then he is seriously mistaken."
- Catholic theologian Ceslaus Spicq declared that *agape* is "completely different" in meaning from erotic love.
- Karl Barth took the thought further by claiming that there is an "antithesis" between *agape* and every other type of love.
- Denis de Rougemont, in his acclaimed *Love in the Western World*, divorces *agape* from the emotions.
- Anders Nygren's seminal work *Agape and Eros* holds the most sway on the issue. He contends that human love is egocentric and possessive, while Christian love "has nothing to do with desire and longing."
- Biblical dictionaries and lexicons assume a clear distinction between *agape* and *eros*. All of the above are indicated in William Phipps's article "The Sensuousness of Agape."

- YHWH experiences hurt when his love is rejected. Jeremiah's poetic language describes it so:
  a bridegroom now abandoned (2:2)
  a wounded, betrayed father (3:19)

- The Lord is saddened over lost opportunities:

  I thought how I would set you among my sons, and give you a pleasant land, a heritage most beauteous of all the nations. And I thought you would call me, My Father, and would not turn from following me.
  Jeremiah 3:19

  O Jerusalem, Jerusalem, killing the prophets and stoning those who are sent to you! How often would I have gathered your children together as a hen gathers her brood under her wings, and you would not!
  Luke 13:34

- He has hopes, yearnings, and love for his people. When they are dashed, he is anguished, disappointed, and feels betrayed:

  Is Ephraim my dear son?
  Is he my darling child?
  For as often as I speak against him,
  I do remember him still
  Therefore my heart yearns for him.
  I will surely have mercy on him, says the Lord.
  Jeremiah 31:20

- The Lord doesn't always exude "unconditional positive regard" to people, he can discriminate:

  With the loyal thou dost show thyself loyal;
  with the blameless man thou dost show thyself blameless;
  with the pure thou dost show thyself pure,
  and with the crooked thou dost show thyself perverse.
  2 Samuel 22:26–27

- YHWH has empathy for humans, but can become an enemy if hurt:

  In all their affliction he was afflicted,
  and the angel of his presence saved them;
  in his love and in his pity he redeemed them;
  he lifted them up and carried them all the days of old.
  But they rebelled and grieved his holy Spirit;
  therefore he turned to be their enemy,
  and himself fought against them.
  Isaiah 63:9-10

- The Lord can briefly turn his back on humans, but his overriding stance is compassion:

  > For a brief moment I forsook you,
  > but with great compassion I will gather you.
  > In overflowing wrath for a moment I hid my face from you,
  > but with everlasting love I will have compassion on you,
  > says the Lord, your Redeemer.
  > Isaiah 54:7–8

- The door is always open, the Lord wants to have intimate fellowship with humans:

  > Behold, I stand at the door and knock; if any one hears my voice and opens the door, I will come in to him and eat with him, and he with me.
  > Revelation 3:20

YHWH is deeply invested in relations with humans and is vulnerable to rejection and neglect. (Philosophers and many theologians would cringe at this statement.) He reacts to human responses, sometimes turning on them ("depart from me into the eternal fire prepared for the devil and his angels," Matt 25:41), but his overarching stance is compassion (*hesed*). YHWH's attachment to humans is covenanted and preordained, yet not a settled matter. He is demanding. His love is persistent. The human response can be tragic, as sometimes the more he pursues, the more we run away (Hos 11:2).

Ironically, it is liberal thinker Jack Miles who brings to Christians a more biblical understanding of YHWH. He takes seriously the references to YHWH's emotions and personhood. Sophisticated Bible readers routinely discount these by saying that YHWH is only "pretending" to be emotional.

Though the Bible was written by different authors over many generations, it owes its amazing unity to the singularity of its Protagonist, YHWH. Miles dares to explore territory where Christians fear to tread: *Who* exactly is this YHWH? *What is he really like?* In Miles's observation—unburdened about debates of what is meant literally and what is intended to be figurative—a Person emerges who is revealed, yet concealed; who is torn by conflicting urges; who creates and destroys; who is tender and, on occasion, fierce; powerful, yet powerless; all-knowing, but sometimes unsure of outcomes. Taking seriously the entire self-revelation of YHWH and allowing his character to emerge from the pages of the Bible, YHWH appears as "constant,"[2] independent, and self-sufficient *but also* relational,

---

2. I use the word "constant," agreeing with Bruce Ware's claim that God is

self-involving, dependent, and vulnerable. YHWH, the all-powerful and all-knowing, willingly involves himself with flakey self-willed humans and, respecting their autonomy, makes himself seemingly powerless and unsure because he does not fore-know *all* human responses. Maybe we can say he is more a macro-manager than a micro-manager. (Nevertheless, he may micro-manage aspects of life: he knows the number of hairs on your head, Luke 12:6–7; he fore-knew micro-aspects of Joseph and Daniel's life.) Life is a somewhat open-ended drama, in which humans are actors *with* YHWH. In this drama we see ourselves reflected in YHWH's very personal and humanlike responses. We experience his jealousy, love, disappointment, joy, intentionality, anger, thinking, sadness, communicating, consciousness,[3] complaining,[4] attachment, and so forth. Consequently, we share the same frame of reference. What emerges is a mirror—we see ourselves reflected in YHWH, even though he is transcendent. (To repeat, being "image bearers" gives us reason to believe in this direction.)

We share likeness with YHWH. Miles speculates and presents YHWH as "an amalgam of several personalities in one character. Tension among these personalities makes Yahweh difficult, but it also makes Him compelling, even addictive."[5] Stories of the Bible reveal that YHWH and humans share similarities of personality and character. The term "personality" indicates that which displays conscious intentions, certain qualities, personal modes of expression or behavior or movements of a living being. The term "character" implies having a unity and integrity of person. Though YHWH may manifest what we call different personalities, he is one ("Hear, O Israel, the Lord our God is one"). Further, "character" implies a combination of qualities that distinguishes a person or the combined moral and ethical structure of the person.

The Older Testament depicts the Holy One as alive and responsive, not as a mild saint but a gritty character. Like the protagonist in a drama, he undergoes character development. To be specific, in Genesis 6:6, he learns a disappointing thing about humans and changes his tactics.[6] Miles adds,

---

"ontologically immutable in his being." "An Evangelical Reexamination of the Doctrine of the Immutability of God," 442.

3. Genesis 6:6–7.

4. The book of Numbers, particularly, records Moses complaining to YHWH, YHWH complaining to Moses, the people complaining to Moses, Moses complaining to the people, the people complaining to YHWH, and YHWH complaining about their complaining. On this mutual irritability, see Miles, *God: A Biography*, 133.

5. *God: A Biography*, 6.

6. The "evolution" of God from the OT to the NT is partially true; however, YHWH's character stays constant from the Older to the Newer Testament.

"Experience shapes character, and character determines action."[7] YHWH is gritty because he involves himself in the messiness of broken human lives. He has chosen to enter time and be impacted by human actions and attitudes. This is apparent in the Older Testament, but exemplified most clearly in the person of Yeshua. Like the Protagonist of the Older Testament, Yeshua is loving, demanding,[8] persuadable,[9] vulnerable,[10] gritty,[11] and primarily concerned with the human-divine relationship. Judaic scholar Wyschogrod echoes this outline of Hashem's personality:

> He [Hashem] is a Person. He is one of the characters who appears in the stories told in the Bible. He has a personality that undergoes development in the course of the story. He creates humans with certain expectations, which are apparently disappointed, and he is then sorry that he has created them. He is subject to the emotions of anger, and jealousy, among others. He is also filled with burning love, particularly toward Abraham and his descendants. He desires certain things and detests others. He is faithful in the sense of keeping his promises, even when for long periods of time it seems that he has forgotten them and has no intention of keeping them.[12]

Let us unpack this more "earthly" love that is "inappropriate" of YHWH. It involves jealousy, hate, anger, judgment, and vengeance. William Phipps, in his article "The Sensuousness of Agape," contends that the Greek Bible (Septuagint) refutes the common assumption that *agape* should be defined in a way that stands in contrast to ordinary human love.[13] The Bible's main word for love, *agape* (or *agapan*, verb) is assumed to mean a nonaffectual love distinct from the sensual or *eros* love. Scholars generally maintain that the translators and authors of the Greek Bible arbitrarily selected the word *agape* in order to avoid the sensual association of *eros*.[14] At that time, however, *agape* was a generic, nondescript word for love. Theologians later infused the word with the unconditional, nonaffectual spin. The

---

7. *God: A Biography*, 87.

8. He said if your eye offends you, cut it out (Matt 5:29).

9. He was persuaded by the centurion seeking healing for his servant (Matt 8:5–13), by the two blind men (Matt 9:27–31), and by his mother to provide wine at the Cana wedding (Matt 8:5–13).

10. He cried at the tomb of Lazarus (John 11:35).

11. Overturning the moneychangers' tables in the temple was gritty (Mark 11:15).

12. Wyschogrod, *Body of Faith*, 84.

13. Phipps, "The Sensuousness of Agape," 370–79.

14. Ibid.

Septuagint Bible uses only one word for love—*agape* or *agapan*—which is used in connection with "loving" sex, church, food, money, spouse, people, God, covenant, and so forth.

> The Lord said to me, "Go again, love [*agapan*] a woman who is beloved of a paramour and is an adulteress; even as the Lord loves [*agapan*] the people of Israel."
> Hosea 3:1

> I found him whom I love [*agapan*]. I held him, and would not let him go . . .
> Love [*agape*] is strong as death . . .
> Many waters cannot quench love [*agape*]
> Neither can floods drown it.
> Song of Songs 3:4; 8:6, 7

David speaks of Jonathan's love:

> "Your love [*agape*] to me was wonderful,
> Passing the love [*agape*] of women."
> 2 Samuel 1:26

> Husbands, love [*agape*] your wives, as Christ loved [*agapan*] the church.
> Ephesians 5:25; cf. Colossians 3:19

Jesus commands:

> "Love [*agapan*] one another even as I have loved [*agapan*] you."
> John 13:34

In the last two Scriptures, Jesus erases the difference between the horizontal and the vertical kinds of love to emphasize that YHWH and humans experience the same love and share the same frame of reference. In Benjamin B. Warfield's study on love in the Newer Testament, he reinforces the notion that *agape* is merely a general term for love:

> The highly preponderating use of *agapan*, *agape*, in the New Testament is not due primarily to the deliberate selection of these terms by the writers of the New Testament as the fittest to express the high idea of love to which they had to give expression . . . . it is due primarily to the currency of these terms in the Greek native to the New Testament writers as the general terms for love . . . . There can be little doubt that, had the New Testament writers had occasion to speak at large of sexual love—to write, e.g., a series of narratives like those of Gen. 24 and Judg.

16 and I Sam. 13—they would have employed *agapan* and *agape* in them just as the writers of the Septuagint had done.[15]

Rodney Clapp echoes:

> The ancient Jews did not attempt to separate neatly the sacred from the profane. The Hebrew term *ahabah* and the Greek term *agape* are like the English term love in that they were used to apply to everything from a sensualist's carnal appetite to a martyr's courageous self-sacrifice.[16]

Dante Alighieri, the Christian Italian playwright (d. 1321), believed that human romantic love, the phenomenon of "falling in love," and the accompanying shock of intense personal feeling is a glimpse of how YHWH loves us. Dante was deeply affected by falling in love with the girl Beatrice at the young age of nine. So profound was the experience that even after she married someone else and prematurely died, his love for her continued with him into old age and was evidenced in his many plays. To him, this romantic love was a *true vision* and, combined with the other expressions of varied love, "its pages were bound up in one volume."[17] It is remarkable that Dante is better known for his descriptions of hell than of love. (*The Divine Comedy* gives a vivid portrayal of how people end up in the inferno or hell.) His understanding of hell came with the anguish in his pursuit of love—love denied, tragically misdirected, and inescapably leading to misery and the eternal prison of hell.[18]

Charles Williams built his "theology of romantic love"[19] on Dante's foundation. As a personal friend of C. S. Lewis and J. R. Tolkien, Williams was among those Oxford Christians known as the Inklings. To Williams, the body was not intrinsically evil and had not fallen any "farther than the soul."[20] For Williams, the romantic vision was not confused but illuminating. The lover sees through the beloved's flaws to the image of God. Romantic love reveals the true person, drawing him out of himself and evidencing his sorry half-life up to the moment he fell in love. The one in love realizes how much her wholeness depends on someone outside herself. Romantic love is "not merely a childish infatuation, but a true call, an echo from heaven."[21]

15. Warfield, "The Terminology of Love in the New Testament," 182–83.
16. "What Hollywood Doesn't Know About Romantic Love."
17. Dante, *Paradise*, 33, 85.
18. Williams, *Outlines of Romantic Theology*, 100–101.
19. Ibid.
20. Clapp, "What Hollywood Doesn't Know about Romantic Love."
21. Ibid.

Therefore, when reading the Song of Solomon we need not allegorize or sanitize the display of passion. It articulates the similar love of YHWH:

> ... for love is strong as death,
> jealousy is cruel as the grave.
> Its flashes are flashes of fire,
> a most vehement flame.
> Many waters cannot quench love,
> neither can floods drown it.
> 8:6–7

C. S. Lewis guessed that all earthly experiences (sensory and emotional) might vanish in heaven "not as a candle flame that is put out but as a candle flame which becomes invisible because someone has pulled up the blind, thrown open the shutters, and let in the blaze of the risen sun."[22] Even though human passion often falls short and can be tainted, it still gives us a valid sense about YHWH's intense passion for us.

Jealousy

Believing YHWH to be jealous—as we know jealousy—is a concept rejected out of hand in today's culture. At best it is consigned to the quaint "Old" Testament, which absorbed the surrounding cultures' mentality of portraying their deities as tribal, temperamental, warlike, and territorial. In spite of this, the personalist theology I am promoting takes seriously YHWH's depicted emotions. Jealousy is a vibrant part of YHWH's love—jealousy as an attendant emotion to love, guarding love, showing the intensity of the human-divine bond. Just so:

> For you shall worship no other god, for the Lord, whose name is Jealous, is a jealous God.[23]
> Exodus 34:14

> For the Lord your God is a devouring fire, a jealous God.
> Deuteronomy 4:24

YHWH supports jealousy between a husband and wife (Num 5:11–31). Jealousy is not to be condemned but is right and normal. Even if the jealousy is groundless, it is to be respected until proven wrong. Proverbs furthers this view:

---

22. Lewis, *The Weight of Glory*, 111.
23. Also compare the mysterious "image of jealousy, which provokes to jealousy" found in Ezek 8:1–14.

> For jealousy makes a man furious,
> and he will not spare when he takes revenge.
> He will accept no compensation,
> nor be appeased though you multiply gifts.
> Proverbs 6:34, 35

Our relationship with YHWH mirrors human romance and marriage with its incumbent joys and hurts. YHWH's love is unwavering, and when thwarted, it elicits the same agitated emotions that accompany human spouse betrayal, abandonment, and divorce:

> Not like the covenant which I made with their fathers when I took them by the hand to bring them out of the land of Egypt, my covenant which they broke, though *I was their husband*, says the Lord.
> Jeremiah 31:32 (italics added)

> For *as a young man marries a virgin,*
> *so shall your sons marry you,*
> *and as the bridegroom rejoices over the bride,*
> *so shall your God rejoice over you.*
> Isaiah 62:5

> For *your Maker is your husband . . .*
> For the Lord has called you
> *like a wife forsaken and grieved in spirit,*
> *like a wife of youth when she is cast off,*
> says your God.
> Isaiah 54:5–6

> *Adulterous wife*, who receives strangers instead of her husband! Men give gifts to all harlots; but you gave your gifts to all your lovers, bribing them to come to you from every side for your harlotries. So you were different from other women in your harlotries: none solicited you to play the harlot; and you gave hire, while no hire was given to you; therefore you were different. Wherefore, O harlot, hear the word of the Lord: Thus says the Lord God, Because your shame was laid bare and your nakedness uncovered in your harlotries with your lovers, and because of all your idols, and because of the blood of your children that you gave to them, therefore, behold, I will gather all your lovers, with whom you took pleasure, all those you loved and all those you loathed; I will gather them against you from every side, and will uncover your nakedness to them, that they may see all your nakedness. And *I will judge you as women who break wedlock*

and shed blood are judged, and bring upon you the blood of wrath and jealousy.
Ezekiel 16:32–38

The Newer Testament continues the use of sexual and marriage metaphors to show the Holy One's feelings of joy, disappointment, and anger with his beloved (Rev 2:22–23; 17; 19; Eph 5:25–33). George Stratton points out that jealousy is not just about hurt love, but serves as a *positive, generative impetus* to guard the integrity of the self of the human as well as the self of YHWH. He says:

> Unjealous love, unchecked, brings union, complete fusion of separate persons into one and can comingle the lover and beloved, blurring the lines of individuality. Jealousy is the guardian of honoring individuality, it is restorative and watchful over the undertaking of love—an essential ingredient—needed to keep the demarcation clear between what is "mine and Thine" and "me and Thee."[24]

Like human romantic stories, YHWH is also subject to "falling in love" and feeling deep passion, and is also exposed to tragic love triangles and the love-anger-jealousy-hate-forgiveness dynamic that attends all intimate relationships. Apathy as a divine response is a rarity—perhaps this happened in the last ten books of the Older Testament? Rather, the extremes of anger and vengeance persist with YHWH. (A strange phenomenon in our world is that murders are perpetrated often by someone who knew the victim intimately—this is the love-jealousy-anger-hate dynamic at work. Seldom is it the case that someone is murdered by a complete stranger.) Oddly too, Anthony Hanson, in *The Wrath of the Lamb*, says the Older Testament describes YHWH as *more angry with His chosen, beloved people* than with the unchosen. Hanson's study of YHWH's judgment suggests, radically, that his wrath could be considered inappropriate for those who were *not* among his beloved, because he would not so directly deal with them.[25] There are two limited references to YHWH's anger with the unchosen: Exodus 15:7 and Deuteronomy 32:27, 35. Being in the path of his dogged love can be dangerous, as some Holocaust survivors testify. Poet Kadia Molodowsky defiantly cries:

> O God of Mercy
> For the time being
> Choose another people.

24. Stratton, *Anger*, 212–13.
25. Hanson, *Wrath of the Lamb*, 12.

> We are tired of death, tired of corpses,
> We have no more prayers.
> For the time being
> Choose another people . . .
> God of Mercy
> Sanctify another land . . .
> Grant us one more blessing—
> Take back the gift of our separateness.[26]

Closer acquaintance with YHWH brings great sweetness to life, but sometimes it brings a greater potential for his wrath. This is the warning given to Christians in Hebrews:

> For if we sin deliberately after receiving the knowledge of the truth, there no longer remains a sacrifice for sins, but a fearful prospect of judgment, and a fury of fire which will consume the adversaries. A man who has violated the Law of Moses dies without mercy at the testimony of two or three witnesses. *How much worse punishment* do you think will be deserved by the man who has spurned the Son of God, and profaned the blood of the covenant by which he was sanctified, and outraged the Spirit of grace? For we know him who said, *"Vengeance is mine, I will repay."* And again, *"The Lord will judge his people." It is a fearful thing to fall into the hands of the living God.*
> Hebrews 10:26–31 (italics added)

Rejecting YHWH's pursuing love elicits a fierce response. (The relationship also brings vigorous joy to YHWH, though this is not the focus of my book.) Wrath is an impassioned response to his injured love that is designed to force the relationship back on track. Theologian Jürgen Moltmann shows the link between his engaging love and his wrath:

> [YHWH's] wrath is injured love and therefore a mode of his reaction to men. Love is the source and the basis of the possibility of the wrath of God. The opposite of love is not wrath, but indifference. Indifference towards justice and injustice would be a retreat on the part of God from the covenant.[27]

YHWH's fierce love and concern sometimes *necessitates* a response of divine anger. He is angered and hurt by squandered human life, social evil, lost opportunities, and wasted resources. Speaking about oppressed African Americans, theologian James Cone proclaims, "A God without wrath does

---

26. Laytner, *Arguing with God*, 207–8.
27. Moltmann, *The Crucified God*, 272.

not plan to do much liberating, for the two concepts (wrath and love) belong together. A God minus wrath seems to be a God who is basically not against anybody."[28]

In 1988 Bill Moyers hosted Joseph Campbell's "The Power of Myth" on PBS. In it, Campbell plainly consigned this annoying god-wrath stuff to the quaint, bygone "Old-Testament-god." "That god" was tribal, temperamental, warlike, and territorial. The New Testament God in Jesus is more respectable; he is nice and well tempered. However, a case can be made to the contrary: Jesus is more terrible and "ill-mannered" than the God of the Older Testament. Jesus represents a more "dipolar" God—he is more gentle, kind, and forgiving (the Lamb) but simultaneously brings more judgment and vengeance upon the earth (the Lion)—if not now, then in the kingdom to come. These higher stakes and more severe judgments can be attributed to the brighter revelation of truth in the cross (the argument in Heb 10:26–31). How far do we take the warning in Hebrews? Will the reprobate Christian, having greater revelation, suffer greater judgment than the people who lived in the Older Testament time, or suffer greater judgment than today's secularist, Hindu, Muslim, or Jew? It remains to be seen.

The Bible claims that those in Christ are no longer under condemnation (Rom 8:1), yet reprobate *followers* of Christ can be cast from his presence (Matt 5:40–46)—another paradox.[29] This overused promise to Christians (Rom 8:1) says that we are no longer under judgment, whereas the "outsider" is condemned. The Older Testament indicates that even the elect can come under YHWH's judgment. Can this carry over into the Newer Testament? First Corinthians 11:27–30 seems to say so: It warns that those who partake of the Lord's table in an unworthy manner can bring judgment upon themselves. Compare Amos 3:2, "You only have I known of all the families of the earth; therefore I will punish you for all your iniquities."

When other seducing lovers and idols come between YHWH and his people (sex, money, and power), he does not ooze continual positive regard, impersonally overlooking attachments to other lovers; rather, he is hurt, jealous, and even vengeful. These other "gods" are real, competing for attention, eliciting YHWH's outrage:

> The Lord is a jealous God and avenging,
> the Lord is avenging and wrathful;
> Nahum 1:2a

---

28. Cone, *A Black Theology of Liberation*, 131.

29. In Matthew 7:22, some Christians will say, "Lord, Lord" ("Lord" being said twice indicates they are emotionally attached to the Holy One). They believe in the divinity of the Messiah and they do miracles in his name, but they are condemned to hell!?

Then the anger of the Lord was kindled against his people,
and he abhorred his heritage;
he gave them into the hand of the nations,
so that those who hated them ruled over them.
Their enemies oppressed them,
and they were brought into subjection under their power.
Many times he delivered them,
but they were rebellious in their purposes,
and were brought low through their iniquity.
Psalm 106:40–43

And as the Lord took delight in doing you good and multiplying you, so *the Lord will take delight in bringing ruin upon you and destroying you*; and you shall be plucked off the land which you are entering to take possession of it.
Deuteronomy 28:63

The verses above are regularly dismissed as merely anthropomorphic or symbolic. But the question still remains: *What are they supposed to symbolize then?*

Christians who are unaccustomed to biblical paradox have overemphasized Jesus's admonition not to hate[30] and Paul's censor on jealousy[31] and anger.[32] As a consequence, love is in danger of being sentimentalized when the *attendant emotions* of jealousy and anger are not incorporated. Lowell Colson shows the inevitability of judgment in the phenomenon of love, "To relate to another person in love is already to insert a dimension of judgment. It is to say, in effect, 'I believe you are worth my attention,' or, 'I am addressing you and am expecting a response from you.' . . . Judgment when taken into love carries with it involvement."[33] The popular concept of "judgment" usually has a negative meaning, that of criticism or condemnation. Colson reminds us, "judgment is derived from the Latin words *ius* (right) and *dicere* (to speak), meaning, literally, 'to speak or say right.' It is 'the condition of

---

30. Matthew 5:43: "You have heard that it was said, 'You shall love your neighbor and *hate* your enemy.'" Matthew 5:44: "But I say to you, love your enemies and pray for those who persecute you." John 12:25: "Those who love their life lose it, and those who hate their life in this world will keep it for eternal life."

31. Galatians 5:19–21: "Now the works of the flesh are obvious: fornication, impurity, licentiousness, idolatry, sorcery, enmities, strife, jealousy, anger, quarrels, dissensions, factions, envy, drunkenness, carousing, and things like these. I am warning you, as I warned you before: those who do such things will not inherit the kingdom of God."

32. Colossians 3:8: "But now you must get rid of all such things—anger, wrath, malice, slander, and abusive language from your mouth."

33. Colson, *Judgment in Pastoral Counseling*, 17.

right speaking,' or 'the act of saying what is right.'"[34] An example of this is YHWH's "right speaking" to those in relationship with him, evidenced through the prophets and Yeshua, such as: "you are beloved," or "you anger me with your distractions by material things, fame, illicit sex, and power," or "I am jealous for your love."

Hate

Our culture conveniently rejects any kind of hate as immoral. Even Christians are reluctant to hate evildoers like the Holy One does. There has been a softening of Christianity in the Western world, a reluctance to use strong words such as evil, sin, wickedness, and perversion. Public attitudes toward criminals has softened too: the media may refer to a violent killer as "Mr. So-and-So," or as a "gentleman," which fifty years ago was not the case. In suicide bombing tragedies, the bomber is included as one of the "victims" in the body count. Criminals are less likely to be held accountable for heinous actions, as they are often explained by a "sickness," a set of circumstances, or a "mistake" of ignorance. There is a Jewish saying from the Talmud that says if you are kind to the cruel it will lead you to be cruel to the kind. In the above examples, the suffering of the victim is increased when this soft language is used.[35] To be specific, in South Africa, my country of origin, after capital punishment was abolished there in the early nineties (that is, more *kindness* was shown to murderers), the murder and rape rate has increased fivefold. Thus, more *cruelty* has been dispensed to more innocent people.

The Bible is emphatic about hating evil:

> The Lord loves those who hate evil. Psalm 97:10a
>
> The fear of the Lord is hatred of evil. Proverbs 8:13a
>
> Hate the evil and love the good. Amos 5:15a
>
> Woe to those who call evil good and good evil. Isaiah 5:20a
>
> I [King David] hate them with perfect hatred; I count them my enemies. Psalm 139:22
> Let love be genuine; hate what is evil, hold fast to what is good. Romans 12:9

---

34. Ibid., 18.

35. Violence is similar. There is moral violence (the Allies fighting against Nazism) and immoral violence (the senseless torturing or blowing up of innocent people). Dennis Prager and Rabbi Shmuley Boteach have helped me think through this hate section (talk-radio and newspaper articles).

Hatred is a valid emotion, and it is the appropriate moral response to inhuman cruelty. Mass murderers must elicit our deepest hatred and contempt. It is not our business to forgive them. Only the victim(s) and the Holy One can do that.

Today, the desire to be tolerant, even toward evil, can produce insane results. People are more concerned about destroying the eggs of the endangered American Bald eagle than killing human fetuses. People who belong to PETA (People for the Ethical Treatment of Animals) say that the barbecuing of chicken is the same as Jews burning in the Holocaust. Berkeley, California, has now banned all hate from its city. It feels good to do this, but it is not thought through. Theoretically, a religious Jew, Muslim, or Christian could be prosecuted for hating some evil in that city. Berkeley's council members may be sincere and well intentioned, but truly naive. Is there no hate for the unrepentant serial sexual predator, the perpetual drunk driver, or the maniac who goes on a shooting rampage at a preschool? Evil must be recognized and confronted with a steady bearing of hate. It will not necessarily disappear by legislating it away, ignoring it, deeming its threat unreal, or believing it will be weeded out by impersonal evolutionary mechanisms (bad karma).

Following the behavior of YHWH, we are encouraged to be angry about the right things. Like Paul we can say, "I have fought the good fight" (2 Tim 4:7). The good fight needs to be waged not only within oneself, but also against others and the spiritual forces influencing humans. "For our struggle is not against enemies of blood and flesh, but against the rulers, against the authorities, against the cosmic powers of this present darkness, against the spiritual forces of evil in the heavenly places" (Eph 6:12). George Stratton asks the question, "Should anger and hate only be directed against certain qualities or abstractions?" as in the cliché, "love the sinner but hate the sin."[36] Evil is not only found in governments, systems, ideologies or other abstractions but sometimes emanates from *persons* with ill will. For example, Paul experienced direct evil from Alexander (2 Tim 4:14). Stratton may be on to something—that anger and hate is not directed against impersonal abstractions *alone*. Hate, like love, is directed against *persons*, just as one cannot love a spouse in an impersonal way, merely loving abstract qualities without loving personally. Likewise, we cannot hate in impersonal ways. The metaphysician may counter that we should not hate the substance of the enemy but only the form; we fight against the spirit of individuals or the spirit of collective individuals. Yet the responsibility for the ill will does not lie out there somewhere in the society-at-large or the "system," but comes

---

36. Stratton, *Anger*, 262.

from conscious, misguided individuals.[37] *Hate* is not an accepted word in our politically correct culture. We avoid the idea that "YHWH loved Isaac and *hated* Esau."[38] We would rather rewrite this to read, "YHWH loved Isaac and *had apathy* for Esau." Personally, I would rather YHWH *hate* me than be *apathetic* to me. Hate means impassioned engagement, while apathy means unconcern, inattention, and detachment.

Jealousy, hatred, and anger are useful forces in the human and the divine—not one of them can be spared. Even the Holy One uses "ignoble" jealousy and anger to further his purposes, as Paul indicates:

- Moses says regarding Israel: "I will make you *jealous* of those who are not a nation; with a foolish nation I will make you angry" (Rom 10:19).
- "salvation has come to the Gentiles, so as to make Israel *jealous*" (Rom 11:11).

It seems degrading for YHWH to be using base jealousy to promote salvation, but so he does. It is not within the scope of this book to go into greater detail on this issue; however, the unpleasant emotions of jealousy, anger, and hate that are attendant to love need to be channeled, ordered, and, obviously, sometimes suppressed and negated as recommended by some Scriptures and other authors. Plato gave some good advice on how to channel anger: Direct your anger with the right amount, at the right time, to the right target. If this is not done, the anger bleeds out to undeserving innocent bystanders—like kicking the dog.

Anger, Unbecoming of Deity

Philo, a Jewish thinker at the time of Jesus, said anger was unbecoming of Deity, "we invent for Him hands and feet, incoming and outgoing, enmities, aversions, estrangements, anger, in fact, such parts and passion as can never belong to the Cause (God); . . .[as] a mere crutch for our weakness."[39] Second-century theologians Clement and Origen said the language of the Bible was adapted to allow for the shortcomings of humankind. The Bible is not meant to be taken literally when it speaks of God's anger and repentance, but merely employs inadequate but recognizable analogies for humans who are unable to grasp the total otherness of God. Instances of divine wrath are

37. Ibid., 264–65.
38. Romans 9:13. Much has been written to soften the word "hate" here; some suggest it signifies only the element of degree, i.e., God loved Isaac *more* than Esau. I side with the majority of biblical translators in choosing "hate."
39. A. Heschel, *The Prophets*, 2:59–60.

allegorized, or if it is conceded, it is distanced from God by attributing this dirty work to the "angels of destruction" of the Bible.[40] Another theologian who disparaged any vestige of passion in God was Arnobius (b. 260), who defined anger as the passion "closest to wild animals and beasts" and, therefore, blasphemous to ascribe to God.[41]

Modern theologians, embarrassed by the passions of God, effectively deconstruct them through the logic of historical criticism.[42] By arguing that humankind has evolved in sophistication of thought, they say that in ancient times the Hebrews saw God as angry and terrible, but now—with the revelation of the Newer Testament—we realize God is decent, good, and kind. Therefore the Newer Testament cancels out the Older Testament rather than fulfilling and completing it. Another way to circumvent the perceived "problem" of YHWH's wrath is to split matters: YHWH is personal in love, but impersonal in wrath; or the Father is demanding, but the Son is kind; or the *human* nature of Jesus experiences anger, but not his *divine* nature[43] (an artificial split born of Greek thought and unsupportable by Scripture). This approach undermines consistency and strains patience: for example, the same people who vehemently argue that God fully embodies the *emotion* of love just as vehemently deny that he might experience the *emotions* of sadness, anger, jealousy, and pain (which characteristically accompany love). The Hebraic worldview challenges these splits and insists on a holistic though paradoxical approach.

Routinely in church culture today, the passion of anger is denounced in humans and disallowed in God, as it is associated with the urge for retaliation, vengeance, the desire to inflict pain on others, and the temporary loss of self-control. Anger—and particularly its extreme manifestation of rage or extenuated wrath—is seen as a prompting of evil. However, anger can be shown to be a benign tool like gunpowder, used for evil or good, and a necessary tool to live life in a fallen universe.

MADD (Mothers Against Drunk Driving) is a cause born of anguish and propelled by anger. Without the ongoing "fire" of anger, the activists would likely capitulate to the evil done by drunk drivers. Behind the anger

---

40. Ibid., 2:60. Palestinian rebbes of the third century also promoted this idea.

41. Ibid., 2:80.

42. Walter Brueggemann, in *Old Testament Theology*, shows a shift away from historical criticism and adopts what he calls a rhetorical approach, which focuses on Israel's speech about God (117–18). He says, "in a practical way, speech leads reality in the Old Testament. Speech constitutes reality, and who God turns out to be in Israel depends on the utterance" (65). Historicity and ontology take a lesser important role.

43. Similarly, Weinandy agrees with Thomas Aquinas that God only suffered in Jesus's *human* nature and not in his *divine* nature.

of MADD is reverence and love for human life.[44] In this context, doing nothing or being indifferent to evil can be more insidious than the doing of evil. So anger can be a force for good, but unbridled or misdirected anger can be evil. From the relentless cycle of retaliation between gang-bangers in east Los Angeles to the revenge wars between the Hutus and Tutsis in Rwanda, the postmodern world does not lack examples of anger gone wrong. The fine line is defined by the admonition to "be angry but do not sin" (Eph 4:26). The Bible itself gives ample evidence of the dual nature of anger. Denunciations of anger include these:

> Cursed be their anger, for it is fierce,
> and their wrath, for it is cruel!
> I will divide them in Jacob,
> and scatter them in Israel.
> Genesis 49:7

> Thus says the Lord:
> For three transgressions of Edom,
> and for four, I will not revoke the punishment;
> because he pursued his brother with the sword
> and cast off all pity;
> he maintained his anger perpetually,
> and kept his wrath forever.
> Amos 1:11

> For as pressing milk produces curds,
> and pressing the nose produces blood,
> so pressing anger produces strife.
> Proverbs 30:33

> Refrain from anger, and forsake wrath.
> Do not fret—it leads only to evil.
> Psalm 37:8

Yet the condoning of anger is also evident in the Bible, using YHWH as the implicit defender of "good" anger:

> And when they came to the threshing floor of Nacon, Uzzah put out his hand to the ark of God and took hold of it, for the oxen stumbled. *And the anger of the Lord was kindled against Uzzah; and God smote him there because he put forth his hand to the ark; and he died there beside the ark of God.*
> 2 Samuel 6:6–7 (italics added)

---

44. I heard on the radio that 40 percent of all traffic fatalities in the US are caused by alcohol use.

> Still the Lord did not turn from the *fierceness of his great wrath*, by which his anger was kindled against Judah, because of all the provocations with which Manasseh had provoked him.
> 2 Kings 23:26

> Indeed, Jerusalem and Judah so *angered the Lord* that he expelled them from his presence.
> 2 Kings 24:20

> He [Jesus] looked around at them *with anger; he was grieved* at their hardness of heart and said to the man, "Stretch out your hand." He stretched it out, and his hand was restored.
> Mark 3:5

> But when Jesus saw this, *he was indignant* and said to them, "Let the little children come to me; do not stop them; for it is to such as these that the kingdom of God belongs.
> Mark 10:14

At times the presence of YHWH inspired anger in its recipients:

> I did not sit in the company of merrymakers,
> nor did I rejoice; under the weight of your hand I sat alone,
> for *you* [the Lord] *had filled me with indignation.*
> Jeremiah 15:17

> And the spirit of God came upon Saul in power when he heard these words, and his *anger* was greatly kindled.
> 1 Samuel 11:6

Anger and willfulness are necessary ingredients in YHWH's engagement with humans. Anger is intimately linked to love. Usually YHWH's anger is triggered by sin and spurred on by concern to repair the human-divine relationship, but it is also brought on by the Israelites wanting to go back to Egypt (Num 11:1); the faithless report of the spies (Num 32:10), Miriam's challenging of Moses's authority (Num 12:9); and the people's complaining (Deut 1:34).

Use with Extreme Caution and Skepticism

Extreme caution and a good measure of skepticism needs to be taken handling this anger and wrath stuff or if we are tempted to mimic the Holy One's anger. To be clear, YHWH's anger is not an absolute attribute but a transient, fleeting condition. Abraham Heschel warns, "The prophets never identify God's pathos [anger] with His essence, because it is for them not something absolute, but a form of relation."[45] As plenty of Scriptures affirm, his anger is for a moment, however his love goes on forever. YHWH is patient and slow to anger.[46] YHWH's judgment, which accompanies his anger, is never inevitable but always revocable through repentance[47] and prayer.[48] Simply put, YHWH's judgment is *fair* rather than "just." "Just" is too rigid, not subject to the mercies that frequently mediate YHWH's judgments. He never compulsively pursues the letter of even his own Law, but allows the relationship to influence him through dialogue.[49] In other words, the Law is not an external force that requires blind obedience—on the part of the Holy One or the human.[50] Fretheim offers, "In terms of straight forward legal thinking, God is much too lenient."[51] Consider Acts 17:30: In times of ignorance God "overlooks" evil, but now he calls for repentance. Finally, the escalation of the Holy One's anger can at times be simultaneously an invitation to cancel his anger:

> For a brief moment I forsook you,
> but with great compassion I will gather you.
> In overflowing wrath for a moment
> I hid my face from you,
> but with everlasting love I will have compassion on you,
> says the Lord, your Redeemer.
> Isaiah 54:7–8

---

45. A. Heschel, *Between God and Man*, 119.

46. Exod 34:6; Num 14:18; Neh 9:17; Ps 86:15; Jer 15:15; Joel 2:13; Jonah 4:2.

47. Jer 7:5–7; 18:11; 26:13; Jonah 4:2.

48. Deuteronomy 9:19: "For I was afraid that the anger that the Lord bore against you was so fierce that he would destroy you. But the Lord listened to me that time also."

49. See the dialogues between Abraham, Moses, Jacob and YHWH.

50. Blumenthal, *Facing the Abusing God*, 15. The way "impersonal Law" would work could be likened to the way much of governmental bureaucracy works in the contemporary world (i.e., in an impersonal system, no one takes direct responsibility for anything, with the excuse being impersonal, governmental "policy"). Sometimes YHWH withholds judgment merely for "his name's sake." For example, Ezek 20:21, 22 (italics added): "But the children rebelled against me; they did not follow my statutes, and were not careful to observe my ordinances, by whose observance everyone shall live; they profaned my sabbaths. *Then I thought I would pour out my wrath upon them and spend my anger against them in the wilderness.* But I withheld my hand, and acted *for the sake of my name*, so that it should not be profaned in the sight of the nations, in whose sight I had brought them out." Thus justice is not meted out in a deterministic manner.

51. Fretheim and Thompson, *God, Evil, and Suffering*, 24.

In sum, the Holy One's anger and wrath are rational, they are planned, forewarned, and are a direct result of intransigent human sin. Its purpose is to put the human-divine relationship back on track. Yet in some obscure instances, his wrath is irrational or suprarational.[52] Why did YHWH kill thousands of Israelites because David took a census (2 Sam 24:15)? A little fear lingers for this reader.

Direct Judgment from the Son

Voicing judgment, hell, and eternal damnation can be depressing and alienating. It is like playing a piece of music an octave too high. People have been psychologically harmed by church people throwing these realities around indiscriminately. However, they come directly from Yeshua and ought to be voiced in certain situations. They are of particular comfort to victims of murder, rape, genocide, or some irreparable evil. C. S. Lewis diffuses some of the abhorrence to the subject when he suggests that humans will send *themselves* to hell by insisting on their own way. When YHWH meets them, he will ask, "Your will or my will." To which seemingly many people will reply "my will be done." Hell will be the enjoyment of their way forever. So YHWH respects their dignity by giving them over to their own misdirected appetites.[53]

With the incarnation of Yeshua comes the simultaneous declaration of salvation *and judgment*. Yeshua invites everyone to participate in the "already" and "not yet" kingdom of God.[54] He attacked those scribes and Pharisees who hindered this objective, calling them "hypocrites," "blind guides," "fools," "sons of hell," and "destined for hell."[55] Seemingly, Jesus got most of his opposition from religious people (this applies for today too). To them he said: "You brood of vipers! Who warned you to flee from the *wrath to come*"? He challenged them to "bear fruit worthy of repentance" (Matt 3:7-8). Jesus was not as the world would say today—a "nice person"—*He spoke more about judgment and hell than any other person in the Bible!* First, evidence of implicit judgment arises in his parables:

52. Examples include the killing of Uzzah for touching the Ark (2 Sam 6:6–9), YHWH's attempt to kill Moses (Exod 4:24), the Lord's killing Aaron's sons for inappropriately playing with fire (Lev 10:1–2), and the story of Job. At the end of Job the Lord gives no reason why all the suffering befell him. Was Job's suffering caused merely by the wager the Lord had with Satan?

53. Romans 1:26.

54. Jesus sometimes stated that the kingdom of God was present then (Matt 12:28), whereas in other instances he said the kingdom of God is in the future (Mark 14:25).

55. Matthew 3:7; 23:13.

- In the parable about the vineyard, the owner kept sending servants to collect fruit, but the tenants abused them until finally he sent his own son, whom they killed. Jesus concludes: "He [the owner] will come and *destroy those tenants* and give the vineyard to others. When they heard this, they said, 'Heaven forbid!'" (Luke 20:16).

- In the parable about the servant who would not forgive a small debt even though he'd been forgiven a huge one, Jesus condemns: "And in *anger his lord* handed him over to be *tortured* until he would pay his entire debt" (Matt 18:34).

- The parable of the king's wedding banquet shows deliberate judgment. Some of the invited guests murdered the king's servants who brought the invitation. In response, "*The king was enraged. He sent his troops, destroyed those murderers, and burned their city.*" Because invited guests were unable to come to the banquet for different reasons, the invitation was extended to those "both good and bad" in the streets. The banquet proceeded with guests from the street, but then another nasty thing happened: "the king . . . noticed a man there who was not wearing a wedding robe, and he said to him, *'Friend, how did you get in here without a wedding robe?' And he was speechless. Then the king said to the attendants, 'Bind him hand and foot, and throw him into the outer darkness, where there will be weeping and gnashing of teeth'*" (Matt 22:1–14).

In the Older Testament, YHWH struck people dead in judgment. On rare occasions, this is continued in the Newer Testament:

- Because of blasphemy Herod is struck dead by the Lord: "And immediately, because he had not given the glory to God, an angel of the Lord struck him down, and he was eaten by worms and died" (Acts 12:23). By the way, Josephus, a Jewish historian at the time, records this event.

- Early Christians Ananias and his wife, Sapphira, are struck dead for lying to the Holy Spirit (Acts 5:1–5).

- Paul warns that "the Lord can be *provoked to jealousy*" (1 Cor 10:21, 22). Those who partake of the Lord's table in an unworthy way may be subject to premature death, as Paul testifies, "For this reason many of you are weak and ill, and some have *died*" (1 Cor 11:30).

The apostles carry on the simultaneous force of the forgiveness *and* judgment of Yeshua. Peter speaks harshly to Simon who wants the power of the Holy Spirit for financial gain: "May your silver *perish with you* . . . repent therefore of this wickedness . . . for I see that you are *in the gall of bitterness and the chains of wickedness*" (Acts 8:20–23). Paul's letters use jarring language: "we were by nature children of *wrath*" (Eph 2:3); "Let no one deceive you with empty words, for because of these things *the wrath of God comes on those who are disobedient*" (Eph 5:6). "Beloved, never avenge yourselves, but leave room for the *wrath* of God; for it is written, '*Vengeance is mine*, I will repay, says the Lord'" (Rom 12:19). "For the *wrath* of God is revealed from heaven against all ungodliness and wickedness of those who by their wickedness suppress the truth" (Rom 1:18). And lastly, Hebrews 3:7—4:13 cites examples of YHWH's wrath (i.e., anger for forty years) because of Israel's rebellion in the wilderness, serving as a warning to Newer Testament times (this last reference challenges Dispensationalism, which alleges that we are now living in the dispensation of grace, and not wrath).

Anthony Hanson observes that the wrath of God is implicit in the Newer Testament, and only becomes explicit through symbol and myth in Revelation.[56] Certainly there will be eschatological (end-of-the-world) wrath: "wait for his Son from heaven, whom he raised from the dead—Jesus, who rescues us from the *wrath that is coming*" (1 Thess 1:10). This wrath will come directly from the Son, not the Father: "the Father judges no one but has given all judgment to the Son" (John 5:22). Judgment is done by the Son, and one's relationship to the Son is pivotal to God's wrath: "Whoever believes in the Son has eternal life; whoever disobeys the Son will not see life, but must endure God's *wrath*" (John 3:36). The book of Revelation, considered by some, as an "un-Christian" book due to the vengeance exhibited, portrays Jesus rendering explicit judgment. Revelation—essentially a book of symbols—can be a heretic's paradise, where symbols can be bent whichever way suits. A vivid picture in Revelation (chapters 1–3) is of the Son of God, or Son of Man, who "has eyes like a flame of fire," and "whose feet are like burnished bronze . . . who was dead and came to life," and from whose mouth "comes a sharp, two-edged sword." "He has the keys to Death and Hades," and calls himself "the one who searches minds and hearts," and says, "I will give to each of you as your works deserve."

Kings, generals, the rich, the powerful, slave and free hide in the caves and among the rocks of the mountains, calling upon them to "Fall on us and hide us from the face of the one seated on the throne and from the wrath of the Lamb for the great day of their wrath has come, and who is able to stand?" (Rev 6:15–17). Here "the Lamb"—which is normally linked with the forgiving, sacrificial lamb, the Messiah—is associated with wrath, echoing Paul's warning of how increased revelation brings greater judgment on those who reject it.

---

56. *Wrath of the Lamb*, 200.

Next—skipping over much detail—"the angel" swings his sickle over the earth and gathers the vintage of the earth, throwing it into the great wine press of the *wrath of God*. The wine press is trodden outside the city, and blood flows from it, as high as a horse's bridle, for a distance of about two hundred miles (Rev 14:19–20). "The angel" is undoubtedly the "Son of Man" mentioned earlier (v. 14) who seems intimately involved in the administration of God's wrath, since the reprobate have consciously denied Yeshua's redemption offer in the cross.

John's revelation continues to describe a rider on a white horse, "who judges and makes war." (This is reminiscent of the "Lord of Armies" in the Older Testament who judges and wages war.) He is clothed in a "robe dipped in blood" (presumably not his own blood, as here he is the slayer, not the slain), and his name is called "the Word of God," "King of Kings and Lord of Lords." He strikes down the nations and treads the *wine press of the fury of the wrath of God* the Almighty (Rev 19:11–16). Thus, Yeshua is intimately involved in vengeance.

If these explicit references to Jesus's enactment of vengeance are summarily discounted because they are from "the book of symbols" (Revelation) the question needs to be asked again: if all this is merely symbolic, what does it represent anyway? Surely it says that evil will be punished—a very comforting thought to those who have suffered at the hand of strong-willed, unrepentant, evil people.

I have observed that movies showing punishment of evil are perennial crowd-pleasers, such as *Man on Fire*, *Inglorious Bastards*, and kid-superhero movies (this also includes best-selling computer games). They unknowingly bring gratification even to atheists or people who don't believe in judgment. People who don't have a strong after-death-judgment theology and who have been severely wronged in this life can only rely on justice this side of death, which is usually inconsistent or lacking. Having assurance that there is a severe accounting of evil, in the next world, brings relief to the sufferer.

YHWH's wrath is usually mediated through human agency (e.g., foreign invasion, war, crime), acts of nature (e.g., drought, famine), or sickness (e.g., premature death, physical and psychological ailments). These "evils" commonly happen to the best of us; they come through impersonal mechanisms in nature; or call it "bad karma"—you reap what you sow. Some may come through bad luck or chance.[57] But some come directly from YHWH:

---

57. Ecclesiastes 9:11 (NRSV): "Again I saw that under the sun the race is not to the swift, nor the battle to the strong, nor bread to the wise, nor riches to the intelligent, nor favor to the skillful; but time and chance happen to them all."

> Ah, Assyria, the rod of my anger—the club in their hands is my fury!
> Isaiah 10:5

> So the Lord raises adversaries against them,
> and stirs up their enemies.
> The Syrians on the east and the Philistines on the west
> Isaiah 9:11–12a

Explain 9/11?

Is the Son's judgment experienced today? I use the 9/11 tragedy to explore this question. Consider four explanations:

- *History is haphazard.* Without meaning or ultimate purpose, 9/11 occurred by blind chance, orchestrated by misguided humans.
- *Cause and effect.* "America had it coming" as a reaction to her actions, that is, America provoked militant Muslims through bad foreign policy (overt support for Israel), economic exploitation, and offensive immorality (sexual promiscuity and hedonism as witnessed through the media). In this secularist option, God is not included.
- *Impersonal moral retribution.* Ultimately coming from God's laws, built into the world, God is indirectly implicated in the action. A matter of "bad karma."
- *Specific, direct, and intentional judgment from the Son.*

The first option, *history is haphazard*, will be dismissed in a world given to uniformity and order, which is easily recognizable. Even the person who declares, "life is chaotic and meaningless" is self-refuting, the statement uses an ordered and meaningful system of language to communicate meaninglessness. A consistent argument would employ meaningless language—"blau-jas bla bla aaa daa" and fail to make its point.[58] Linguist Noam Chomsky concedes that "all children are born with a knowledge of the principles of the grammatical structure of all languages, and this inborn knowledge explains the success and speed with which they learn language." Indeed, it is in our DNA that the world is meaningful, to paraphrase a concept of Norm Chomsky: "the child is born with the sentence, the surrounding community supplies the words."[59]

---

58. Thanks to Francis Schaeffer for this point.

59. http://www.sk.com.br/sk-chom.html. I also heard this somewhere on a Krista Tippett podcast.

The second option, *cause and effect*, has strong explanatory power and works well for secularists; however, it is reductionistic and has a cruel determinism as we cannot escape what is due to us. We are *trapped* in our world, at the mercy of impersonal evolutionary forces and of the bad and good of ourselves and others. We live in a deterministic world. There is no atonement, no possibility of a merciful God intervening on our behalf.

The third option of *impersonal moral retribution* is similar to the second option but allows God into the equation. This option has appeal because it acknowledges judgment ultimately coming from God, but distances him enough from an alleged "bad" deed of vengeance to maintain comfort. In practice, probably, most Christians adhere to this option. In practice, they refrain from attributing much, if anything, to YHWH's direct judgment in life or the world. Rather, they emphasize that people are punished or rewarded through impersonal mechanisms built by God into the human and the world. This position is an easy sell: wrath comes from moral retribution that arises from the impersonal law of God, whereas love comes directly from God.

Scripture does bear out that mechanisms built into reality punish sin,[60] such as "your sins will find you out" and "you reap what you sow" (Prov 22:8; Gal 6:7). Said another way: "God gave them up in the lusts of their hearts to impurity, to the degrading of their bodies among themselves . . . received in their own persons the due penalty for their error" (Rom 1:24–28). When sin is not confessed, a stricken conscience can affect the body and mind detrimentally:

> While I kept silence, my body wasted away
> through my groaning all day long.
> For day and night your hand was heavy upon me;
> my strength was dried up as by the heat of summer.
> Psalm 32:3–4

With these seemingly impersonal enactments of judgment, sometimes the righteous are indiscriminately included, and inversely, sometimes the wicked are blessed along with the righteous. All of life is interconnected, so much so that the weeds are allowed to grow up with the wheat. If the weeds are pulled, the wheat is uprooted in the process (Matt 24:24–30). The Bible even says nature is interwoven with judgment and blessing.[61]

To complicate matters further, YHWH's wrath can go forth, as a decree, in an impersonal manner:

---

60. I have found Fretheim and Thompson's treatment on the topic to be helpful: *God, Evil, and Suffering*, 21–32.

61. Isa 24; Jer 4:23–26; 9:10–11; 12:4, 7–13; Hos 4:1–3; Rom 8:18–22.

wrath has gone out
Numbers 16:46

wrath goes forth
Jeremiah 4:4

Look, the storm of the Lord!
Wrath has gone forth, a whirling tempest;
it will burst upon the head of the wicked
Jeremiah 23:19

This third option, left to stand with these Scriptures, resembles the principle of *karma* in orthodox Hinduism where reward and punishment come through impersonal means. Brahma (God) cannot change *karma* and is independent of *karma*.[62] Reward follows good works, and punishment follows sin with no intervention of God; there is no grace, no repentance, and *no atonement*. I find this kind of determinism wretched. There is a problem to all this: If judgment (or perceived anger) is not *directly* from YHWH but from an impersonal system that punishes sin, then we have to accept that there is an eternal dualism between God and his own law. Further, this option does not account for Scriptures that declare vengeance coming *directly* from YHWH. Many Scriptures in this third option effectively show YHWH not to be directly involved in judgment; however, paradoxical Scriptures support a fourth option.

The fourth option, *direct judgment from Yeshua,* makes use of Scriptures already mentioned about YHWH's jealousy and anger culminating in the "wrath of the Lamb." This option emphasizes the human-divine relationship. Anger and vengeance are a direct response to the human's preoccupation with other lovers. Attributing direct judgment from the Holy One can be a hazardous undertaking in our postmodern world, as Pat Robertson and Jerry Falwell quickly found out.[63] I would agree with Robertson and Falwell partly, but posit a different reason for the curse of 9/11: it was not necessarily brought on by liberal or secular elements in our society (homosexuals, abortionists, etc.), but by a church that has stopped being "salt" in the culture, and, therefore, "good for nothing, to be thrown out and trampled under foot" (Matt 5:13).[64] These are harsh words from Yeshua. The sequence

---

62. For a more detailed discussion on *karma*, see Hanson, *Wrath of the Lamb*, 215–23.

63. Soon after 9/11, Falwell and Robertson declared on Christian TV (which was then carried to the other TV networks) that 9/11 was judgment from God against the secular liberal elements in American society, namely, homosexuality, abortion, no prayer in the public schools, etc.

64. Matthew 5:13: "You are the salt of the earth; but if salt has lost its taste, how

of judgment in the Bible usually starts with the elect (Israel, the church) and then goes to the surrounding culture. The events of 9/11 *can be* considered a curse[65] coming directly from YHWH. To be specific,

> *Because you did not serve the Lord your God* joyfully and with gladness of heart for the abundance of everything, *therefore you shall serve your enemies whom the Lord will send against you* . . . .
> *The Lord will bring a nation from far away,* from the end of the earth, to swoop down on you like an eagle, a nation whose language you do not understand . . .
> Deuteronomy 28:47–49 NRSV

America has been blessed with peace and prosperity, bringing wealth to more people than any nation in human history. I can testify to this, as a recent immigrant. Is the tide changing? Perhaps. Is YHWH using militant Muslims to punish the decadent West, as he used Nebuchadnezzar to punish unfaithful Israel? YHWH spoke thus, "Nebuchadnezzar, my servant" (Jer 25:9; 27:6; 43:10), who brings judgment to Israel. YHWH is intimately involved in the pillage of Israel—"I [YHWH] will punish that nation with the sword, with famine, and with pestilence, says the Lord, until I have completed its destruction by his [Nebuchadnezzar's] hand" (Jer 27:8).[66]

As a critical realist I believe there is an objective truth about this matter, but it has to be subjectively apprehended by humans. Other believers are needed to confirm this fourth option. No matter how uncomfortable the option of YHWH's direct punishment of America is, it needs to be kept on the table. If Americans glibly invoke God to bless America, then they need to have caution that YHWH, the God of all nations, could hold demands in return. George Washington, who often invoked God's name and blessing on America, saw this connection. He simultaneously feared God's judgment on America, especially when he observed the immorality of his soldiers.

This section on YHWH's wrath is not meant to be a complete and comprehensive study. YHWH's judgment can be paradoxical and varied: He imposes punishment for a specific sin that is elsewhere ignored; he mediates the consequences of sin that are intrinsic to it, and yet the wicked sometimes prosper (Jer 12:1), the innocent sometimes suffer (Job), and often there is an

---

can its saltiness be restored? It is no longer good for anything, but is thrown out and trampled under foot."

65. For a list of curses see Deut 28:15–68. America's becoming a borrowing nation is considered a curse (v. 44).

66. Nebuchadnezzar is no puppet of YHWH because the narrative shows that Nebuchadnezzar overreaches his judgmental activity, but YHWH corrects this (Isa 47:5–7; Jer 25:11–14; Zech 1:15).

element of chance in how judgment is meted out (Eccl 9:11). The Holy One will not necessarily hold to divine rules, and will override them if it benefits the relationship (Jer 26:3, 13, 19). Fretheim and Thompson appropriately describe this fluid approach as having no "tight causal weave."[67] YHWH always engages to heal breaches in his relationship with humans, as he *wants life, not death* (Ezek 18:23).

Questions

1. Klitsie claims that YHWH's love is similar (not identical) to human love as we are image bearers. He does not accept the *agape/eros* divide. Do you agree?
2. Give examples where jealousy and anger can indicate love.
3. Hebrews 10:26–31 argues that with more revelation through Yeshua comes greater judgment. Does this apply to "Christian" nations?
4. What do you think of the idea that 9/11 could be direct judgment from the Son of God?

---

67. *God, Evil, and Suffering*, 28.

5

APPLYING MULTIFACETED THEOLOGY

Apprehend over Comprehend

WE ARE IN PERPETUAL danger of giving primacy to concepts or dogmas about the Holy One that give the impression of knowing or possessing him, instead of settling with the less safe and raw insights of his nature. Going with raw, angular—sometimes mismatched—Scripture requires more faith and effort than going with settled, smooth church dogmas. Of course, dogmas are needed—but can, at times, encumber our relationship with YHWH. We do not so much comprehend him as we *apprehend* him in each particular historical situation. Luther said that the greatest evil was not fighting the battle where the battle currently is, and he deplored fighting yesteryear's battle. In Luther's time, he battled for "being saved by faith and not works." For Jonathan Edwards it was "humans in the hands of an angry God." For Wesley it was "holiness now," and for post–World War II Christians it was "be born again, receive the baptism of the Holy Spirit, and praise and clap your hands." Recently it has been calling men to be "Promise Keepers."[1] All of these particular emphases were required to meet the needs of their time. I believe YHWH is impressing on the church today—post-Holocaust (after the Shoah)—to be in touch with his fierce, gentle, but dangerous love. Theologians both Jewish and Christian are beginning to tackle this heavy topic.[2]

1. Promise Keepers (PK) is an organization started by a football coach who saw a need for men to be affirmed and encouraged. This call has gone all around the world.

2. See Sweeney, *Reading the Hebrew Bible after the Shoah*.

Robert Banks, a long-time theologian from Australia, observes that theologians can live in a bubble, believing that they—only they—have special access in knowing who God *really* is, through their knowledge of Hebrew, special textual criticism, contextual knowledge, and so forth. This is akin to the elitism of the Gnostics who believed that they—and only they—had secret access in knowing God through their *enlightened* knowledge.[3] The Bible attests the contrary, claiming that sensitivity and attachment to YHWH is accessible to the common person; actually education may hinder this:

> For this commandment which I command you this day is not too hard for you, neither is it far off. It is not in heaven, that you should say, "Who will go up for us to heaven, and bring it to us, that we may hear it and do it?" Neither is it beyond the sea, that you should say, "Who will go over the sea for us, and bring it to us, that we may hear it and do it?" But the word is very near you; it is in your mouth and in your heart, so that you can do it. Deuteronomy 30:11–14

Though the Bible is complicated, it is still accessible to the eager and uninitiated. Conversely, the Bible is inaccessible to the unattached, judgmental, and those too attached to their unexamined, inherited, cherished dogmas. The Person of the Bible remains hidden to the spiritual tourist—he/she may get the story, the idea, or the concept but miss the pathos and realness of YHWH. As with the parables of Yeshua, many people got the story but missed the secrets of the kingdom of God embedded in them, not because they lacked intelligence but *heart*. Isaiah 42:20 says, "He sees many things, but does not observe them; his ears are open, but he does not hear." "Do and you shall know" is Kierkegaard's paraphrase of John 7:17: "Anyone who resolves to do the will of God will know whether the teaching is from God or whether I am speaking on my own."[4] We educate ourselves about YHWH not through study alone but through existential living. We know by doing. At Mt. Sinai the Hebrews said, "We shall do and then we shall listen/understand" (Exod 19:8, *na'aseh v'nishma*).[5] This is where the rubber hits the road: inner appropriation, intuition combined with apprehending

---

3. Robert Banks gave this challenge in a course on Practical Theology at Fuller Theological Seminary, Pasadena, 2000.

4. Fretheim and Thompson, *God, Evil, and Suffering*, 7.

5. Exodus 19:8: "And all the people answered together and said, 'All that the Lord has spoken we will do.' And Moses reported the words of the people to the Lord." Jacobs, "Do First, Understand Later."

the Person of the Bible. Psalm 34:8 says, "O taste and see that the Lord is good"—a whole-body-person encounter.

Inspiration and Participation

Christians can fall into a pious trap by overstating that the Bible is solely a divine work. It seems safe: how can one go wrong overstating this? Yet this phony piety of how "high" you view Scripture, reminds me of my Catholic days where we were required to believe beyond what the Bible states: We believed that the Virgin Mary never had other children besides Jesus, and she did not die, because "she was assumed into heaven." The downside of a "too high" view of Scripture is that it flattens our multidimensional world because it neglects the contribution of the human. This has a direct effect on our everyday relations with YHWH. To be sure, the Bible is YHWH's revealed Word, but we need to acknowledge a partnership between the human and the divine. Two extremes need to be avoided: On one extreme, Scripture is considered solely supernatural in origin, its writers were mechanically controlled, to the letter. The Qur'an is viewed in this way, Allah dictated it word for word, so much so that one can only find its true meaning by studying it in its original "perfect" Arabic. The other extreme says that Scripture is reducible to human fabrication, made up through subjective, personal, or cultural phenomenon. Abraham Heschel brings balance to the extremes: Scripture originated from the interplay between a divine *situation* and a human *situation*.[6] It is a *situation,* because Hashem is a conscious, thinking, feeling Actor, relating to conscious, thinking, feeling humans. Hashem, the Protagonist, interacts with humans, which propels the sacred drama of the Bible. For example, in this passage from Isaiah 5, notice the interplay between the prophet's and Hashem's thoughts and feelings: they share a similar frame of reference of concerns and burdens:[7]

> 1 Let me sing for my beloved
> a love song concerning his vineyard:
> My beloved had a vineyard
> on a very fertile hill.
> 2 He digged it and cleared it of stones,
> and planted it with choice vines;
> he built a watchtower in the midst of it,

---

6. A. Heschel, *Between God and Man*, 243.

7. Heschel believes that thought and feeling are intertwined. He says, "thought is part of emotion . . . . Emotion may be defined as the consciousness of being moved. Emotion is inseparable from being filled with the spirit." *The Prophets*, 2:96.

and hewed out a wine vat in it;
and he looked for it to yield grapes,
but it yielded wild grapes.
3 And now, O inhabitants of Jerusalem
and men of Judah,
judge, I pray you, between me
and my vineyard.
4 What more was there to do for my vineyard,
that I have not done in it?
When I looked for it to yield grapes,
why did it yield wild grapes?
5 And now I will tell you
what I will do to my vineyard.
I will remove its hedge,
and it shall be devoured;
I will break down its wall,
and it shall be trampled down.
6 I will make it a waste;
it shall not be pruned or hoed,
and briers and thorns shall grow up;
I will also command the clouds
that they rain no rain upon it.
7 For the vineyard of the Lord of hosts
is the house of Israel,
and the men of Judah
are his pleasant planting;
and he looked for justice,
but behold, bloodshed;
for righteousness,
but behold, a cry!

Note the "mixture of response, of receptivity and spontaneity, of event and experience" in this song.[8] The prophet speaks first in his own name (vv. 1–2), then the Lord's voice is heard (vv. 3–6) and then his own name again (v. 7). There is a co-mingling of the human and the divine, where both thoughts and feelings are communicated. It is a human event and a divine event: The prophet has emotional solidarity with the Lord, and the Lord identifies with the human situation. The prophet has compassion for humans and the Lord communicates his message with thought and passion. The outcome of this interplay is prophecy. In this manner, Heschel says prophecy is not simply the application of timeless standards to particular

---

8. A. Heschel, *The Prophets*, 2:ix.

human situations, but rather an interpretation of a particular moment in history, a divine understanding of a human situation.[9]

This understanding has direct bearing on us in the church today, where we, as priests,[10] can receive a word or feeling from the Lord that addresses a specific *situation* in our world (cf. Paul's encouragement to this effect in 1 Cor 12–14). The Christian therapist can receive a thought or feeling about her client; the praying truck driver can receive a thought on how to speak to his wayward son; a women's fellowship may receive a burden to help unmarried mothers; and a screenwriter may receive a human story that directly depicts the thwarted love of YHWH. Of course, people can abuse the claim that they "received a word or feeling from the Lord"; however, mature Christians can discern when "a word" is merely made up in one's mind, originating from a malicious spirit, or truly coming from YHWH. Increased problems (yet with great benefits) can be expected when people are encouraged to follow this calm quiet voice from YHWH, but "where there is life there are problems." Conversely, where there is death, there is tranquility: the cemetery is a very quiet place. Often churches that do not have problems are very dead places.

To restate, Judeo-Christianity can be likened to be an ellipse (not a circle with only one center). An ellipse has two centers of interest and energy—YHWH and humankind. Lopsided theology can arise if we focus too much on humankind or even too much on YHWH—a balance is needed. For example, some hymns sound like this, "I am a nothing, *a nothing*, a mere worm. You Lord are everything, *everything*." These are humble, pious words, but uncalled for as the Bible ennobles and encourages us to sing, "I am a something, *a something*, together and because of you, YHWH." (I think that watching a Monty Python movie making fun of high pious church mannerisms might help some of us laugh at ourselves.)

The inspiration of Scripture is not some other-worldly magical thing, but comes out of historical situations where YHWH communicates or demonstrates, through events, thoughts, and feelings to sympathetic humans, though sometimes YHWH/Yeshua acts against the will of a person, for

---

9. Ibid., 2:xiv.

10. 1 Peter 2:5: "Like living stones, let your selves be built into a spiritual house, to be a holy priesthood, to offer spiritual sacrifices acceptable to God through Jesus Christ." 1 Peter 2:9: "But you are a chosen race, a royal priesthood, a holy nation, God's own people, in order that you may proclaim the mighty acts of him who called you out of darkness into his marvelous light."

example, Jeremiah[11] or Paul.[12] To gain insight into what YHWH may be saying to one's community today, one needs to simultaneously have compassion for one's community and sympathy with YHWH (the latter develops by reading the Bible, especially the Prophets). We can define sympathy as a state of openness to the presence of another person. Like the prophets, who were open to the presence of the Holy Spirit, we may sense the thoughts and pathos of YHWH, which may calm, frustrate, delight, anger, empower, or even overwhelm us. Paul communicates the dynamic of receiving the Holy Spirit's feelings,

> we ourselves, who have the first fruits of the Spirit, groan inwardly as we wait for adoption as sons . . . . Likewise the Spirit helps us in our weakness; for we do not know how to pray as we ought, but the Spirit himself intercedes for us *with sighs too deep for words.*
> Romans 8:23, 26 (italics added)

If all this has a ring of hocus pocus, Heschel grounds the thought, "just as clairvoyants may see the future, the religious man comes to sense the *present moment.*"[13] For the religious "seer" today, the insight may be merely seeing the human situation *as it really is* (from Hashem's point of view). The sympathizer then makes Hashem's concern his or her own.[14] When Hashem speaks to us, he reflects a realism about our situation—a truth by which we are invited to grow and mature. We can call this orientation critical realism or "common-sensism." Heschel contends that the biblical term *da'at elohim*—which is usually translated as "knowledge of God"—ought to be rendered as "understanding" or "sympathy for God" and,

> owing to the nature of the divine pathos as an ever-changing reaction of the Deity to human behavior, understanding for God—unlike "knowledge of God"—cannot, once attained, remain man's permanent and safe possession. *The voice speaks to man not in timeless abstraction but in singular moments of life and history.*[15]

---

11. Jeremiah 20:7: "O Lord, You have deceived me and I was deceived; You have overcome me and prevailed. I have become a laughingstock all day long; Everyone mocks me" (NASB). Heschel says the operative Hebrew words in this passage are sexual: Jeremiah was "seduced" (not deceived) and "raped" (not overcome) by YHWH.

12. Paul's life was interrupted on the Damascus road, unbidden.

13. A. Heschel, *Between God and Man*, 71.

14. A. Heschel, *The Prophets*, 1:25.

15. A. Heschel, *Between God and Man*, 25 (italics added). The root *yada'* means "to know" as well as "to have sexual intercourse" in most Semitic languages.

So where does the Bible's authority and power come from? It does not simply come from humans steadfastly declaring that it is the Word of God. Terence Fretheim says, "the Bible's authority is derivative, that is, it derives its authority from the God to whom it witnesses."[16] Its authority arises from reception, participation, experience, and growing trust within our community of faith.

Gutsy Prayer

With multifaceted theology we stay with traditional theology (like Reformed theology) but add the neglected minority reports: YHWH can be grieved (Gen 6:6; cf. John 11:35), can change his mind (Exod 32:14), can resort to alternative plans (Exod 4:14; John 11:5), can be open and responsive to what humans do (Jer 8:6–10), can be surprised at what people have done (Jer 3:7; 32:35; cf. Luke 7:9), and can even make himself dependent on our prayers (Jas 4:2). Therefore, prayer gains an added dimension. Notably, several consequences result if YHWH has pathos and is impacted by humans:

1. We can wrestle with him.
2. We can at odd times bargain with him.[17]
3. We can on rare occasions change his mind.
4. Taking YHWH's pathos seriously, we may feel his pain, sadness (Rom 8:26), tender kindness, anger, and winning joy.
5. Events are not all predetermined, but are somewhat open-ended. There is wiggle room.
6. As participants with him, we can significantly affect the future positively, but we can also botch things. So YHWH takes some risk with our contribution.

Erich Fromm identifies the empowerment humans received after YHWH entered a covenantal relationship with them:[18]

---

16. Fretheim and Froehlich, *The Bible as Word of God*, 126.

17. For example, Genesis 28:20–21: "Then Jacob made a vow, saying, 'If God will be with me, and will keep me in this way that I go, and will give me bread to eat and clothing to wear, so that I come again to my father's house in peace, then the Lord shall be my God.'"

18. One can perhaps identify four different covenants made between Hashem and humans: (1) Adamic, (2) Abrahamic, (3) Mosaic, and (4) Yeshua-church covenant.

> With the conclusion of the covenant, God ceases to be the absolute ruler. He and man have become partners in a treaty. *God is transformed from an "absolute" into a "constitutional" monarch.* He is bound, as man is bound, to the conditions of the constitution. God has lost his freedom to be arbitrary, and man has gained the freedom of being able to challenge God in the name of God's own promises, of the principles laid down in the covenant.[19]

Continuing in the Newer Testament, Yeshua also gave up some power to humans. Humans are invited to participate in making history: "I give you the keys to the kingdom," "Ask anything in my name," "You are my friends," "I give you all authority," "You will do even greater miracles than I did," "If you keep asking you will get what you want," and yet "There are things that are beyond you which you cannot attain, know, or change." Thus, in this active personalist relationship, the door is opened for gutsy, demanding prayer—praying with *chutzpah*.

Exaggerating to make a point, YHWH can be banished from a community by continued indifference and persistent sin. Yes, Scripture says he will never forsake us or leave us—individually and corporately; yet some Scriptures indicate he can be forced into exile. Rabbi Heschel explains: "The will of God is to be here, manifest and near; but when the doors of this world are slammed on Him, His truth betrayed, His will defied, He withdraws, leaving man to himself. God did not depart of His own volition; He was expelled. God is in exile."[20] One thinks of the Lord's Prayer: "Thy kingdom come, Thy will be done on earth as it is in heaven . . ." There is a *differential* in play, when humans are not invoking the Lord to rule in their domain or world, the Lord, who is the perfect "gentleman," may retreat. Humans have an inescapable responsibility to call down the Lord's reign. Human indifference may inhibit him. This can be a grim diagnosis for the believer as YHWH can be in exile even in our churches or synagogues. I use the word "differential" above and not "causality" because the relationship between the human and YHWH is *not stiffly causal*, not mechanical, not tit for tat, but Person to person(s).

To digress a bit, in Greek tragedies, the gods also participate in the drama of human life, but everything, all gods and humans, are subject to *Moira* or inevitable Fate.[21] Consequently, the Greeks believed that history is predetermined by Fate. That is, even Zeus, the supreme Greek god, was

---

19. Fromm, *You Shall Be Gods*, 23 (italics added).
20. A. Heschel, *Man Is Not Alone*, 398.
21. A. Heschel, *The Prophets*, 2:18–20.

subject to and fearful of Fate. Fate was a blind, immutable, impersonal power that predetermined the life of the gods and humans to either calamity or well-being. "Fate was the ultimate power, the ultimate mystery to the Greeks." Perhaps Fate was guided by intelligence, perhaps not, but neither the gods nor humans could argue with Fate—it was an irrational brute. Jack Miles, in *God: A Biography*, insists that there is no third option in the Bible of an impersonal alternative: no Fate, no Nature, no Cosmos, no Ground of Being, no Collective Unconscious—*just YHWH*. YHWH as Person cuts across impersonal Fate, making human destiny open-ended, contingent, and makeshift, depending on our relationship with the ultimate Protagonist, YHWH. This is why the prophets were so intense about how humans interact with YHWH to unfold history. It ratchets up the human-divine drama—loss and gain are amplified in our lives.

Our churches usually shy away from Scriptures that show YHWH changing his mind, show raw divine pathos, and show the high stakes of loss and gain—revealing that history is not all predetermined and settled. Many a lay person has raised the perennial question, "Why do we need to pray if everything is already meticulously predetermined by God?" A woman posed this question to Ambrose, the bishop of Milan, in A.D. 233:

> First, if God foreknows what will come to be and if it must happen, then prayer is in vain. Second, if everything happens according to God's will and if what He wills is fixed and no one of the things He wills can be changed, then prayer is in vain.[22]

In the abstract, predestination and free-willism are contradictory. For instance, "YHWH hardened Pharaoh's heart," and simultaneously "Pharaoh hardened his heart." Yet in real life they involve each other. Biblical texts should be viewed as partial elements of a greater whole, and should not be totalized but allowed to dialogue with other texts on the same theme. Predestination and free-will enthusiasts can dial down. German theologian Zenger suggests this: "If the Bible, as revelation of God, is to confront the variety and multiplicity of life with God, the complexity of the individual biblical texts within the whole of the biblical canon must remain vital and valid."[23] Multifaceted theology facilitates conversation, it has an easiness with incorporating a wider variety of Scriptures and tolerating paradox. And so, it can embrace all the rich Christian traditions of the differing views of the Calvinists, Barthians, Thomists, Molinists, Redemptive Interventionists, Church Dominionists, and adherents to the Openness model. It is not

---

22. This question was raised to Origen by Ambrose. See *Origen: An Exhortation to Martyrdom*, 92.

23. Zenger, *A God of Vengeance*, 86.

my intention to go into detail about these models (which Terrance Tiessen so aptly does in his comprehensive book on prayer),[24] but to merely show how a postmodern attitude can weave through them *all*. Varied prayer is needed because human situations are so varied. Sooner or later, working concepts of how YHWH acts in the larger world will not align with specific events. YHWH may act in the world in a seemingly contradictory way; consequently, Tiessen concludes, "we may find ourselves affirming statements derived from Scripture that are *logically incoherent.*"[25] Specific, preconceived structures for prayer permit simplification, but they can telescope the way we think YHWH acts in the world and think of our corresponding responsibility. It is better to draw from the general impression given by the entire canon of Scripture, with room for minority reports that may contradict the overall thrust of the biblical narrative. Any attempt to codify YHWH's behavior ignores the reality that we necessarily engage only small portions of him through different models at different times.

For example, on peculiar occasions we should refrain from praying, as YHWH has already withdrawn himself from the situation. Consider Jeremiah 14:11, "The Lord said to me: 'Do not pray for the welfare of this people.'" Instead, the people are commanded to be quiet and repentant (Jer 7:16; 11:14). In other situations, Isaiah urges YHWH not to intercede or forgive the house of Jacob (2:9b)! This is a disengaged position. At other times we need to find rest in the fact that YHWH has unilaterally preordained elements of our lives (Eph 1:4; 5:10; 2 Tim 1:9–10; 1 Pet 1:20). Here prayers conform best to a Calvinist model. The detail of YHWH's providence is evidenced in Jesus's sayings about feeding the birds (Matt 6:26) and knowing the number of hairs on each head (Luke 12:6–7). In such a light, praying for somebody who is terminally ill may be futile, and even self-indulgent. The story of Joseph's life, spelled out by a preordained dream, gives further credence to the Calvinist model.

Yet going in the opposite direction, on some occasions we may pray like Moses or Abraham who "rudely" bargained with YHWH and recommended a novel line of action—the Openness model. Here the Lord may change his plans concerning 10,000 people or more in response to the tenacious prayer of one person. The Lord was willing to spare Sodom and Gomorrah because of the prayer of Abraham. And likewise the Lord was willing to spare the Hebrews in the wilderness when Moses pleaded. A contemporary example of this happened in South Africa in the early 1990s

---

24. Terrance Tiessen gives a complete discussion of each of these traditions in his book *Providence and Prayer*.

25. Ibid., 18.

when it was on the brink of a bloody civil war. According to evangelist Michael Cassidy, who mobilized the surprisingly over-attended prayer rallies across South Africa, the faithful prayers of a few hundred thousand Christians interceding on behalf of the rest of the country's forty million people precariously saved South Africa from ruin.[26] The church dominion model may be appropriate when expelling demons. We do not pray, "Lord, if it is your will, make the demon go away." Rather, we take a dominion approach, *we* presumptively do the banishing of the demon through the authority we have in Jesus Christ. The success of the exorcism might be contingent on *our* faith. Consider Jesus's statement, "these will only come out by much fasting and praying."

YHWH's acting is often coupled with human expectancy, just as Jesus's miracles were curbed by the nonexpectancy of people in Nazareth, where he did not do any great miracles (Matt 13:58). James 4:2 says, "you have not because you ask not," furthering the notion that sometimes YHWH does not move alone, but awaits human participation. He takes human agency seriously, even when granting something, which may not be in our best interest. YHWH gave Israel a king because they insisted on being like the other nations. This was not the best choice for Israel (1 Sam 8). Similarly, when YHWH wanted Moses to be the spokesperson for the Hebrews, YHWH was swayed by Moses to allow Aaron to speak for him (Exod 4:14). John Sanders believes that YHWH accommodated these requests in the hope that the people would mature in their relationship with him so they could later move on to greater depth.[27] Sometimes we need to persevere in prayer even though nothing may happen for a very long time (Dan 10:13). On a rare occasion, when in deep trouble, do not even mention God or pray, just hang on in faith. The righteous hero Esther (in the book of Esther), did just so, where YHWH faithfully acted behind the scenes unilaterally.

Here is an uncomfortable way to handle things—contrary to today's church culture—when violated by someone, allow yourself to vent, don't camouflage your feelings; allow yourself to be a little paranoid; say this "primitive" prayer:

> Appoint a wicked man against him;
> let an accuser bring him to trial.
> When he is tried, let him come forth guilty;
> let his prayer be counted as sin!
> May his days be few;
> may another seize his goods!

26. Cassidy, *A Witness For Ever*.
27. Sanders, *The God Who Risks*, 273.

> May his children be fatherless,
> and his wife a widow!
> May his children wander about and beg;
> may they be driven out of the ruins they inhabit!
> May the creditor seize all that he has;
> may strangers plunder the fruits of his toil!
> Let there be none to extend kindness to him,
> nor any to pity his fatherless children!
> May his posterity be cut off;
> may his name be blotted out in the second generation!
> May the iniquity of his fathers be remembered before the Lord,
> and let not the sin of his mother be blotted out!
> Let them be before the Lord continually;
> and may his memory be cut off from the earth!
> Psalm 109:6–15

Commonly and rightfully, Christians reflexively go with Yeshua's injunction to forgive. But distortion can happen. For instance, after a shooting spree in, say, Los Angeles, pastor so-and-so in Minnesota gets on the media and says as Christians we need to forgive the perpetrator. First, it is none of pastor so-and-so's business, and second, only YHWH and the victim can grant that forgiveness. Brueggemann contents that, at times, we need to hold on to our anger and not be too quick to forgive. We should be honest with our emotions; not deny them; speak honestly, but don't take action. The psalm gives permission to show forth our humanness under duress; but in the middle (v. 21) and the end of the psalm (v. 31), the grievance is entrusted to YHWH, "a trustworthy conversation partner"[28] and ultimate judge. In a word, Brueggemann says that

> the Psalms offer a script whereby that ugly, unruly underside [of ourselves] is handed over to the majesty and wisdom of God, who knows and takes seriously our wounded speech and who then acts in the freedom that belongs only to God.[29]

At times we may implement the audacious stance of arguing, bargaining, and wrestling with the Holy One, a model familiar to Hebrew culture. Anson Laytner, in *Arguing with God*, enlightens Christians to the Hebrew way of dialoguing with Hashem. It is structured on the law-court pattern: address, argument, petition, and verdict. This can be detected throughout the Older Testament, with examples from Abraham's argument with Hashem

---

28. Brueggemann, *From Whom No Secrets Are Hid*, 95.
29. Ibid., 99.

over Sodom and Gomorrah (Gen 18:23–32),[30] Jeremiah,[31] Psalms,[32] Lamentations, and Job. Laytner observes that in the Torah, Hashem is understood as the judge (Abraham and Moses), but in the Prophets and Writings,[33] he is addressed both as judge and defendant. Argument with Hashem is thus widened, and the way is opened for the ordinary person to do the same, that is, hold Hashem accountable as judge and defendant. Arguing with Hashem is a sign of faith, not doubt; it takes seriously that YHWH is there as judge and mediator, that one is invited to participate, even wrestle, with him.[34]

John Sanders says YHWH may grant us something *because of* and *in response to* our requests. In 2 Kings 20:1–6, YHWH proclaimed through the prophet Isaiah that King Hezekiah would die. When Hezekiah begged the Lord not to end his life, YHWH changed his mind. If Hezekiah had not so prayed, biblical history would have been different. Strangely, this incident illustrates both the Openness model (Hezekiah changed YHWH's mind); and the Calvinist model (verse 6, Hezekiah was "preordained" to live another 15 years). YHWH genuinely takes our desires into account, yet sometimes *he*

---

30. Also see Exodus 5:22–23; 32:32; and 1 Kings 18:37.

31. Jeremiah shows the arguing with YHWH motif in a the law-court pattern:
Address: 11:20a . . . Lord of Hosts
Argument: 11:18–19 . . . against the wicked: YHWH is judge
Petition: 11:20 . . . let me see your vengeance
Divine Response: 11:21–23 . . . I will punish them

32. The law-court pattern can be shown in the Psalms:
Address: 44:2
Argument: 44:10–17
Recollection of God's Past Deeds: 44:2–4
Expression of Trust and Faithfulness / Assertion of Innocence: 44:5–9
Petition/Supplication: 44:24–27

33. Psalms, Proverbs, Job, Song of Songs, Ruth, Lamentations, Ecclesiastes, Esther, Daniel, Ezra, Nehemiah, and 1–2 Chronicles.

34. A common issue that arises when wrestling with Hashem is how much of human suffering is deserved or undeserved. Rabbis have compiled a prayer, using Cain's appeal and protest to Hashem (this can apply to Christians too, as reflected by Paul's lament in Rom 7:24): "Today you have driven me away from the soil, and I shall be hidden from your face; I shall be a fugitive and a wanderer on the earth, and anyone who meets me may kill me!" (Gen 4:14). The corporate prayer shares the responsibility for the generation of sin and its removal with Hashem himself:
Address: Master of the Universe!
Accusation: You created the evil inclination in us from our youth [as it says in Gen 8:21], and it causes us to sin against you, but you do not remove the cause of sin from us.
Petition: We beg of you, remove it from us in order that we may do your will.
Divine Response: God said to them: So shall I do in the future [to come] as it is said: "In that day, says the Lord, I will assemble the lame and gather those who have been driven away, and those whom I have afflicted" (Mic 4:6).

prevails over us, changing our thinking and even sending us in a direction never considered. When we pray, "we open a window of opportunity for the Spirit's work in our lives, creating new possibilities for God to carry out His project."[35] YHWH takes our prayers seriously and is impacted by them—so much so that he has actually instructed people to stop praying (Jer 7:16; 11:14; 14:11; 15:1). Prayer makes a difference in our lives but also in the life of YHWH. Allowing for exaggeration, Rabbi Heschel claims that Hashem's presence is banished from our world by sin. Thus, "to pray means to bring God back into the world . . . to expand His presence. . . . His being immanent in the world depends on us."[36] Likewise, Rabbi Simon ben Yohai overstates for effect: "If you are my witnesses, I am God; if you are not my witnesses, I am not God."[37] YHWH makes our concerns his concerns, weaving our petitions into his purposes and actions for the world. YHWH calls us to make our requests known to him (Phil 4:6; 1 John 5:14–15), encouraging us to ask for our desires in Yeshua's name (John 14:13–14), even though he will not always grant those that are impure or misdirected.

Fellowship with YHWH gains added meaning, as Sanders asserts, because he wants us "to be his partners not because he needs our wisdom but because he wants *our fellowship* . . . the relationship is not one of domination or manipulation but of *participation*. Wherein we become collaborators with God (1 Cor 3:9)."[38] Prayer is a dialogue, an interaction, and even an argument with YHWH. Gowan describes this reciprocity:

> The picture of God presented to us throughout the Old Testament is that of a God who has chosen to work *with*, rather than just *upon* human beings, so that humans (in this case Moses) are given the chance, if they will accept the responsibility, to contribute to a future that will be different from what it would have been, had they remained passive.[39]

If YHWH was influenced by Moses, then the future of the Hebrews is not solely in the hands of YHWH. Moses did have a say in the outcome of Israel's unfolding history—a genuine divine-human partnership existed. With such partnership comes risk. For example, he risks a bungling of the Great Commission (the Newer Testament charge to proclaim the gospel to all the world). The contemporary church cringes at a history, of say, missionaries in Africa forcing female African converts to wear bras, sing Western

---

35. Sanders, *The God Who Risks*, 273.
36. A. Heschel, *The Insecurity of Freedom*, 258.
37. A. Heschel, *Moral Grandeur and Spiritual Audacity*, 163.
38. Sanders, *The God Who Risks*, 272.
39. Gowan, *Theology in Exodus*, 231–32.

hymns, or use organ music. Despite these and many more unnecessary externals, the gospel still amazingly propagates. Opennness theology argues that YHWH does not hold total control over everything that happens in the world but allows some control to humans. YHWH sets the general parameters of history but allows "space" for humans to exercise free will. David Basinger argues that YHWH is *just* such a risk-taker: "God adopts certain overall strategies—for example, the granting of significant freedom—that create the potential for the occurrence of individual instances of evil which are, as such, pure loss and not a means to any greater good."[40] This freedom allows humans to move away from the desires of YHWH, thus thwarting his way. This seems to be a real loss to YHWH's project on earth; however, he is resourceful enough to use other means to further his goals. Conversely, Sanders reasons that the only way for YHWH to avoid risk is to affirm theological determinism or an exhaustive sovereignty that renders it impossible for humans to frustrate the plans of YHWH, even down to the least significant event.[41]

Clark Pinnock makes an interesting observation about Openness theology:

> [It] resonates deeply with the *traditional Christian devotional life*. Biblical personalism is widespread among believers, for it allows for a real relationship with God. When we address God in prayer we commonly believe that we are entering a genuine dialogue and that the future is not settled. Yet traditional theology has had a difficult time allowing for such a dialogue.[42]

Christians (usually the Reformed type) who oppose the Openness model sometimes unknowingly attest to its validity in practice. Professor Terrance Tiessen observes that some of his students (Calvinists) who believe in meticulous providence, sometimes pray in faith for YHWH to change his mind, especially pertaining to the salvation of a lost soul.[43] Also, people who explain that evil comes from the "free-will" decisions of humans contradict themselves in prayer by calling upon YHWH to prevent it, thus overriding the free moral agency of humans. Disparity between belief and practice is apparent. Also I have found that people who view God as "Omni" usually, in practice, perceive only Jesus empathizing and suffering with humanity and conceive of the Father as distant. Thus, lopsided praying to

---

40. Basinger, "Middle Knowledge and Divine Control," 135.
41. Sanders, *The God Who Risks*, 171.
42. Pinnock, *The Openness of God*, 7.
43. Tiessen, *Providence and Prayer*, 14.

Jesus arises.[44] Jesus seems more accessible since only he manifests empathy through his "human side." This is the thinking of Aquinas (1225–1274) and of contemporary promoters of the immutability of God such as Weinandy. Jesus is artificially split into man-made distinctions: his "human" and "divine" sides.[45] We need to be reminded of Yeshua's injunction to pray to the Father ("Our Father, Who art in heaven . . ."). Also, Yeshua generally deflected attention from himself to the Father. Consider his saying, "I am the Way, the Truth and the Life." Of this we ask: the Way to what? The answer is the Father. Thus, prayer ought to be primarily directed to the Father.

With the "presentism" I am highlighting, we need not "ascend to heaven" when we pray because YHWH (and not just Yeshua) is already descended into our world. In this manner, Judeo-Christianity uniquely affirms our material world. If the world is important to YHWH, it ought to be important to us. Although this world is not our ultimate home, we are encouraged to engage culture. We partner with YHWH in wrestling for the coming of his kingdom—this makes prayer fiercely meaningful. In this way, the biblical characters *prayed boldly* and understood that they were *working with YHWH to determine the future.*[46] Watchman Nee puts it this way, "the church is to restore to God His own omnipotence."[47]

Exodus 22 shows the chilling immediacy of YHWH's action:

> You shall not wrong or oppress a resident alien, for you were aliens in the land of Egypt. You shall not abuse any widow or orphan. If you do abuse them, *when they cry out to me, I will surely heed their cry*; my wrath will burn, and I will kill you with the sword, and your wives shall become widows and your children orphans.
> Exodus 22:21–24 (italics added)

According to Judaic scholar James Kugel, the text implies that Hashem does not always know what is going on; it denies his absolute knowledge over all things in the world. What Hashem *does not* miss is the *cry* of the afflicted. What arouses Hashem to action is not primarily injustice but the *cry* of the abused. He is uniquely moved by suffering. Hashem *must* act.[48] Theology that solely works from generalities, systems, and concepts tends

---

44. Bernard Cooke, in *The Distancing of God*, posits that God the Father has become a stranger.

45. Weinandy, *Does God Suffer?* 213, 225.

46. Sanders, *The God Who Risks*, 272.

47. Nee, *What Shall This Man Do?* 148.

48. Kugel, *The God of Old*, 112, 119, 123. For further evidence, see Exod 3:7–9; 15:24–25; Num 20:16; Judg 10:12; Neh 9:27; Job 34:28; Ps 12:5; 34:17; 79:11; Isa 19:20.

to flatten reality, whereas respecting the sometimes-embarrassing particularities of the Bible revitalizes the living, personal YHWH who responds to our varied lives. The Bible shows YHWH freely but not consistently sharing himself with us. Voluntarism is evident on both sides. Sometimes humans are unpredictable, but on rare occasions YHWH can be too.[49] Sometimes YHWH chooses to be close and present: "The Lord used to speak to Moses face to face, as one speaks to a friend" (Exod 33:11). Other times, YHWH is absent: "How long, O Lord? Will you forget me forever? How long will you hide your face from me?" (Ps 13:1). A similar tension exists for Newer Testament believers: closeness ("you are my friends," John 15:14; I will never leave you, Heb 13:5) and distance (there are things you cannot know, John 3:8; 4:32; 8:14; 14:5; 16:18; I will withdraw from you, to test what is in your heart, 2 Chron 32:31; Jas 1:2–4).

In short, the reality that we share the same frame of reference as YHWH encourages reciprocal addressability and mutual demand.

Lament without Giving Up

Pastoral theologian Ottmar Fuchs observes that Christians haven't allowed for lamentation in prayer. In lamentable situations, he claims, the Christian turns all too quickly to trusting petitions of surrender and prayers for endurance. The absence of lament in certain situations can leave the sufferer calmed but depressed.[50] When confrontation between YHWH and the sufferer is suppressed, the strained relationship prevents catharsis, prayer becomes tame and domesticated. To address this problem, Zenger suggests integrating the scandalous, it's-okay-to-feel-bad Psalms into regular church services:

> In a liturgical presentation, the psalms of enmity could be deliberately integrated into the canonical textual context in which they now *de facto* appear. The difficult psalm 137 would unfold its dynamic as prayer especially if it were prayed in sequence between Psalm 136 and Psalm 138.[51]

Psalm 136 proclaims a fundamental hope in God, while Psalm 138 opens with thanksgiving and affirmation of God's faithfulness. Sandwiching

---

49. In the Older Testament, YHWH can be unpredictable: he killed Uzzah for touching the Ark; here, David was "afraid" of YHWH (2 Sam 6:6–9). Early Christians Ananias and his wife, Sapphira, were struck dead for lying to the Holy Spirit (Acts 5:1–5)—and the church was struck with fear.

50. Zenger, *A God of Vengeance*, 89.

51. Ibid., 93.

Psalm 137 with its lamenting voice in this manner portrays a more complex—*and accurate*—view of the human condition. The book of Psalms reflects the human condition with its wide range of human experiences: lament, praise, doubt, thanksgiving, petition, and worship side-by-side in a colorful mixture.

Bob Dylan sheds some light on how to handle despair. His song "Not Dark Yet" sets a mood on how to "lament without resignation," as Jeff Keuss puts it. Keuss discerns that in past Christian culture, *certainty* was aligned with *faith*, and that's wrong. Something new is happening, *faith* is the destination, *not certainty*. Faith is a following after, regardless where it goes. There has been a generation who overplayed the idea of Jesus as an anchor (staying in one place and never moving). Rather, Yeshua is the keel of a ship; amid storms it keeps you upright to get you to this or that shore. The Abrahamic call led to places Abraham had no idea of. Dylan's song identifies the dusk of his life, he has no idea how the story will end: We live our lives beyond the map. What to do next? In the song he waits patiently, discovers this contemplative space, laments without reservation, admits life is full of sorrow. He "cannot even murmur a prayer"—all he can do is offer himself. Nigel Goodwin adds to Keuss's observations that there is paradox in life—thesis and antithesis. This is reflected in Dylan's words: "behind every beautiful thing there's been some kind of pain." He continues, "It's getting dark," to which Goodwin says, "something/someone is still there, it's not about how I am feeling existentially but what is true. It has to get dark before it gets light—compare a seed falling into the ground and dying before it can rise and live."[52]

Mother Teresa, who worked in the slums of Calcutta, shares a similar mood. Publicly she would attest the joy of Christ, but her interior environment was a different matter. The last half-century of her life she felt *no* presence of God—she felt "darkness," "loneliness," "dryness," "emptiness" and "torture." She was even driven to doubt the existence of heaven and God. To this, atheist Christopher Hitchens, said "ha ha, told you so"; religion is nothing but a "fabrication." In a letter to a spiritual confidant, the Rev. Michael van der Peet, Mother Teresa wrote of a different Christ, an *absent one*. "Jesus has a very special love for you," she assured Van der Peet. "[But] as for me, the silence and the emptiness is so great, that I look and do not see,—Listen and do not hear—the tongue moves [in prayer] but does not speak . . . . I want you to pray for me—that I let Him have [a] free hand."[53]

---

52. "Theology of Music," podcast on *The Kindlings Muse,* 3/26/09, at 54:00 minutes. The Bob Dylan song, "Not Dark Yet," is on the album *Out of Mind.*

53. Van Biema, "Mother Teresa's Crisis of Faith." The article further informs: "The church anticipates spiritually fallow periods. Indeed, the Spanish mystic St. John of

The confessions of Mother Teresa give encouragement to the disheartened believer; perhaps that is why YHWH decided to withhold his presence from her all those years. Here is one of her prayers:

> Lord, my God, who am I that You should forsake me? The Child of your Love—and now become as the most hated one—the one—You have thrown away as unwanted—unloved. I call, I cling, I want—and there is no One to answer—no One on Whom I can cling—no, No One.—Alone . . . Where is my Faith—even deep down right in there is nothing, but emptiness & darkness—My God—how painful is this unknown pain—I have no Faith—I dare not utter the words & thoughts that crowd in my heart—& make me suffer untold agony. So many unanswered questions live within me afraid to uncover them—because of the blasphemy—If there be God—please forgive me—When I try to raise my thoughts to Heaven—there is such convicting emptiness that those very thoughts return like sharp knives & hurt my very soul—I am told God loves me—and yet the reality of darkness & coldness & emptiness is so great that nothing touches my soul. Did I make a mistake in surrendering blindly to the Call of the Sacred Heart?[54]

Mother Teresa was heroic, sticking to her faith and work to the end. However, perhaps, she was too lopsided, too self-emptying and identifying too much with the pain of Jesus, as she wrote: "I want to . . . drink ONLY [her emphasis] from His chalice of pain."[55] Timothy Keller grounds our tears so: We do not deny or embrace our tears, neither do we stuff or bow to them. Rather we invest them. As believers in YHWH, we can expect tears, even more so as we get a new sensitized heart of flesh (Ezek 11:19) and because we empathize with YHWH, who suffers-with-humanity. All this has a hopeful end. We invest our tears in him, and in the end we reap joy (Ps 126).[56]

---

the Cross in the 16th century coined the term the 'dark night' of the soul to describe a characteristic stage in the growth of some spiritual masters. Teresa's may be the most extensive such case on record. (The 'dark night' of the 18th century mystic St. Paul of the Cross lasted 45 years; he ultimately recovered.) Teresa found ways, starting in the early 1960s, to live with it and abandoned neither her belief nor her work."

54. Ibid., 3.

55. Ibid., 4.

56. Timothy Keller, "Praying Our Tears," podcast on iTunes (last accessed May 2010).

YHWH Suffers With Us

> *In all their affliction he was afflicted*,
> and the angel of his presence saved them;
> in his love and in his pity he redeemed them;
> he lifted them up and carried them all the days of old.
> But they rebelled
> and *grieved his holy Spirit*;
> therefore he turned to be their enemy,
> and himself fought against them.
> Isaiah 63:9–10 (italics added)

Christians in miserable situations often feel compelled to pray with resignation, "Thy will be done." However, a theology that seriously considers the Father and Spirit as also suffering (not just Jesus) gives "Thy will be done" new meaning. The Lord's will can mean that he *weeps* over his creation, *avenges* evil, or *feels* remorse over evil in the world. If YHWH suffers with us, it makes human lamentation meaningful. Erich Zenger says that if he is personally touched by injustice, then we can reflect *YHWH's own self*.[57] The victims of violence need not be speechless and apathetic because YHWH is not speechless or apathetic to their plight. The YHWH-human relationship is a two-way street, bringing with it the related emotions of disappointment and joy in both directions.

There is little courage today to voice the vengeance and punishment of YHWH. However, it can be of great comfort to those afflicted by grotesque evil. The comfort comes because it says that this current life is not the only arena for justice. In the kingdom to come, YHWH will judge unrepentant evildoers. For catharsis, the sufferer can pray the Psalms of vengeance. The victim of injustice relies on YHWH—who is by nature just and fair—to impose their vengeance. Prayers of vengeance are recommended to be prayed by a God-fearing person within the believing community on behalf of the afflicted. This is to be done to restore and defend the damaged order of law. Praying this way presupposes that YHWH is personally touched by injustice and that the prayer also voices YHWH's grief.[58] One must keep in mind when praying such a prayer, though, that the answer may be that YHWH will suspend the punishment due to an evildoer, as when he mercifully abandoned the punishment due to the inhabitants of Nineveh. Prayers of vengeance can be very short, as Martin Buber illustrates in his direct translation of Psalm

---

57. Zenger, *A God of Vengeance*, 72.
58. Ibid., 72.

94:1: "God of punishments, appear!" The longer prayers of vengeance could include this well-known passage:

> The Spirit of the Lord God is upon me,
> because the Lord has anointed me
> to bring good tidings to the afflicted;
> he has sent me to bind up the brokenhearted,
> to proclaim liberty to the captives,
> and the opening of the prison to those who are bound;
> to proclaim the year of the Lord's favor,
> and the *day of vengeance of our God*;
> to comfort all who mourn;
> to grant to those who mourn in Zion—
> to give them a garland instead of ashes,
> the oil of gladness instead of mourning,
> the mantle of praise instead of a faint spirit;
> that they may be called oaks of righteousness,
> the planting of the Lord, that he may be glorified.
> Isaiah 61:1–3

Respecting the anthropomorphisms in the Bible gives credence to the notion that YHWH is doing battle *with* and *about* his loved ones. The psalms of vengeance[59] take seriously YHWH's enactment of justice against evil, which can be appropriated by the victims of evil. Zenger, in *A God of Vengeance*, states that these psalms were not concocted in a harmonious state, but "*in the midst of* a world that is often felt to be hostile, *in the midst of* enemies, against whom those at prayer are defending themselves, not least by bringing God forward as their protector and companion in battle."[60] Zenger boldly tackles the difficult passages in the Psalms that portray God as vengeful. The Psalms that reflect God's vengeance are 12, 44, 58, 83, 109, 137, and 139. (Psalms 58, 83, and 109 are omitted from the Roman Catholic Church's Liturgy of the Hours because they show the violence and vengeance of God too much.) These difficult Psalms not only demonstrate an outcry *against* violence, but also a crying *for* violence—that YHWH would avenge and destroy in retaliation against the enemies of the righteous. Using the Psalms of vengeance can be difficult, awkward, and foreign to our sensitivities; they can be rendered "pre-Christian," "un-Christian," or "less than Christian," as clinical psychologist Franz Buggle contends:

> what the psalms really are: in large part, and to a degree seldom encountered otherwise, a text dominated by primitive and

---

59. Ibid., 26, 11.
60. Ibid., 11.

uncontrolled feelings of hatred, desire for vengeance, and self-righteousness . . . . I have not read any text so marked by excessive and unbridled hatred and thirst for revenge.[61]

Nevertheless, these Psalms are particularly helpful: "the psalms of vengeance are a passionate clinging to God when everything really speaks *against* God . . . passion for God is aflame in the midst of the ashes of doubt about God . . . they leave everything in God's hands, even feelings of hatred and aggression."[62] Psychology tells us that suppressed fears and repressed aggression do not overcome violence, but further it. Hatred, hostility, violence, retaliation, and even revenge are *not submotifs* in the Psalms, but rather are *substantive* parts of it. We can scarcely be surprised that the Psalms, and the perspective on YHWH therein, have aroused resistance and rejection in Christian theology and psychology, sometimes even leading to rejection of the Older Testament. Having a lively debate with these awkward passages that portray a violence-laden image of YHWH may uncover something about ourselves and the world in which we find ourselves.[63]

Lewis Smedes shows the importance of distinguishing between *suffering* and *longsuffering*:

> To suffer is to be a victim; to be longsuffering is in a sense to be free. To earn the description "longsuffering" we have to make a decision for what we do not want, choose to live indefinitely with what we hate. This paradox . . . makes longsuffering a creative art of living . . .
>
> We are talking about digging in daily, renewing over and over again our decision to accept what we desperately do not want and cannot change, making no bones about not wanting it and yet determining to live with it and rejoice in it . . .
>
> Longsuffering, therefore, is the power to be a creative victim. Longsuffering is not passive. It is a tough, active, aggressive style of life. It takes power of soul to be longsuffering.[64]

Indeed, with "longsuffering" our response to hardship is a conscious, honest aggressive engagement with YHWH—"warts and all." Involvement is encouraged. Despair—a stance of paralysis without hope—is never an option. With multifaceted theology we can adopt a broader spectrum of reality by embracing diversity and contradiction; we can incorporate the marginal references in Psalms, the Prophets, and Lamentations with greater

---

61. Quoted in ibid., 22.
62. Zenger, *A God of Vengeance*, 79.
63. Ibid., 13.
64. Smedes, *Love within Limits*, 2–3.

ease. Sudden mood swings are allowed; intense joy and lament can coexist. We don't always have to act "nicely" and "saintly."

Worldview versus "Loves"

> You become like who you serve. (paraphrase of Jeremiah 2:5)

James Smith suggests we call for a temporary moratorium on the use of "worldview" in Christian dialogue. (In the 1970s Arthur Holmes and Francis Schaeffer popularized this concept.) Worldview talk leaves the impression that humans are primarily animated by ideas, according to Smith. He recommends the more encompassing idea of "loves." Education should primarily be about ordering our loves and not centered around just obtaining information or formulating our ideas because its focus on "objectivity" engenders detachment and freedom from emotion. Put another way, as they are formed, our identities are not primarily ordered by cognitive processes, but rather by what and whom we worship. We are lovers. The goal then is to be held captive by the right lovers.[65]

Paul Ricoeur believes that people are changed not by ethical urging but by a transformed "imagination"[66] or by what we worship. Our imagination about the Holy One, who has dangerous pursuing love, embodies pathos, and is vulnerable to human behavior, changes people more than the immutable, impassible, no-needs "Omni-God." Imagination is important because we become like what we venerate. This is particularly evident in teenagers, who often emulate the dress, mannerisms, and attitudes of music groups they admire. A sad example is the way teens who, imitating Britney Spears, dress and muse like hookers. A more sober example to consider is the devotees of Buddha: Do Buddhists become like the one they worship? Do Buddhists become emotionless, detached from this world of illusion (*maya*) as the Buddha exemplifies? If Buddha isn't concerned about this world of *maya*, why would we expect Buddhists to be? If the Buddha is beyond suffering, feeling, and passion, it would stand to reason that Buddhists consciously or unconsciously try to adopt these characteristics themselves. My purpose here is not to put down Buddhists but merely to describe differences in outlook (some people may prefer the Buddhist approach). I think it is no accident that if we look at Nobel Prize winners in science, 63 percent are Protestant, 23 percent are Jewish, 11 percent are Catholic, and 3 percent are "Other." I say it has little to do with IQ and everything to do with how we

---

65. J. K. A. Smith, *Desiring the Kingdom*, see introduction.
66. Ricoeur, *The Philosophy of Paul Ricoeur*, see chaps. 15 and 16.

view the world. Judeo-Christianity is material-world affirming—this world is *not maya* and is worth investigating—spurring people on to be scientists. Stating the obvious: Genesis declares that YHWH made a real world, YHWH is separate from creation, and YHWH begins science by inviting Adam to name the animals.[67]

What captures our imagination about YHWH influences our demeanor, our very personhood and life. Consequently, if YHWH is intimately, passionately related to our messy world, suffers with us, and involves himself with delinquent humanity, this fact will generate followers who do likewise—people who are urgent, passionate, and engaged with life.

Pathos Is Part of the Image of YHWH

What is the "image of God"? In ancient Mesopotamian literature, only the king was created in God's image: "A (free) man is the shadow of god, the slave is as the shadow of a (free) man; but the king, he is like unto the (very) image of god." Similarly, in ancient Egypt, usually the Pharaoh alone was considered to be created in a god's image, for example, "image of Re" or "image of Atum."[68] The Older Testament is ambiguous about the "form" of YHWH from which the "image" is taken. On the one hand, references indicate that YHWH has no form: at Horeb the Israelites "heard the sound of words, but saw no form" (Deut 4:12). The prophet asks, "to whom then will you liken YHWH, or what likeness compare with him?" (Isa 40:18). On the other hand, references show that YHWH does have some physical form: "Seated above the likeness of a throne was the likeness as it were a human form" (Ezek 1:26).

The Bible's open-ended term "image of YHWH" has allowed for a myriad of interpretations. Generally, prevailing philosophical and cultural trends have influenced the outcome of those interpretations. Karl Barth shows, through a historical survey, the influence that anthropology (the study of the human) and the theology of the time have had on the interpretation of the image of God.[69] For example, Augustine, animated by Greek, Neo-Platonic philosophy, would say: "For *not in the body* but in the mind was humanity made in the image of God." For Ambrose (339–397), the bishop of Milan, the *soul* was the image; for Athanasius (354–430), the bishop of Alexandria, Egypt, it was *rationality*. For the Reformers like Luther,

---

67. The beginning of science is taxonomy.
68. Clines, *On the Way to the Postmodern*, 479, 480.
69. Barth, *Church Dogmatics*, III/1, 192–94.

the image was the *original righteousness* enjoyed by Adam before the Fall.[70] Which is the correct interpretation of the image? The dominant and common interpretation of the "image" throughout history is that the *spiritual part* of humanity resembles the *spirit* of YHWH.[71] Scholars usually identify the quality shared with YHWH as nonphysical, such as *reason* (Heinisch), *personality* (Procksch, Sellin), *vitality and innate nobility* (B. Jacob), *intelligence and power* (Duncker), *self-consciousness and self-determination* (Festorazzi), *spiritual nature* (Rowley), or *thought and conscience* (Cassuto).[72]

Without question, love is consistently included in the "image" throughout history, but not its attendant emotions: jealousy and anger. They are awkward and base. *Pathos* or passion is conveniently omitted in the above sweep of history—maybe because men did all the theologizing and were prejudiced against feelings and passion. Indeed, feelings can be misleading and destructive, when mishandled. The more thinking stuff—which is safe—is preferred. Plainly what we put into the "image" depends on which era we live in and which pastor/theologian/philosopher influences our thinking. If we go with "YHWH-of-the-Prophets" and Yeshua—over the "Omni-God-of-the-philosophers"—and take seriously the anthropomorphisms of the Bible, we should include all of the above interpretations—plus *pathos*. *Pathos* involves love (which is an easy sell in our "limitless mercy culture"), but it also includes transitory sadness, joy, anger, compassion, jealousy, and even hate, that is, hate of evil. David Brooks from the *New York Times* holds that, even today—in our enlightened postmodern world—passions and feelings are downgraded:

> Reason, which is trustworthy, is separate from the emotions, which are suspect. Society progresses to the extent that reason can suppress the passions. This has created a distortion in our culture. We emphasize things that are rational and conscious and are inarticulate about the processes down below. We are really good at talking about material things but bad at talking about emotion. When we raise our kids, we focus on the traits measured by grades, IQ, and SAT scores. But when it comes to the most important things like character and how to build

---

70. "Wherefore, when we now attempt to speak of that image, we speak of a thing unknown; an image which we not only have never experienced, but the contrary to which we have experienced all our lives, and experience still. Of this image therefore all we now possess are the mere terms—the image of God! . . . But there was Adam, an illumined reason, a true knowledge of God and a will the most upright to love both God, and his neighbour." Luther, *The Creation*, 91.

71. Clines, *On the Way to the Postmodern*, 451.

72. Ibid., 449–50, 454.

relationships, we often have nothing to say. Many of our public policies are proposed by experts who are comfortable only with correlations that can be measured, appropriated, and quantified, and ignore everything else . . . . [Instead] emotion is not opposed to reason; our emotions assign value to things and are the basis of reason."[73]

Pathos needs to be identified and valued as an important part of the "image" even though it can be a risky, volatile force, deep within the human. To the prophets, sin was a lack of passion or *pathos*. Or sin was *pathos* misdirected.

Do we have a physical resemblance to YHWH? This less-appreciated interpretation is promoted by theologians Edmond Jacob and Gerhard von Rad: humans share both a spiritual and physical resemblance to YHWH.[74] As already pointed out, the Bible does not split the human into spiritual and physical parts. Humanity is essentially a unity—so the "image" should represent the whole human person. The plain understanding of the "image of YHWH" is that humans are in some way and to some degree like YHWH, though not an exact copy of him. Here lies the limitation of having the *likeness* of YHWH. All human beings are elevated to special status on earth in this way. The Bible's definition of the essence of humanity is that we share some physical resemblance to God. The Hebrew terms *tselem* and *dmus*, usually translated as "image" and "likeness," are basically visual terms. "The image of YHWH" is meant in the same way as children share a likeness to their parents.[75] The writer of Hebrews says that "[the Son] bears the very stamp of [God's] nature" (Heb 1:3). The word "stamp" used to describe God is the Greek word for "character," evoking a sharply defined impression made in clay, wax, or metal by a seal. Though we never see the actual

---

73. Brooks, "The New Humanism."

74. See both von Rad, *Genesis*, 61; and Jacob, *Theology of the Old Testament*, 166–70.

75. The same word is used when Adam sees his "likeness" in his son Seth (Gen 5:3). Only brief mention is made to the image of God in the Bible: Gen 1:26: "Let us make humanity in our image after our likeness." Gen 5:1–2: "God . . . created humankind in the likeness of God." And Gen 9:6: "Whoever sheds the blood of a human, by a human shall his blood be shed; for God made humanity in his own image." In the NT there are two explicit references to the image of God: 1 Cor 11:7 and Jas 3:9. Further mentions of the image in the NT are developments of this idea. Christ is recognized as the full image of God, the last Adam, "who is the likeness of God" (1 Cor 4:4–6), "the image of the invisible God" (Col 1:15). The NT asserts that believers are brought into "conformity" to the image of Christ/God by faith in Christ (Rom 8:28). The NT also highlights the fallen nature of humanity and the need for redemption in Christ. In this way, only those who appropriate the work of Christ can more fully realize the image of God.

seal (God) we do receive an accurate idea of the seal itself. Furthermore, Yeshua is the Word of God, the living expression of the living God (John 1:1, 14, 18). Thus, looking at the Son, we obtain an accurate representation of YHWH. Yeshua showed *pathos*: frustration, empathy, anger, hatred of evil, sadness, and of course strong-willed love.

Celebrating Personhood

> God is the premier person, the first and chief exemplar of personhood . . . and the properties most important for an understanding of our personhood are properties we share with him.[76]

The book of Genesis features the making of humankind. Humans are the pinnacle, the climax of YHWH's attention. Man and woman are to be YHWH's image bearers on earth and are to be the sole creatures showing forth his invisible nature. The human, therefore, is created with the express purpose of revealing to all other creatures the invisible and infinite substance of YHWH.[77] Illingsworth says that the highest avenue through which to conceive God is studying human personality, and this personality representing God is a synthetic unity of reason, will, and love.[78] Since we are image bearers, arguing in reverse, we assume that YHWH shares our likeness in emotions, reason, personhood, and perhaps even physicality.

In this light, Morton Kelsey emphasizes, YHWH is not an object to be studied, but a Person to be apprehended:

> Learning about God is more like learning about another human being than about things, and human beings seldom reveal themselves until the conditions are right. If God had been able to communicate himself through a law or prescription, he very likely would have done so.[79]

The personhood of the human is inextricably linked to the personhood of YHWH. YHWH is a Subject to be related to, not a mere Object to be reckoned with. When Nietzsche proclaimed that "God is dead,"[80] Nietzsche, a bright and insightful man, realized the tragic consequences:

---

76. Plantinga, "Advice to Christian Philosophers," 264–65.
77. Graham McFarlane's thoughts, in Schwöbel and Gunton, *Persons, Divine and Human*, 99.
78. Illingworth, *Personality*, vii-viii, 8.
79. Kelsey, *Encounter with God*, 239.
80. Nietzsche, *Thus Spoke Zarathustra*.

man is therefore dead and, subsequently, all human meaning, purpose, and morals are ultimately arbitrary—temporary human fabrications. Conversely, if YHWH is alive, then the human is alive; humans are infused with direction, meaning, and purpose—for the life and passion of the human soul relies ultimately on its Source, YHWH. As Francis Schaeffer pointed out, if there is no *personal* God, humans are doomed. If we are merely products of an impersonal universe of matter and energy, then we as personal beings are "cosmic freaks." Our sense of personhood or importance as a soul is baseless romanticism and ultimately unfulfillable, as everything in the end of time will either dissolve into matter and energy (the materialist conclusion) or be subsumed into an *impersonal*, Cosmic-Mind-Energy-Force (pan-everything-ism).[81] Muhammad, who conversed with Christians and Jews in his caravan journeys across the Arabian Peninsula, defined Allah as all-merciful, all-sufficient, but without companions or children—no sons, no daughters, and no friends. Muhammad made this clear, to oppose the Christians' belief of a Father, Son, and Holy Spirit, and the Jewish belief of Hashem being a "husband" to Israel.[82] The Bible shows the personal attachment and deep intimacy of Hashem to the Jews: Israel is his "son," originating from his very loins (Hos 11:1). The same intimacy is extended to the church—we are YHWH's "bride," "son," and "friend."

If YHWH is the premier Person, the chief exemplar of our personhood, we have much to look forward to in expanded communication, love, unique identity, fellowship, and joy in this and the next life. The exhortation in Ephesians 4:24[83] teaches that our new self is being transformed to YHWH's likeness in righteousness and holiness; that is, complete personhood, available in Christ, is "already here" and "not yet." Paradox again. Still, YHWH's aim is to fortify and solidify our personhood in this life and the next.

Bishop Tutu of South Africa claims that the biggest mistake the white man made in South Africa was giving the Bible to the black man. This seemingly harmless book is subversive, able to doom the white man's dominance. The Bible raises the self-assertiveness, self-worth, and energy of the reader and practitioner. Consequently, the majority of the people of South Africa—comprised of black Christians—demanded better treatment. Fortunately, the predominately Christian white minority population listened to

---

81. I heard this explained when visiting Francis Schaeffer at L'Abri, Switzerland, 1981. Also note that I do not use the word *pantheism*, because it unduly implies that there is a "theos," a self-conscious communicating personal deity.

82. Stratton, *Anger,* 223.

83. Ephesians 4:24: "and put on the new nature, created after the likeness of God in true righteousness and holiness."

their consciences, relented, and ushered in the bloodless revolution of 1990, releasing Nelson Mandela after 27 years in prison, and then voted him in as president.

If I may generalize, Hinduism, Buddhism, and most forms of pantheism lack grounding in the value of the self. Their "deities"[84] have wandering affections, while YHWH is jealous for and concerned about human attachment. The Eastern religions lack a strong polarity between good and evil and between self and *Om* (Brahman). *Om* includes all, accepts all, rejects and hates nothing. In this life we are temporally differentiated from Brahman, but in the end of time, everything will be absorbed back into Brahman. All individuals vanish, losing all sense of identity, by being collapsed into Brahman—a form of nihilism. An analogy often used to illustrate this view is that we are like drops of water as individuals but when we die (or attain release from the cycle of reincarnations), the drops of water are absorbed into the ocean of Brahman. Thus the individual drop of water loses all sense of identity and self-consciousness.

In comparison, Judeo-Christianity has a strong sense of boundary between creature and Creator. The soul retains its identity even into eternity, as Yeshua said: "as for the resurrection of the dead, have you not read what was said to you by God, 'I am the God of Abraham, and the God of Isaac, and the God of Jacob?' He is not God of the dead, but of the living" (Matt 22:31–32). This Scripture indicates that these unique individuals—Abraham, Isaac, and Jacob—retain their identity with YHWH in the next life. It is no accident that the science of psychology was born out of a Judeo-Christian culture (Sigmund Freud was a Jew; Carl Jung, the son of a pastor; and Carl Rogers came from a church background). Relationship with YHWH or exposure to church/synagogue culture aggrandizes the person. To use Martin Buber's argument, if there is a "Thou," then there is an "I"; if there is only an impersonal "It" for God, then the person degenerates into an "it" as well. According to the principle of the "survival of the fittest" in evolution, the individual has no lasting value either: the individual human is only there in the chain of ancestry to propagate the species—nothing more. If one is to live honestly and consistently with the notion that we are nothing but an evolved organism—as in *atheistic* evolution—then we must desist from relishing all poetry, songs, and art that celebrate the splendor of the human, of love, and so forth. To be intellectually honest, all these aspirations to the nobility of the soul/person and its eternal continuance, in some manner, should cease. Ultimately, all these are wishful thinking having no basis in

---

84. Buddhism neither denies nor asserts the existence of God or gods; Hinduism maintains the existence of millions of deities.

the nothing-but-an-evolved-universe narrative. Again, we become like the one we worship: if YHWH is personal, fierce in love, and jealous over human affections, we become like him—willful, self-valuing, and jealous over personal relationships and circumspect of our affections. Like our Creator, we become directed, principled, and discriminating with our energies and emotions.

Buddhism says all suffering comes from *desire,* from human attachment to other humans or things. The Buddha showed the way to enlightenment by negating all desire, thus attaining bliss. Similarly in Tao ("the divine way") we need to rid ourselves of all conflict, passion, desire, and greed because the divine way is everlasting calm, eternal silence, and the place of unchangingness.[85] The Bible goes in the opposite direction—it emphasizes *attachment and desire.* Though agreeing with Buddhism that desire is a sure recipe for heartache and suffering, the Jew and Christian nevertheless embrace desire and attachment, but with qualifications. We are called by Hashem to attach to him with our whole soul, heart, and mind. Attachment and passion have built-in liabilities of disappointment and suffering, yet they yield huge benefits. Psalms and Lamentations are entirely dedicated to dealing with the heartache and pain associated with dashed attachment to YHWH, humans, and things. We do not tune out pain, but rather go directly to and through it. So there is a place for anger, compassion, disappointment, elation, jealousy, sadness, and joy in the midst of attachment.

Alongside YHWH's patience and mercy, witnessed in Scripture, his irritability demonstrates his desire to attach to us; it makes us aware of the seriousness of the battle for our mind, soul, and body. It heightens the value of the human, and intensifies the responsibilities we have in directing life here on earth. Heschel says Hashem is "all-personal and all-subject."[86] His primary concern is not to make nice, but have relationships with humans.

"Masculine" Love Deficit

My Catholic upbringing emphasized Jesus as meek, mild, and nice. If a priest, nun, or monk got angry or frustrated with us students, it was considered a boo-boo requiring an apology. In their words, they had failed to copy Jesus, who was passive, endlessly merciful, and forever receptive as portrayed in the Beatitudes (Matt 5:3–12). "Masculine" love was lacking. It is safe to say that the Western church is effeminate. The church is primarily

---

85. A. Heschel, *Between God and Man,* 119.
86. A. Heschel, *The Prophets,* 1:218.

filled with women and children and predominantly portrays God as nice, tolerant, limitlessly merciful, and domesticated.

Feminist criticism of patriarchy in Western culture makes a good case much of the time, with warranted but inaccurate conclusions. The men's movement—particularly propounded by Robert Bly, Robert Moore, and Douglas Gillette—acknowledges that men have been tyrannical, abusive, weak, manipulative, masochistic, sadistic, detached, addictive, and impotent. However, these should be viewed as the *shadow* of the masculine soul, the result of immature grown-up boys who are self-interested and self-involved, who seldom or never act for the greater good of humanity. Never outgrowing the childish self, they pass on wounded masculinity to their children. (By the way, women are not exempt from weakness; their *shadow* sides can be witchy, manipulating, betraying, helpless, and codependent.)

In his book *Wild at Heart*, John Eldredge thinks too many Christian men have become docile and timid. He holds up Mister Rogers—the soft-spoken TV character, now deceased, Fred Rogers—as an example of what many Christians believe they should emulate, the soft nice guy. Eldredge insists that men need a battle to fight, a beauty to rescue, and an adventure to live.[87] Popular movies such as *Gladiator*, *Braveheart*, and *Lord of the Rings* reveal what the male heart longs for: bravery, integrity, courage, and goodness. These movies make men (and women) come alive—there is a battle to fight, where the enemy can be within and without.

The instinct to fight is deep in the heart of YHWH. Exodus 15:3 reminds us that "YHWH is a warrior, YHWH is his name." He is "the Lord of armies," "the Angel of YHWH," "the Redeeming Angel," and "the Man" who fights with Joshua to gain the Promised Land. In Isaiah 53, YHWH wears bloodstained clothes, and "the Spirit of the Lord" upon Samson kills a lion with his bare hands and a thousand men with the jawbone of a donkey (Judg 15:14). Yeshua confirms this capacity for aggression: "From the days of John the Baptist until now the kingdom of heaven has suffered violence, and the violent take it by force" (Matt 11:12). The fierce love of YHWH takes risks and validates the goodness of aggression in certain situations. YHWH is *angry* about what has happened to us; he is not angry with us—he is angry *for* us.

So what does a "godly" man look like? Church culture abounds with duties and obligations for men, while a better way to mobilize them is to make them come alive to what is already in their hearts—the desire "to fight, to rescue a beauty, and to live an adventure." Personalist theology heightens the danger and adventure of having a relationship with YHWH. In contrast,

---

87. *Wild at Heart*, 8.

generic theology can produce men who abstractly and dutifully adhere to biblical principles and laws. However, life should be entered as a mystery—a sacred drama. The Person of the Bible is to be sought, apprehended, and engaged—this adventure lures us. In the process, a man is called out, takes on a dangerous journey, and gets a new name (e.g., Abram, Jacob, and Saul of Tarsus become Abraham, Israel, and Paul, respectively).[88] Multifaceted theology allows YHWH the warrior to be appropriated, on occasion, and allows the judgment of Jesus to be voiced, at times, to counter the lopsided "niceness" of Jesus. Allen Bloom, a secular university professor, identifies and decries the "niceness" of today's students, who, like spineless jellyfish, avoid all conflict, avoid making value judgments, and accommodate so much to the prevailing culture that they are like mirrors merely reflecting it back.[89]

YHWH is the king, the warrior, the priest, and the lover.[90] The warrior aspect of Yeshua is particularly neglected in our church culture. The Bible shows the balance between withholding and engaging, anger and gentleness, firmness and forgiveness, warrior and friend, and cursing and blessing. This is how men are to model themselves—they are to have a weathered skin to bear living in our fallen universe. When men take up this challenge, women will be freed to drop their compensatory stances of being the hopeless one, the witch, the overly petite, the manipulative, or the domineering.

88. Ibid., 118.

89. Bloom, *Closing of the American Mind*, 25–43.

90. Moore and Gillette, *King, Warrior, Magician, Lover*, xvii. Moore and Gillette identify the archetypes (primordial images) of masculinity, the real image of man: the *warrior*, the *king*, the *magician* (priest), and the *lover*. I prefer to use the biblical notion of priest instead of magician. These need to be called forth and restored. I have described the *warrior* somewhat in the above text. They define the *king* as ordering, bringing fertility, and blessing (p. 52). The *king* organizes law out of chaos and stimulates outpourings of creativity and generativity—he is a good steward of nature. The king is to behold, to make the beholden feel valued (today's men are starving for affirmation from older men), and to be generative (this is particularly embodied in the stories of the shepherd, the gardener, the husband, and the vinedresser in the Bible). When the king archetype is distorted, the tyrant and weakling appear, the shadow of the strong generative king. The *priest* understands the hidden dynamics of human life, is able to bless or curse, sees through denial, is a "bullshit detector," sees evil masquerading as good, and has the capacity to detach from the outer or inner storms of life to connect with deep inner truths (p. 108). He is able to utilize raw emotional energy, and transform and channel this into life-enhancing self-expression (p. 117). In other words, he is able to channel primal emotions. The shadow of the priest is the manipulator. The *lover* is deeply sensual, shows gentle appreciation, feels and sees without shame, wants to be related to, can feel hidden motives that can be painful, feels the painfulness of being alive, and is deeply pained by idolatry. The shadow of the lover is apathy, aimlessness, and depression.

This order of behavior is Paul's reasoning in Ephesians 5. Yeshua manifested the ideal masculine archetypes of warrior, priest, king, and lover. Church culture adequately portrays YHWH as lover, priest, and king, but is mute about the aggressive warrior side of his goodness. George Stratton argues for the correct balance that Yeshua had in "meanness" and tenderness:

> For Jesus is not the fanatic warrior Muhammad; nor is he the Buddha, seated under the Bodhi tree, studying how he may lose the last trace of passion. Jesus is not an emotionalist, but he showed emotion; he loved, he wept, he lost heart, he grew angry, he attacked . . . . His anger is detached from all selfish interest; he is enraged against those who have had opportunity and yet remain opponents of the truth and of mercy.[91]

At the beginning of Yeshua's ministry he proclaimed his warrior intent (Luke 4:17) by quoting Isaiah's war cry:

> The spirit of the Lord God is upon me,
> because the Lord has anointed me;
> he has sent me to bring good news to the oppressed,
> to bind up the brokenhearted,
> to proclaim liberty to the captives,
> and release to the prisoners;
> to proclaim the year of the Lord's favor.
> (Isaiah 61:1–2a)

Contrary to the feminist demand for less masculine power in the world, more is needed, that is, less *immature* masculinity and more *mature* masculinity. Men need to selectively copy YHWH's way of loving, which is routinely forgiving, sometimes demanding, tender, sometimes dangerous and "terrible."[92] Warrior love will not tiptoe around controversial issues, but will go straight into the hornets' nest if necessary to speak truth. Perhaps, for example, a young man can be dissuaded from acting out on his same sex attraction if the truth is spoken to him early enough, helping him see an alternative. (The media has displayed this adrenalin-producing topic as black and white—they fail to show the tremendous elasticity of human sexuality.) A warrior-commander, instead of bombing a city filled with innocent civilians, may choose a harder fight on the ground, door-to-door, risking more casualties among his soldiers. A warrior-employer may confront and correct an employee without firing him/her from the job. And so on.

91. Stratton, *Anger*, 129.

92. 2 Samuel 6:9: "David was *afraid* of the Lord that day; he said, 'How can the ark of the Lord come into my care?'"

Moore and Gillette say this is the age of the "soft masculine"[93] (think Tom Cruise), where many are uncomfortable with the masculine energy of the warrior. When the warrior is repressed, that instinct goes "underground" and resurfaces as inordinate emotional and physical violence.[94] Some men even fight the wrong battle—as did King Saul who tried to kill David, or Saul who persecuted the early church.[95] The Christian warrior should be animated by things that lie beyond his own concerns and personal gain. He is alert, discerning, clear in thinking, focused in mind and body, knowing one's limitations yet not romantic about vulnerability. Many things in the world need to be destroyed by Christian warriors: deceit, camouflage, lies, pretense, corruption, tyranny, oppression, and injustice. In the current cultural war, in the United States—to echo Eldredge—Christians need to pick up the sword and rush into the abyss, bringing light and destruction to the darkness.

Divine Guidance

Multifaceted theology with paradox challenges popular theology's tidy rendition of divine guidance. There is wiggle room. Matters can be established, open, pre-ordained, messy, and varied. We wrestle with YHWH; tension is okay; risk exists. Pure gain and pure loss are possible in life. "Work out your salvation with fear and trembling" and "you have not because you ask not." The focus shifts from God's having a perfect, preordained plan for your life, which can happen for parts of your life, to a more varied and fluid arrangement. Unilateral predestination dictated by YHWH can happen, as happened to me when I was in the South African Army in Namibia. I was "hand-picked" by an officer to join another military group, sending me to another location where life-changing events happened to me. I use Calvinist language to describe these events—I felt YHWH's preordained, providential election. YHWH calls us and has plans for our unique selves, but there is elasticity—his plans can change because he is *influenced by us*. Things are malleable. People who overplay predestination provide unconvincing support for the notion of free will.[96] They believe that God always has some-

---

93. Moore and Gillette, *King, Warrior, Magician, Lover*, 75.

94. A similar phenomenon happens when a culture is overly materialistic and suppresses any notion of the supernatural (angels, demons, and Satan)—it inadvertently resurfaces in the popularity of psychic/witchcraft/horror movies and TV shows in that culture.

95. Eldredge, *Wild at Heart*, 168.

96. With this broad sweep about predestination I do not intend to include all

thing specific he wants us to accomplish: God has a master blueprint for our lives, which we can either find for our lives, or miss out on. Divine guidance in this model is merely a matter of finding God's already preordained path for our lives. It emphasizes God's "perfect" will for one's life. To concede some ground, however, multifaceted theology can be paradoxical and accommodate specific predestination, as was the case of Joseph and his brothers. Joseph was given specific details in a dream of how he would rule over his brothers one day, and these prophecies were specifically fulfilled. Yeshua also lets on that even when a sparrow falls, he knows.

I believe the biblical word "perfect" has been pushed too much in the direction of Greek philosophy. (For Aristotle, God is absolutely perfect—*actus purus*—he has no need to change for the better and cannot change for the worse.[97]) It is not my intention to go into an in-depth analysis on the word "perfect" as it has been translated in both the Older and Newer Testaments; however, I suggest that its meaning leans more in the direction of being complete, whole, and without blemish rather than incapable of change.[98] Rabbi Heschel argues that the word "holy" better fits the original intent of "perfect" in the Older Testament,[99] having more latitude to it. Though words are not exactly defined in the Bible, we can deduce their meaning from different contexts: holy can mean different, whole, awesome, just, merciful, terrible, faithful, complete, or without blemish. When the word "perfect" is applied to God, it tends to place him in a narrow mold, where his ways cannot be swayed or changed. According to Heschel, "The notion of God as a perfect being is not Biblical . . . . It is the product not of prophetic religion but of Greek philosophy; a postulate of reason . . . perfection is a term of praise which we may utter in pouring forth emotion . . . . We are never told: 'Hear, O Israel, God is perfect!' It is an attribution which is strikingly absent in both the Biblical and rabbinic literature."[100]

Multifaceted theology allows more latitude. YHWH voluntarily involves himself with risk, "failure,"[101] untidiness, and waste. Thus, the more malleable word "holy" fits better for messy human situations. Consequently, YHWH rules unilaterally, but with some input from humans on how to guide the world. In divine guidance, many different routes are open to us;

Calvinists and those in the Reformed tradition.

97. Weinandy, *Does God Suffer?* 71.

98. Leviticus 11:44: "be holy, for I am holy"; and Matthew 5:48: "be perfect, as your heavenly Father is perfect."

99. A. Heschel, *Moral Grandeur and Spiritual Audacity*, 129.

100. A. Heschel, *Between God and Man*, 98.

101. Wyschogrod, *Body of Faith*, 14–17.

matters are not always "perfectly" predetermined. YHWH, who is endlessly resourceful, adjusts his plans to fit in with human decisions. However, to qualify, there is a general predestined plan he adheres to in curbing human destiny. In some cases he may have a very specific task one needs to carry out; for example, YHWH asked Gideon to tear down the altars of Baal (Judg 6:25). Yet we should assume there is leeway for different options in our life. Here I differ with John Sanders, who adheres to Openness theology, in that he believes specific directions from the Lord are "rare" and Christians should assume that there is no specific lifelong plan.[102]

I like Openness theology's core emphasis: YHWH wants *fellowship* with humans. Consequently, our guidance comes—or the unfolding of our life happens—as we pursue fellowship with YHWH. Love is his main interest. Sanders adds: "As a lover and friend, God works with us, wherever we go and whatever we do. To a large extent our future is open and we are to determine what it will be in dialogue with God."[103] We are not called to seek God's "perfect" will for our lives, but to seek God's *wisdom* for our lives (Jas 1:5) and his will in general.[104]

This wisdom comes by reading the Bible, seeking counsel from wise people, and seeking the leading of the Holy Spirit. Our focus with this model is not that we are searching for a vocation, place to live, spouse or no spouse, but that we are pursuing a *relationship* with YHWH—in this way, life's details unfold as a byproduct. Jesus said, "Seek first the kingdom of God and all these things will be added unto you" (Matt 6:33). Seek first the kingdom of God then everything else comes. The relationship with YHWH is dynamic and living. The Holy Spirit leads us. If we abide in Christ, we bear much fruit (John 15:5). We are not puppets. Sometimes we may be perplexed;[105] sometimes we may be in lockstep with the Holy Spirit; sometimes tired, and sometimes energized. At times, the action of the Holy Spirit in us can be thwarted and frustrated (Eph 4:30), making his plans appear "fallible." To compare, Aquinas describes God as an "immovable pillar" around which humans move. Similarly, in "hyper-sovereignty" (ultra-Calvinism) God can

---

102. *The God Who Risks*, 276.

103. Ibid., 277.

104. Romans 12:2: "Do not be conformed to this world but be transformed by the renewal of your mind, that you may prove what is the will of God, what is good and acceptable and perfect." Colossians 4:12b: "that you may stand mature and fully assured in all the will of God." Hebrews 13:21: "equip you with everything good that you may do his will, working in you that which is pleasing in his sight, through Jesus Christ; to whom be glory for ever and ever. Amen."

105. 2 Corinthians 4:8a, "We are afflicted in every way, but not crushed; *perplexed*, but not driven to despair."

be an all-controlling despot who cannot tolerate any resistance (to be fair, even Calvin himself would have a problem with the theology developed by those who claim his name). With these examples, the love of God is a one-way benevolence with no place for receptivity and passion on God's part. Here God's love is not dependent.

I have relied heavily on Openness theology in this section, even though I do not agree with all of its assertions. I am not sure I go along with some of its conclusions, especially pertaining to chance events and accidents, which can mix in with our lives.[106] I would rather leave such matters to mystery. Although traditional theology affirms the Openness model's main assertion of seeing persons in loving relation with each other and with YHWH as a reliable way to seek guidance, the Openness model puts flesh to bone in its promotion.

Worship

"The-God-of-the-philosophers" is the Unmoved Mover, with no needs. "Yahweh-of-the-Prophets-and-Moses" is the Most Moved Mover, who needs and pursues humans. He is vulnerable to rejection and suffering. This adds another dimension to the act of worship. He has condescended to our world (not just Yeshua); we share the same frame of reference. The human and divine are intimately intertwined. We share his concerns, his pain *and* his joy. God is not "up there" while we are "down here." We are his temple, we move together in the same space. To be "spiritual" is to be in the here and now. Life is not divided into spiritual and physical. The Hebrew word for "worship" (*abodah*) is the same word used for "work" or "service." Therefore worship is concrete. It's a *whole person* thing, using everything we got: voice, musical instruments, dance, clapping, filmmaking, science, architecture, decor, visuals, mime, and silence. So, all our doings and work are worship when done with the right intention.

Today, Hasidism (ultra-orthodox Judaism) exemplifies the aforementioned, giving insight to Christian worship and piety. Life is indivisible—action and thought are inextricably bound together. Worship applies to *all* areas of life. Life is concrete and historic; nothing is trivial; no act is trite; every moment is extraordinary. Therefore, worship and living are not separate actions. Even going to the bathroom can be sacred! (A Hasid can pray, "Blessed are you Lord who made the workings of the body.") All life is shot through with significance and meaning. The tables in our homes are sacred altars where we offer "sacrifice." Heschel explains, "the Hebrew

---

106. Sanders, *The God Who Risks*, 277.

verb to sacrifice means literally to come near, to approach. Our task is not to renounce life but to bring it close to Him."[107] All our seemingly trivial activities are brought close to him, dedicated to him by consciously living in his presence. Worship is extremely concrete; we shape our lives to his image by copying him in joy, creating, sadness, intentional communication, compassion, sometimes anger, and sometimes letting things go. Incidentally, the Bible divulges little or nothing about YHWH's *being*, but concerns itself with his acts, movement, and pathos. In Jewish thought, *being* and *doing* are not separated; in fact, biblical ontology does not separate the two. Simply put, *what is, acts.*[108] I believe this is what James is trying to say in his epistle about the "faith alone" versus "works" split. They are inseparable.

YHWH is jealous of humanity's deceiving lovers and joyed by humanity's attention. Voluntary, conscious worship and praise from humans brings him pleasure. The human-divine relationship is voluntary and reciprocal. Authentic relationship occurs because both parties speak, sing (yes, YHWH sings over us too, Isa 5:1; 27:2), and act in freedom and candor.

Why a Chosen People?

Why did Hashem choose a particular tribe, Israel, to reveal himself? Why did he come up with the idea of a Promised Land?[109] Having lived in Israel, I asked these questions many times because of all the strife it causes. Initially, when the Israelites took possession of the Land it was occupied, and they had to drive out—even kill the Canaanites for their evil of routine child sacrifice.[110] The Land was "spewing" them out. (Likewise the rebellious Jews would later be "spewed out" themselves.) Today irresolvable conflict is produced by displacing Palestinians. Jews even acknowledge that the whole idea of being "the apple of God's eye," has aroused much resentment and anti-Semitism all through history among the rest of us, the "unchosen."[111]

---

107. A. Heschel, *God in Search of Man*, 399.

108. A. Heschel, *The Prophets*, 2:44.

109. There are people who say the promise of this land is not applicable today as the Jews have not kept their side of the bargain—being a righteous nation. There is scriptural backing for this position. However, I do not believe this position can be sustained as there are numerous other references attesting that the land is unconditionally promised to them.

110. Were the Aztecs conquered by the Spanish and Portuguese Conquistadors (15th–17th centuries) because the Aztecs routinely sacrificed their children and young virgins on alters to their bloodthirsty gods? Maybe the same explanation can be given: YHWH "ordained" it.

111. See Prager and Telushkin, *Why the Jews?* Some of my thoughts: Does the Lord

And further, why does Hashem, who is omni-present, favor Jerusalem as his Holy City, intensifying conflict over a place?[112]

Today, the three monotheisms compete for real estate in Jerusalem. Jerusalem is the third most holy place for Islam (a legend arose that Muhammad, in a dream, ascended to heaven from Jerusalem). Next, Christianity and Judaism compete for the same sites in the Holy City. These three religions are equally triumphalist: Islam will triumph with the coming of the mahdi; Christianity will triumph with the second coming of Yeshua; and Judaism will triumph with its coming messianic age/messiah. It seems that unavoidable conflict awaits the future of Jerusalem. Zechariah intensifies the thought, "On that day I will make Jerusalem a heavy stone for all the peoples; all who lift it shall grievously hurt themselves. And all the nations of the earth shall come together against it" (12:3). Intellectually, I don't like all this—the chosen people, the Promised Land, and the Holy City of Jerusalem—it does not feel right either. And yet it is. Generally, evangelical Christians concede the above, but with qualifications, one being that we do not have to agree with everything the Israeli government does.

The Holocaust and "Omni-God"

After the Holocaust, both Jewish and Christian thinkers are adjusting the generic "Omni-God" assumption to a more biblical view: Rabbi Dan Cohn-Sherbok, who has reflected on the Holocaust for fifty years, documents this trend. In his book *Holocaust Theology*, he shows the different reactions people take. Jewish scholar Richard Rubenstein and Sherwin Wine, the founder of humanistic Judaism, tell us to abandon all belief in a supernatural Deity. God is silent. God is dead.[113] Jonathan Sacks, the chief rabbi of Great Britain, says it's a mistake to blame God; the Holocaust was the result of human free will.[114]

---

use "hunters" (Nazism) and anti-Semitism to bring the Jews back to Israel? I have often asked these questions. Jeremiah 16:16 can be applied to further this line of thought. "I am now sending for many fishermen, says the Lord, and they shall catch them; and afterward I will send for many hunters, and they shall hunt them from every mountain and every hill, and out of the clefts of the rocks." The "fishermen" can be considered the Zionists who went about pre-Hitler Europe urging the Jews to emigrate to Palestine. The "hunters" can be considered the pogroms, Nazism, and Stalinism that forced a mass emigration to Israel and the United States.

112. Psalm 135:21: "Blessed be the Lord from Zion, he who resides in Jerusalem. Praise the Lord!"

113. Cohn-Sherbok, *Holocaust Theology*, 2.

114. Ibid., 10.

David Blumenthal categorically insists that the Jews have absolutely no responsibility for the Holocaust (it would be as if blaming the victim). Hashem is solely responsible: He is the Perpetrator.[115] Hence, Jews are justified in keeping their distance from him, clinging tenaciously to their rage, and telling the ugly truth that he is the "Abuser" and the "Perpetrator" of the Holocaust atrocities. Blumenthal demands that *God* must repent and return to the Jewish people.[116] If we line up Blumenthal's ruthless honesty with Job 42:7, YHWH is not offended. He can take it. One has to commend Blumenthal: Unlike those who are indifferent to God, he has a robust relationship with Hashem. Though he is angry, there is room for movement. (However, using the word "Abuser" may be too strong, as it implies deliberate evil on the part of the Perpetrator. Also, in abuse cases, the victim—as a rule—is innocent.)

Abraham Heschel, an orthodox Jew, also engages the problem of Hashem's involvement front on, but he addresses the Holocaust indirectly through his commentary on Isaiah—judgment happens and the victims are not all innocent.[117] Traditional Jewish theology has always maintained that every major catastrophe that happened to the Jews is Hashem's punishment. Jewish theologian Ignaz Maybaum says the Holocaust was God's plan to destroy the medieval Jewish institutions in Europe and drive Jews to reconstruct their lives into the next century. So Hitler was Hashem's instrument.[118] Indeed, the establishment of Israel is a consequence and step towards the redemption of the world. The Messiah will come. These ideas are obscene to many. Rabbi Anson Laytner, a self-identified agnostic mystic, like many contemporary secular Jews, believes Hashem is in exile and withdrawn from the midst of his people for an unspecified period of time. There is a perceived loss of physical intimacy with Hashem.[119] This position evades any direct explanation. Christian theologian Ulrich Simon offers that the Holocaust was a sacrifice to God. Like Christ's death, the murder of millions of Jews is akin to a sacrificial offering.[120] The Jews suffer to eventually bring something good to the rest of humanity.

Elie Wiesel as a young boy witnessed the hanging of another young boy in one of the death camps in Europe by the Nazis. The hanging boy, looking into the eyes of the other inmates, took half an hour to die. Wiesel

---

115. Blumenthal, *Facing the Abusing God*, 266.
116. Ibid., 266–67.
117. *The Prophets*, 1:147, 187.
118. Cohn-Sherbok, *Holocaust Theology*, 6.
119. Laytner, *Arguing with God*, 233.
120. *Holocaust Theology*, 8.

heard a man behind him ask: "Where is God now?" A voice within Wiesel answered: "Where is He? He is—He is hanging here on this gallows."[121] Psalm 91:15 says, "I will be with them in distress," and Isaiah 63:9 says, "In all their troubles he was troubled" (compare Ps 23:4; 139). The accepted "Omni-God" presumption, who is unaffected by human pain, has lost credibility. Instead, what explains more is YHWH who voluntarily involves himself and silently suffers with the afflicted. Christian philosopher Marcel Jacques Dubois says the suffering of Israel in the Holocaust converges with the suffering of Yeshua.[122] Christian theologian Paul Fiddes, empathizing with the suffering of Holocaust victims, says YHWH freely chooses to limit himself, endure pain and death while remaining the living God.[123] YHWH's love suffers with us. Commonly, religious people don't want a suffering-servant God, as depicted by Isaiah 53 (the suffering servant represents Yeshua or Israel)—they want triumphant-omni-God-now.

In the Bible stories, on occasion, Hashem turns away angry. In his wrath, he may temporally abandon his people. And yes, there are innocent victims. In this regard, we can respect the outrage of survivors of such atrocities and avoid quick answers to their tension: YHWH is awesome—yet sometimes awful. Blumenthal says victims left with abandonment and loss need courage to revisit and dissipate their psychic pain. The cruel fact is, therapy can risk re-victimization.[124] He recommends the following steps in religious healing:

- Recognize and state one's fear, anger, and even rage (Psalms 44 and 109).
- Recall moments of connectedness and closeness to God.
- Reaffirm God's saving power and one's desire for it.
- Acknowledge one's helplessness and vulnerability.
- Actively call on God for help.
- Acknowledge one's doubt.
- Resume spiritual relatedness to God.[125]

The psychic severance, the disconnect between the Jews and Hashem, needs to be addressed. The process of psychic healing involves mood swings

---

121. Wiesel, *Night*, 61–62. In typical Jewish fashion Wiesel is ambiguous about Hashem's presence in the world. Is Hashem vigorously present or absent?

122. Cohn-Sherbok, *Holocaust Theology*, 146.

123. Ibid., 8.

124. Blumenthal, *Facing the Abusing God*, 238.

125. Ibid., 257.

between denial and acceptance, numbness and awareness of what has happened. This is coupled with oscillating stances of anger (even rage) and embrace, suspicion and trust, confrontation and bargaining, and anger and adoration toward Hashem. Catharsis, as displayed in many of the Psalms, is not a straight path, but a back and forth process between these opposite poles—all the while moving towards the goal of face-to-Face, presence-to-Presence relatedness to Hashem. Blumenthal continues, "We must have the courage to address God with this truth, and the strength to use ideas that are strange to the heart and words that are alien to an ear sensitized to the traditional liturgy. It takes conviction, and time, to pray these texts."[126] Further, protest is to be done in context, by righteous people and in a circumspect manner.[127] Sample protest prayers include:

> Why dost thou hide thy face?
> Why dost thou forget our affliction and oppression?
> Rise up, come to our help!
> Deliver us for the sake of thy steadfast love!
> Psalm 44:24, 26

Elie Wiesel cries:

> Why, but why should I bless Him? In every fiber I rebelled. Because He had thousands of children burned in His pits? Because He kept six crematories working night and day, on Sundays and feast days? Because in His great might He had created Auschwitz, Birkenau, Buna and so many factories of death? How could I say to Him: "Blessed art Thou, Eternal, Master of the Universe, Who chose us among the races to be tortured day and night, to see our fathers, our mothers, our brothers, end in the crematory? Praised be Thy Holy Name, Who hast chosen us to be butchered on Thine alter?"[128]

As a general rule, mourning, grieving, sorrow, sadness, and lament are *constructive* emotions, taking one in the right direction, whereas bitterness, hopelessness, despair, regret, revenge, unbridled hatred, and inordinate anger are *unhelpful* emotions, carrying one in the wrong direction. In lamenting prayers, Hashem is not rejected but engaged, addressed more intensely, not denied. Walter Brueggemann similarly encourages one not to repress rage but to express it, speak it honestly to God, reject quick forgiveness, but

---

126. Ibid., 285.
127. Ibid., 252.
128. Wiesel, *Night*, 64.

leave the avenging to him.[129] Awfulness is part of Hashem's holiness—we have an intuitive sense of his otherness and sacredness—it overwhelms, compels, and frightens. Interestingly, the Bible does not have commands to love our children, as this is easy. But there are plenty of Scriptures admonishing us to love Hashem—this is obviously difficult. Shlomo Carlabach, a contemporary "singing rabbi," sings about the repulsion and attraction between the divine and the human, and the dynamic tension between holiness and sin. They are lovers; to know one is to know the other; to be attached to one means to cling to the other and the more the Lover of heaven pursues us, the more we run away (cf. Hos 11:2).[130]

Mainstream church culture is currently incapable of including the "terrible" references of YHWH. Claiming the higher moral ground, they assume that dark personalizing depictions of him are "primitive." As already argued, these anthropomorphic depictions ought to be incorporated. One needs to avoid attempts to harmonize or rationalize away these frightening, embarrassing behaviors of YHWH. Again, the Hebrew word for truth, *emet,* is composed of the first, the middle, and the last letter of the alphabet, signifying that it embraces all: the everlasting awesomeness and occasional, fleeting awfulness of YHWH need to be voiced.

Art

There is an overabundance of *sunshine* theology in our churches today, causing artists in the church to only exhibit muted references, if at all, to the shadows, valleys, and negative passions of anger, lament, and hate (that is, hate towards evil and waste). "Good" and "nice" Christians seldom show intense feelings—against the evil of lost lives, ruined marriages, ruined sexuality, wasted opportunities, and squandered resources. By observing their behavior, you would never guess we are engaged in an ever-present war: fighting for the kingdom of God.[131] I think, if King David were alive today, he would feel constricted by our calm church music; he would need to augment his repertoire with rock, classical, black spiritual, maybe some heavy metal and various kinds of dance music. His Psalms plainly lay out this range of mood. All too often Christian artists have confined the experience of YHWH and life to a narrow band where the extreme emotions of

---

129. Brueggemann, *The Message of the Psalms,* 76, 77, 85, 86.

130. I loosely remember these words from one of his songs.

131. The Lord uses trouble in the world to separate those who are for him and those who are against him. Joel 3:14: "Multitudes, multitudes, in the valley of decision! For the day of the Lord is near in the valley of decision."

protest and ecstasy are tempered. Accordingly, much of Christian music is orchestrated within an accepted and recognizable zone of instrumentation and singing. To be specific, church music is usually played in comfortable major keys; and if this is done continually, the translation is boring. This constriction sometimes repels the very wounded seekers that the church means to soothe.

Walter Brueggemann explains the "goodness" problem:

> Well-meaning Christians believing that God is unambiguously good may stifle their feelings of protest when bad things happen. They may think themselves at fault. Their denial and pretense fails to take into account the reality of evil and the depth of the crisis of theodicy. God, to them, may be "perfect," transcendent and omnipotent—preventing any mere person from wrestling with Him. Their worship may be happy, positive, and upbeat, but underneath they may harbor rage against God and people.[132]

Quick and easy sellers of the gospel (some TV evangelists) and theologians have overemphasized YHWH's perfection, goodness, and niceness at the expense of his gritty, demanding holiness, thus sanitizing and domesticating him. Some churchgoers—and their "God"—display little or no passion, anger, or righteous indignation. If I may exaggerate, I believe that hate and anger towards YHWH is better than apathy towards him, because at least the angry hater is engaged. There can be movement. And there is hope of reconciliation.

Steve Turner explains the harm of continual sunshine theology in Christian art:

> By continuously "praising the Lord" the contemporary Christian music artist rarely shows evidence of a comprehensive worldview. In fact, the world is not viewed at all. What is viewed is personal spiritual experience and usually only its beautiful peaks. The valley of the shadow of death is rarely traversed, nor is the valley of indecision. The casual nonbelieving browser is effectively excluded because there is no overlap of experience.[133]

Too easily, pastors and theologians voice the valid transcendence and unchangingness of God but fail to sufficiently voice the differing minority reports. Prominent evangelical writer Millard Erickson asserts God's plans for the world are unaffected by humans and emphasizes the changelessness

---

132. Brueggemann, *Finally Comes the Poet*, 47.
133. Turner, *Imagine*, 52.

of his preordained ways.[134] So too, Stephen Charnock voices the transcendence of God whose ways are immutable and who exercises complete control over the unfolding of history.[135] Again, this theology is not wrong; it is based on Scripture.[136] However, its difficult and unpopular corollary is not expressed: YHWH is impacted by humans, on occasion he changes his mind, the unfolding of history is a bit open-ended, and humans contribute to advancing or hindering the kingdom of God. Multifaceted theology voices competing Scriptures, tries to balance them, thereby making truth a mosaic. YHWH is not only the "Unmoved Mover" who dwells in perfect bliss, essentially unaffected and untouched by the disappointment, sorrow, and suffering of his creatures. No, he is also the "Most Moved Mover."[137]

All of the above encourages artists into genuine conversation with him, which is engaged, varied, and sometimes contradictory. Sometimes we sing "hallelujah," but in terrible situations we lament:

> How long, O Lord? Wilt thou forget me forever?
> How long wilt thou hide thy face from me?
> How long must I bear pain in my soul,
> and have sorrow in my heart all the day?
> How long shall my enemy be exalted over me?
> Psalm 13:1–2

The number of Christian artists who have tapped into this full range of expression—from submissive love to furious protest—is slim.[138]

If I can make a sweeping generalization: *secularism, scientism, abstraction,* and *reductionism* have stripped down the human in Western art. As already mentioned, *secularism* declared "God is dead," consequently "man is dead"; *scientism* made the human individual meaningless, the individual is merely here to propagate the species; *abstraction* makes humanness evaporate as it favors the philosophical or general concept over concrete particulars;[139] and *reductionism* reduces the human to "nothing-but-biochemical-pro-

---

134. Erickson, *Christian Theology*, 1:351–54. Scriptural backing for YHWH's transcendence and unchangingness comes from Exod 15:11; 20:3; Ps 18:31; 24:10; Isa 6:1; 37:16, 46:9; Mal 3:6; 1 Tim 6:15–16.

135. Charnock, *Discourses upon the Existence and Attributes of God*, 1:310–62.

136. Gen 18:14; Num 23:19; 1 Sam 15:29; 2 Chron 20:6; Ps 90:2; 139:4, 16; Isa 46:10.

137. These words come from Clark Pinnock's book title: *The Most Moved Mover*.

138. To name a few artists shining the light of passion and displaying robust humanness: Rembrandt, Michelangelo, and present-day painters Ed Knippers and Jerome Witkin; musicians J. S. Bach, Durufle, U2, Peter Gabriel; sculptor Auguste Rodin, and present-day sculptor George Segal.

139. Sheesley, "Jerome Witkin: A Profile." Sheesley brings our attention to modern art's predominant style of the abstract.

cesses" or love to "nothing-but-the-secretion-of-oxytocin-in-the-blood."[140] Reductionism has the tendency to reduce complex issues of life to one parameter, shrinking it to something less complex. With these atomized scientific explanations, scientists create the illusion that they satisfactorily know how life works. Multifaceted theology can help the artist to combat the above corrosive elements: one can maintain a whole-person encounter with reality and YHWH, can remain multifactorial, not allowing oneself to fall into myopic, narrow depictions of life. In the Western museums I have visited with my wife, a painter (Los Angeles, Washington, DC, Amsterdam, Bern, Johannesburg, and Jerusalem), we have found a monolithic conformity to this reductionism and abstraction motif.

Philosopher John Alexander describes modern art as hollow and shallow. Andy Warhol's Campbell's soup cans say to the viewer: superficial, superficial, and more superficial. We seldom see statues of real people but rather statues of giant clothespins. Also, when great artists paint people, they are likely to paint pictures so abstract they hardly appear human.[141] Mystery and grandeur are lost through reductionism; things are taken for granted; we have failed to retain a wonder, awe, or reverence for life. The human soul has become empty, and the world has become flat.[142] YHWH cautions Job against reductionism:

> Hear this, O Job;
> stop and consider the wondrous works of God.
> Do you know how God lays his command upon them,
> and causes the lightning of his cloud to shine?
> Do you know the balancings of the clouds,
> the wondrous works of him who is perfect in knowledge,
> you whose garments are hot
> when the earth is still because of the south wind?
> Can you, like him, spread out the skies,
> hard as a molten mirror?
> Teach us what we shall say to him;
> we cannot draw up our case because of darkness.
> Shall it be told him that I would speak?
> Did a man ever wish that he would be swallowed up?
> And now men cannot look on the light
> when it is bright in the skies,
> when the wind has passed and cleared them.

---

140. An author whose name I forget called this "nothing-buttery."

141. Alexander, *The Secular Squeeze*, 15.

142. I heard Paul Johnson, a British historian, being interviewed on the radio, describe this.

Out of the north comes golden splendor;
God is clothed with terrible majesty.
Job 37:14–22

Judeo-Christianity has the answer to this void: Copying YHWH, we can be true "humanists" showing forth personhood, engagement, and passion. Unfortunately, our Christian forebears (as documented in previous chapters) have hindered this expression by commonly equating the suppression of passion with good morality. Passion was a disturbance or weakness in the soul and connected to the animal nature, whereas reason was linked to the divine nature. The Bible, specifically the Prophets, go in the opposite direction: misguided passion, lack of passion, "hardness of heart," or callousness are seen as most evil (cf. Eph 4:18).

Lastly, today's art is rife with *disintegration*. Postmodern art can have elements of being spiritual, physical, personal, intellectual, and passionate, but seldom shows all the elements unified, because the secular artist, not having a relationship with YHWH, is unable to do so. They lack a sufficient integration point greater than themselves to which they can direct themselves. The *Shema*[143] directs us to engage reality using all of our faculties: heart, mind, and soul—whole-person encounter. We are encouraged to be who we really are in our unpretending realness. Wyschogrod reminds us how bloody, noisy, and smelly the meeting place of the human and the divine (the temple) really was:

> Sacrificial Judaism brings the truth of human existence into the Temple. It does not leave it outside its portals . . . the bruiting, bleeding, dying animal is brought and shown to God . . . . In the Temple, therefore, it is man who stands before God, not as he would like to be or as he hopes he will be, but as he truly is now, in the realization that he is the object that is his body and that his blood will soon enough flow from his body as well. The subject thus sees himself as dying object. Enlightened religion recoils with horror from the thought of sacrifice, preferring a spotless house of worship filled with organ music and exquisitely polite behavior. The price paid for such decorum is that

---

143. The *Shema* says: "Hear, O Israel: The Lord is our God, the Lord alone. You shall love the Lord your God with all your heart, and with all your soul, and with all your might" (Deut 6:4–5 NRSV), which incidentally, Jesus highlights (Matt 22:37). The *Shema*—a fit-everything-together, how-to-direct-your-love-and-life Scripture—is read every Shabbat in synagogues and Jewish homes around the world. In a world wrought with fragmentation, we can be united in our effort in approaching the world; we are admonished to believe that God is *Echad* (one). The *Shema* says "The Lord your God is *one*"—the same way that Adam and Eve became *echad* (*one* flesh).

the worshiper must leave the most problematic part of his self outside the temple, to reclaim it when the service is over and to live with it unencumbered by sanctification. Religion ought not to demand such a dismemberment of man.[144]

Thus, when the visceral human comes into the presence of YHWH in the temple, the dualism between the sacred and the secular is undone. If modernism can be identified as an emphasis on reason, and postmodernism as an emphasis on feeling, what is called for is not finding a balance between reason and feeling with just a little of each but both a full measure of reason and feeling—both passionately intellectual and passionately emotional. Rembrandt and Bach had the unique ability to inform their work with both passion and theology. Alexander echoes: "We need both halves of ourselves: left brain and right, rigorous logic and passionate intuition, analysis and imagination . . . . We need a synthesis between heart and intellect, between science and art. We must affirm their essential unity."[145] Some of us may be gifted with the potential of being both fully intellectual and fully feeling; others may not have that potential. As a Christian community, however, we can surely manifest both fully. Hence, living in postmodernity presents an exciting opportunity to the Christian artist.

Recapping my idea of critical realism, we affirm the presence of objective truth that is subjectively apprehended. Our "maps" of people, things, and YHWH are only approximations. We do not claim pure objectivity; knowledge is perspectival and approximate—and/or absolute. In this way, at times, Christians can be fragmentary in orientation, defer the gratification of quick resolutions—knowing all along that our security and certainty rests in intimate relatedness to the premier Person, YHWH. Putting into practice Hebrew block logic gives artists certain guideposts to keep their bearings but allows for tension. I hold that the believer in YHWH—the grounder of our personhood—is freed to be disintegrative at times and still remain solidly integrated (this is evident in the "Psalms of disorientation"[146]).

Bach's organ discords vividly illustrate this truth. Some musicologists believe these organ discords are a root of modern rock music. Jeremy Begbie says "tension and resolution" and "deferred gratification" are found in Bach's organ discords, and for that matter, all Western music.[147] Throughout the

---

144. *Body of Faith*, 19.

145. Alexander, *The Secular Squeeze*, 105.

146. Brueggemann says certain Psalms are like this. "The Prophetic Imagination of Walter Brueggemann," podcast, with Krista Tippett, *On Being*, December 22, 2011.

147. Dr. Jeremy Begbie, from Cambridge University, identifies this structure with examples from Beethoven, Mozart, Bach, and Chopin to the Beatles, U2, and Elton

piece there is tremendous discord, distortion, and fragmentation, reflecting the drama of life (it resonates with people because it is not Pollyanna but solid and real); there are attempts to bring the music "home," to find resolution to the discord, but in the short term this fails. In the end, however the music culminates and finally comes "home" firmly, to an integration point—or in other words, to the ultimate hope, Christ. To Bach, "home" was solidly YHWH. To this Begbie asserts that all Western music has this underlying hope (or "coming home") built into its structure because of its strong Judeo-Christian underpinning.

The task of trying to make sense of art is by nature elusive and hazardous. Even more intimidating is fine art; it is elitist in that only the "experts" are qualified to critique it. My wife the artist disagrees with me. Nevertheless, postmodern Christians should trust their gut reaction in critiquing the art around them, and, if applicable, call it for what it is: *the emperor's new clothes are nothing; he is naked.*

Christians Botching Up on Science—Again?

Giordano Bruno (1548–1600), an Italian Dominican friar, philosopher, mathematician, and astronomer, said, "the universe is infinite." He was deemed a heretic by the church and burnt at the stake. The theologians contended that only God can be infinite, while creation is finite. Today this is a total non-issue as science self-corrected itself in 1965 with the big bang theory. Before this the "steady state theory" or "infinite universe theory" reigned. It said that new matter is continuously created as the universe expands; the universe has no beginning and no end. Or simply put, matter is eternal. Today the "big bang" is an established fact, attesting the biblical notion that there was an abrupt beginning (Genesis 1). Stephen Hawking explains the universe as "finite but unbounded." He says that all the stuff generated from the big bang—the entire universe—is finite. However, space travelers would never experience it as finite, they would never come to a boundary as the gravity of all the created matter would keep pulling them into a circle, giving the illusion that space goes on forever.

Here is another example of religious people making an issue out of nothing: An early botanist put forward the idea that there were male and female parts in flowers; he too was deemed a heretic, and if I remember correctly, was burnt at the stake.[148] The church establishment was sure that

---

John. Begbie, "The Sense of an Ending."

148. I am going by memory. I came across this studying botany at the University of Port Elizabeth, South Africa, circa 1977.

only humans were male and female according to Genesis 1:27. Then on another occasion church people steered things in the wrong way: they were sure there was only one ocean, as Genesis 1:9 declares, "the one ocean sea" ("the water was gathered in one place"). So for the longest time explorers were hindered by this incorrect assumption. Added to this, the incorrect belief that after Noah's flood the earth was split into 3 equal sections for the populations of Ham, Shem, and Japheth, with Jerusalem at its center, further thwarted the exploration of the earth—overland explorers and sailing ships only ventured so far. Then there is Martin Luther. He botched up big time, he considered Copernicus (an observant Catholic)—who said the earth revolves around the sun—an idiot. Yes, Luther used that kind of language. In his words, "This fool [Copernicus] wishes to reverse the entire science of astronomy; but sacred Scripture tells us that Joshua commanded the sun to stand still, and not the earth."[149] Again this has proved a complete non-issue. According to the theory of relativity it is impossible to tell if a body is moving or standing still in outer space without an absolute reference point. Since *there is no absolute reference point in space*—as everything is moving—it is irrelevant to say which is moving: the sun or the earth.

Now today. About 45 percent of American Christians see evolution as an enemy to the Bible. I find this troubling, as it means that Christian children's curiosity, speculation, and free scientific inquiry about how the Creator did creation is suppressed. Definitely the *philosophy* of evolution is contrary to the Bible, especially when applied to the social sciences. Notably, Hitler used "the survival of the fittest"—from the *philosophy* of evolution—to justify his crimes against humanity. But how about biological evolution? Should Christians rule out the possibility that YHWH used evolutionary processes in the making of the different species in the Genesis account? The Genesis description is not written like a science textbook (the details and chronologies in chapter 1 and 2 do not match up). Instead it's a Hebrew creation poem, which does not submit to our modernist-rationalist criteria. Concisely, this is Genesis's message: YHWH did it, and humans are created in his image.

Science is about penetrating YHWH's creation; it's about observing the intelligence, complexity, and intricacies built into creation, thus heightening awareness of YHWH's wisdom. Johannes Kepler (1571–1630)—the brilliant mathematician and astronomer—said of his research: "O God, I am thinking thy thoughts after thee."[150] In this light, Kepler experienced science as an act of worship, noting in one of his major works, *Harmonies of the World*:

---

149. Boorstin, *The Discoverers*, 302.
150. Hummel, *The Galileo Connection*, 57.

> I give thanks to Thee, O Lord Creator, who has delighted me with Thy creation. I rejoice in Thy handiwork. Behold! I have now completed the work of my profession . . . I have demonstrated the glory of Thy works . . . My soul, praise the Lord thy Creator, as long as I live . . . . To Him be praise, honor and glory, world without end. Amen.[151]

Having studied and taught science for many years (physics, astronomy, and biochemistry) has influenced the way I read the Bible. As in the field of science, my instinct when reading the Bible is to stay with its raw angular texts and not smooth things over, even if a text may offend my sensibilities. To include the sometimes-disagreeing texts, I employ multifaceted theology. A few examples from science show how to deal with data that does not fit:

1. *Precision and certainty are set alongside a little paradox, fuzziness, and uncertainty.* In Newton's day the universe was perceived to be static, solid, absolute, permanent, and certain. Subatomic particles behaved in predictable patterns like billiard balls colliding on a table (the billiard balls remain intact and collide in predictable ways). Subatomic particles were viewed as indestructible and permanent, and scientists believed they could isolate their exact position and movement in space. Today, however, subatomic particles are viewed in a paradoxical way—they are simultaneously "particle" and "wave" ("particle" implies a precise point in space, whereas "wave" implies a fuzzy field). Irreconcilable paradox exists. Recent research shows subatomic particles in a less certain way: they are not indestructible or stable, but rather are described in a murky way, they are constantly changing energy fields with no exact location. Subatomic particles can appear "out of nothing" and then disappear "into nothing." ("Out of nothing" challenges classical theology's *ex nihilo* creation doctrine, which states that "out of nothing" creation only happened in Genesis 1.) Their behavior and existence inside the atom is a *fuzzy* affair, it might best be compared to standing waves like the different harmonic chords played on a piano. In other words, these particles are packets of energy occupying a changing neighborhood in the atom: They talk, sing, and harmonize with each other, incessantly.

Furthermore, the apparent "hardness" of matter around us gives the illusion that our world is "solid." Actually this is not the case, as matter consists mainly of empty space built with subatomic particles that have no essential substance. The "hardness" of matter is only due to the strong interaction of the subatomic energy fields. For example, to show how insubstantial matter is, electromagnetic waves and neutrinos, say from cell phones and the sun,

---

151. Ibid., 266.

respectively, travel through our bodies—without hindrance—continually. In fact, the building block of the universe, the atom, is so vacuous that the chance of its electrons colliding is compared to the probability of two flies colliding into each other in the Grand Canyon.

In today's world post-Einstein, we no longer view space and time in a straightforward absolute way. Both space and time can be stretched, squeezed, and distorted. Space warps around the strong gravitational fields of stars; time slows down around strong gravitational fields; and objects get shorter and heavier as they approach the speed of light.[152] Because of the warping of space and time, our GPS instruments (Global Positioning System), for instance, have to factor in this new science, otherwise they would become inaccurate within minutes. The universe is no longer perceived as fixed and firm.

When I was studying physics, I came across a physicist who proclaimed that all the major laws of physics had been discovered, and now, the task before us, was only to fine-tune the details. How wrong he was, as nowadays the horizon of our understanding of the universe has been pushed further back. At present, it is established that we do not know 96 percent of the universe, as it is composed of "dark matter." This "dark matter" is invisible and uncommunicative, we cannot detect it or study it with our scientific instruments, but we know it is there through mathematical calculation: It accounts for the missing gravity in the universe. To put it another way, we only know 4 percent of the universe. When you add up all the planets, creatures, plants, humans, stars, galaxies, all the visible luminous stuff is only 4 percent of the universe. We don't know what this "dark matter" is; the term merely serves as a placeholder till we find out what it is. The words *paradox, uncertainty*, and *fuzziness* are now accepted alongside certainty in science; the mature Christian can adopt a similar stance toward theology without compromising one's relationship with YHWH. To add to the idea how of little we know, in biology, the average human consists of 70 trillion cells, each cell has 2 meters of DNA wrapped into it. If we took all the DNA out of one human being, unraveled it, and connected it all end to end, it would be long enough to stretch 500 round trips to the sun.

Galileo (1564–1642), who was both a pioneering scientist and a sincere Christian, put it well when he said that God has given us two books—one

---

152. Einstein's theories have been verified: Huge stars have been shown to bend light through "gravitational lensing," and accelerated particles have been verified to gain mass in particle accelerators. Also, an atomic clock was placed on the top of a high-rise building and another placed in the basement of the building. After an extended time the clock in the basement lost an infinitesimal amount of time due to the stronger gravity (closer to the center of the earth).

of "Nature" and the other "Scripture."[153] To Galileo, the two books God has given us were *complementary* sources of knowledge about God and nature. Studying the book of nature and the Bible[154] requires the attributes of a good investigator, that is, clear thinking, fact-finding, listening to peer reviews, truth telling, and collaborating with others who have expertise. (To repeat, the enterprise of theology, like science, merely creates crude, provisional "maps" about our visible and invisible worlds.) Obviously, one needs intellectual prowess in understanding the Bible and nature. However, one also needs to check one's attitude when "reading" the two books. Both theologians and scientists have been misled in their understanding and reasoning because of subjective factors such as unexamined inherited beliefs, hidden agendas, and pride.

A dictum of modernism was that science dealt with *facts* and theology dealt with matters of *faith*.[155] Science and theology were kept apart because they were viewed as incompatible. In the last decades, however, the reliability and scope of science has been demonstrated *not* to be purely objective. The enterprise of science has not only an intellectual dimension but also incorporates the emotional, volitional, spiritual, and physical dimensions of the scientist. The scientist, as subject, interacts with and is impacted by the world to be investigated; the questions asked and experiments chosen to be done are up to the subjective interaction of the scientist with his/her world. Michael Polanyi says: "We have here an instance of the process described epigrammatically by the Christian church fathers in the words: *fides quaerens intellectum*, faith in search of understanding."[156] It is a mistake to believe science is devoid of faith and that theology is devoid of reason. Both theology and science, in their endeavors to uncover the mysteries of the Bible and nature, require "reasoning faith" and "trusting reason."[157] Recently

---

153. "Both the Holy Scriptures and Nature proceed from the Divine Word, the former as the saying of the Holy Spirit and the latter as the most obedient executrix of God's orders." Peacocke, *Creation and the World of Science*, 3–7.

154. This works for the Bible as it has historical stories; the scientist can verify or falsify the existence of Pharaoh, Moses, Canaan, Jeremiah, Jesus, Paul, and so on. This would not work for a religious book such as the *Bhagavad-Gita*, as any Hindu would openly acknowledge; its stories about Krishna, Vishnu, and Brahman did not happen in our space/time history.

155. This kind of thinking can be traced back to Francis Bacon, who recorded this distinction: "Let no one think or maintain that a man can search too far or be too well studied in the book of God's Word or in the Book of God's Work, divinity or philosophy [nature]. . . . [We should] not unwisely mingle or confound these learnings together." *Essays, Advancement of Learning*, 179.

156. Polanyi, *Science, Faith and Society*, 45–50.

157. Hummel, *The Galileo Connection*, 258.

researchers have confirmed that both religious and nonreligious thought takes place in the same region in the brain, namely, the ventromedial prefrontal cortex, which is an area associated with emotions, rewards, and self-representation. Co-author of this finding Sam Harris says,

> Religious belief may seem to be a unique psychological experience, but a growing body of research shows that thinking about religion is no different from thinking about secular things.... The finding adds to the mounting evidence against the notion, popular in the scientific community as well as among the general public, that religious faith is somehow different from other types of belief.[158]

This last point by Harris leads beautifully to the next point about dealing with data that does not fit: *integrating body, soul, and mind into one.*

2. *The Hebraic paradigm encourages whole-person encounter.* All of the body, soul, and mind engages with Hashem and the universe. All of life—work, sex, going to synagogue/church, mundane activities like washing the dishes, as well as doing science or theology—is holy and worthy of attention: Done with the right intention, *all are acts of worship*. The early scientists Galileo, Kepler, Newton, and Mendel saw little separation between science, theology, and philosophy. In fact, much of their undergraduate studies were in theology and philosophy. We would do well to return to this approach. Science was considered a mere extension of theology. This holistic approach has an orientation of wonder, awe, curiosity, teachability, worship, and employment of all the faculties.

Hummel echoes the importance of whole-person encounter:

> Whole-person encounter with a complex environment neither compartmentalizes life nor reduces explanations of nature to one perspective ... the biblical and scientific descriptions are complementary perspectives—different kinds of maps for the same terrain.[159]

Nancey Murphy puts it this way: theologians have a "top down" view and scientists have a "bottom up" view of our complex world.[160] The domains of science and theology are different yet they overlap slightly. Totalizing statements from either domain should be discouraged. Conclusions do not have to be drawn; tension is in order; whole-person encounter is en-

---

158. Bond, "Belief in the Brain."

159. Hummel, *The Galileo Connection*, 261.

160. I got this idea from Dr. Nancey Murphy, in one of her classes at Fuller Theological Seminary, Pasadena, California.

couraged. Neither science nor theology can be purely objective; both are liable to subjectivism (theology more so)—this acknowledgment encourages conversation.[161] Adopting truth as sometimes absolute, sometimes paradoxical, holding matters in tension, delaying conclusions, and leaving place for mystery can create Christians who are less boastful, less definitive, less triumphalist, and less threatened by science.

In the past, Christians have fallen into the trap of confronting scientists with some unexplained part of the universe, whether that was planet formation, fetus creation, or miracles of the human body. Scientists derogatorily referred to this as "the God of the gaps." Inescapably, with each new scientific discovery, another "gap" was eliminated, and so the Christian retreated and sometimes even abandoned faith in God because his or her faith depended on that unexplained "gap." My position avoids holding on to remaining unexplained "gaps" as evidence for God, and avoids totalizing assertions of how exactly creation happened.

Questions

1. Moving beyond the minority reports, Klitsie argues for adopting a multifaceted theology: try to incorporate and apply all. Can this approach be destructive to our Christian faith? Is it too open-ended, too disjointed?

2. Klitsie emphasizes that we "partner" with YHWH, actually contributing to YHWH's regaining part of his omnipotence! Does this idea bring God down too much, down to our level? Is it sinful humanism?

3. Revelation 12:11 can be read as indicating that Christians overcome the Devil "by the blood of the Lamb" (the work of Christ) *and* "the word of their testimony" (human contribution). What do you think of this reading?

---

161. Both theology and science begin with a belief in their underlying premises; both assume there is a real world characterized by order that is continuous over time; both use human reason to make sense of the world at least in part; both draw on historical experiences. Even though theology and science ask different questions, both try to make sense of the world in which we live. Larry Laudin shows the similarity between science and theology: "there is no fundamental difference in kind between scientific and other forms of intellectual inquiry. All seek to make sense of the world and of our experience. All theories, scientific and otherwise, are subject alike to empirical and conceptual constraints.... The quest for a specifically scientific form of knowledge, or for a demarcation criterion between science and nonscience, has been an unqualified failure." *Beyond Positivism and Relativism*, 85.

CONCLUSION

MAKING GOODNESS THE ULTIMATE characteristic of God is misguided. YHWH has been restrained in a straitjacket of "good" as defined by human standards or Greek philosophy. However, the higher concept of "holy" permits a more visceral depiction of YHWH. Well-intentioned pastors and theologians who insist on the "noble" attributes of God have manicured YHWH instead of vitalizing him. It is erroneously assumed that *holy* is synonymous with *good*.

Under modernity's approach it has been difficult to piece together timely and particular notions of YHWH's wrath, love, vengefulness, mercy, and jealousy with general, universal, and timeless theological concepts. Postmodernism, by comparison, accepts as true that which is particular, local, and timely.[1] Under this paradigm it is easier to voice the competing truths about YHWH.

Christians can be very nervous about where one stands on particular issues: "Once saved always saved" versus "you can lose your salvation"; predestination verses free-willism; the "kingdom of God" focus of Yeshua versus the "justification by faith" focus of Paul; God's omni-attributes versus his self-imposed limitations on power, knowledge, and presence, and so on. Which is it? Multifaceted theology voices and incorporates all—as all are found in Scripture. The "Protestors" or Protestants can stop protesting; the Reformation passed; Catholics are no longer selling indulgences or saying we are saved by "works." Tension is okay. Yes, we are saved by faith alone; yet, employing biblical paradox, we can concede ground to the Catholics: Yeshua said, "bear fruit worthy of repentance" (Matt 3:7–8); Paul implies that we must "keep on" doing good works to get eternal life (Rom 2:7; cf. Phil 2:12; Col 3:23–24; 1 Thess 1:3; 2 Thess 1:5, 11); and James says "faith without works is dead." The authors of the Bible, including Yeshua, used

---

1. Toulmin, *Cosmopolis*, 186–92.

Hebrew block logic (paradox), in presenting information: Yeshua is the Prince of Peace, but simultaneously brings a genocide of baby boys when he is born; he brings "the sword" (Matt 10:34–37), "destruction" (Luke 2:34), and "violence" (Matt 11:12).

Disparity appears between theory and practice. Evangelicals present God as personal, yet in practice it seems only Jesus is approachable. God is placed in a straitjacket—he cannot change, be frustrated, saddened, or impacted by humans as the Bible portrays. In addition, we are tempted to go for the easy sell: Jesus is nice, all-inclusive, non-judgmental, and domesticated. As a result, love becomes emasculated and sentimentalized. Following this, men avoid church because it has become soft and effeminate. In lock step, Christian art generally reflects this overly *sunshine* theology. However, employing multifaceted theology, the attendant emotions of love—anger, judgment, and jealousy—can come into play, making YHWH's love more pursuant and demanding. Thus, a firm, mixed, and messy theology arises that stands on three supports:

1. The Hebrew Paradigm

The Hebraic way can be primitive, clunky, exclusive, scandalous, embarrassing, and paradoxical: Actually, it fits reality better. To compare, the more sophisticated modernist-Western paradigm, which has a love for universally applicable truth, coherence, and non-ambiguity doesn't mesh well with the sacred divine-human drama. Using "Hebrew block logic," we do not synthesize the varied truths presented about YHWH's character in the Bible; we leave them in tension. Truths about YHWH's dealings with humans are *transitory* and *timely,* and/or they are *absolute*. Dealings may vary: "I [the Lord] kill and I make alive; I wound and I heal" (Deut 32:39). His love is *absolute*, yet his anger or wounding is *transitory*. Directives can be time-sensitive, for instance, Yeshua said don't tell people I am the Messiah (Matt 16:20), and yet later, we are mandated to declare the opposite (the Great Commission, Matt 28:19–20). Biblical truths are not always universally applicable and are, on rare occasions, contradictory. Definitely, don't make a graven image to behold (Exod 32:8). Yet, oddly, in Numbers 21:6–9, the opposite is commanded, place a serpent on a pole and behold it, so you may be healed.

As in the raw biblical narrative, I have tried to heighten the idea of YHWH as a dramatic character with a complex personality. I bring attention to the embarrassing, neglected, "shadow side" of YHWH, which once in a while displays hiddenness, suffering, changeability, and "hostility." This brings meaning to the words "God-fearing." YHWH can, on odd occasions, be an enemy with an "oppressive" presence (1 Sam 5:6). Yeshua of the Newer Testament fits a similar pattern. Moreover, Paul brings to light the intensification of mercy *and judgment*. This revelation ought to be incorporated, though it may not sit well with prevailing church culture. The Person who emanates from the biblical narrative is gentle and sometimes gritty and fierce in love.

2. Postmodernism

Commonly and understandably Christians are threatened by postmodernism, but it's not all bad. Its central assertion that there is no meta-story or absolute truth does threaten to relativize Judeo-Christianity into irrelevancy. However, there is good coming out of it, causing some pastors and theologians to reexamine the Bible and—in true postmodern manner—hunt down marginalized, neglected, unpopular Scriptures, including references to YHWH's pathos. Contrary to normal instincts, it benefits the church to embrace these minority reports. Modernism tended to flatten the paradoxical with its emphasis on abstract, propositional theology—it presented the human-divine relationship in a tidy and unambiguous way. By comparison, postmodernism gives a breath of fresh air to the plurality of meanings and paradoxes, which are so indicative of life, the Bible, YHWH, and ourselves. This facilitates a personal, dynamic, and interactive YHWH who is free to act differently with divergent people, depending on the amount of revelation they have, their behavior, locality, and time. Because YHWH is not a Law or Principle that can be adequately captured or homogenized (the modernist tendency), we can leave the varied testimonies about YHWH as they are (the postmodern way)—dangling.

Untrained Bible readers can sometimes have an advantage. Not encumbered by theological frameworks, they work with concrete situations, go with the biblical narrative, and leave loose ends dangling. Unwittingly, this is the postmodern way: Don't give too much attention to grand schemes, go with the raw insights into YHWH's nature and leave some things open ended. YHWH is naturally benevolent, rarely "malevolent," close, rarely absent, forgiving, and scarcely unforgiving. With reflection, a sure and firm theology comes forth, yet parts can be uncertain and checkered.

With this postmodern multifaceted attitude, the difficult attributes of YHWH—his wrath, passion, and vengeance—can be affirmed as they need not be elevated to primacy but accepted as *particular, transitory, timely,* and *local*. The age-old temptation to synthesize and conceptualize the different attributes of YHWH into a neat, grand theological system is decreased, allowing YHWH to be free and personal. Consequently, competing theological claims can be accepted without the need to blend and thereby muddy them. The differing images of YHWH coming from the Bible can all be voiced. First Samuel 2:1–10 demonstrates this hodge-podge vividly: YHWH is forgiving and rarely vengeful, firm and contingent, mother and father, lover and warrior, king and servant, omnipotent and vulnerable; he can raise up the poor and give strength to a king.

3. Openness Theology

Though I have reservations about some of Openness theology's philosophical extrapolations or conclusions (does God know the future exhaustively?), I find it useful because it resurrects and voices the minority reports of the Bible. Our generation is challenged to renew our commitment to Scripture first, then inherited theology second. Much of the opposition to Openness theology from evangelicals is philosophical first and secondarily stems from their featured Scriptures. Opposing Scriptures are dismissed or ignored.

To be specific, Bruce Ware chooses to overlook the Scriptures backing the Openness position and rather makes a philosophical charge that it makes God look weak and, therefore, not worthy of undiminished adoration (taking after the title of his book).[2] One can get around this charge by stating that YHWH has a fondness to humble or empty himself (Phil 2:5–8). His strength is shown in the weakness of suffering (cf. 1 Cor 1:18–31). Ware leaves the impression that YHWH is chiefly concerned about power and control and less about humans being persuaded and voluntarily joining the expansion of YHWH's kingdom on earth—a matter of emphasis. Christians are quick to agree that YHWH totally embodies the emotions of love, joy, and compassion, but balk at voicing that YHWH completely—yet briefly— embodies the pathos of jealousy, anger, and vengeance.[3]

Following the example of the Bereans in Acts 17:11, who examined the Scriptures to see if what Paul said was true, we need to reopen issues, keep them open, include minority reports, hold a plurality of images, and give attention to particulars. We need an organic model that doesn't always

---

2. *God's Lesser Glory: The Diminished God of Open Theism.*

3. Half-"hearted" but thoroughly intellectual theologies have appeared lately in response to Openness theology, proposing a theology "toward" Divine emotion—"God is impassible and impassioned." In effect God is quarantined from suffering. Only an emanation of God seems to experience suffering; it is not from deep within YHWH (ontologically). Lister, *God Is Impassible and Impassioned*, 173, 184.

revert to propositions and keeps a place for poetic expression of YHWH's enigma. Joseph Hallman, in *The Descent of God*, says Christians need not ascend to the divine because the Lord has already descended to the human. Or in other words, we move forward with the divine rather than upward toward it.[4] Philip Yancey says it another way: "Other religions ask humanity to rise above their pain, or perhaps to deny it altogether. In Christianity, we do not rise above our pain; rather, God descends into it."[5] In yet another way of speaking, Judeo-Christianity does not have a God-on-top-of-a-ladder, whom we approach by ascending the steps through acts of virtue. No, YHWH is with us.

And so this makes for a concrete, incarnational, and messy theology.

---

4. Hallman, *The Descent of God*, xiv.
5. Philip Yancey, "Foreword" to Ohlrich, *The Suffering God*, foreword.

Appendix A

PREINCARNATE SON IN THE OLDER TESTAMENT?

How did early Jewish Christians, supposedly strict monotheists, come to worship Yeshua as God so easily? Where did this second Person of the Godhead—Yeshua, the "Word," whom John identifies as the producer of creation and the one who holds all things together—come from? These questions lead one to suspect that the Judaism of Yeshua's time was not strictly monotheistic. The presence of "the man," "the angel of the Lord," "the redeeming angel," and "the Lord of armies" in the Older Testament hints at a second God beside "the Most High God" (referred to as *El Elyon*). Postmodernism, unconcerned with neat theology, allows consideration of the obscure and curious theophanies of "the angel" and "the man" embedded in the Tenach (OT).

Acknowledgment of the Trinity is essential. It is vital that sinful earthlings/humans know the Father, Son, and Holy Spirit to be saved. C. S. Lewis *conjectured* that there may be other planets inhabited by other creatures who are not contaminated with sin and are thus more advanced than our world. If so, they would obviously relate to the Godhead in a different way. Yeshua said, "I have other sheep . . . not of this fold"—one cannot be sure who these "other sheep" are (John 10:16). I had a pastor in South Africa who conjectured: Maybe in the kingdom to come, after the final destruction of sin and Satan, there will be no further need for differentiation into Father, Son, and Holy Spirit—at which time we might relate to an undifferentiated God? One is free to speculate.

Margaret Barker in *The Great Angel: A Study of Israel's Second God*, asks if there was a preexisting pattern of belief about "the angel of the Lord," "the Son of Man," "YHWH," "the Sons of God" and the "Most High God" (*El Elyon*) in pre-Christian Judaism. Barker believes the first Christians fitted Yeshua into an existing pattern of belief established by the theophanies mentioned.[1] Clues that the Hebrew God consists of many Persons are evident in the Bible, a view that deserves some exploration.

Fossils of "Polytheism" in the Bible

Even though God is clearly represented as "one" (*echad* = "one," the same way a man and woman become *echad*, Deut 6:4–5; Matt 22:37), there are cryptic references to God's plurality:[2]

"sons of God"

> *the sons of God* saw that the daughters of men were beautiful; and they took wives for themselves, whomever they chose. (Gen 6:2 NASB)

> *the sons of God* went in to the daughters of men, who bore children to them. These were the heroes that were of old, men of renown. (Gen 6:4b)

> *the sons of God* came to present themselves before the Lord, and Satan came also among them. (Job 1:6)

"gods"

"When the Most High apportioned the nations, when he divided humankind, he fixed the boundaries of the peoples according to the number of the *gods*" (Deut 32:8). The Masoretic Text renders "the number of the *gods*" as the *"sons of Israel,"* but the Qumran text (which represents an earlier Hebrew reading) furnishes it as *"the Sons of God."*[3]

---

1. Barker, *The Great Angel*, 2.

2. The divine name, Elohiym, in Genesis 1:26 is a compound plural word alluding to the plurality of persons in the Godhead.

3. Ibid., 6.

"us"

God said, "Let *us* make humankind in our image." (Gen 1:26)

the Lord God said, "See, the man has become like one of *us*." (Gen 3:22)

Come let *us* go down and confuse their language. (Gen 11:7)

I heard the voice of the Lord saying, "Whom shall I send, and who will go for *us*?" (Isa 6:8)

"holy gods"

At last Daniel came in before me—he who was named Belteshazzar after the name of my god, and who is endowed with a spirit of *the holy gods*—and I told him the dream: "O Belteshazzar, chief of the magicians, I know that you are endowed with a spirit of *the holy gods* and that no mystery is too difficult for you. Hear the dream that I saw; tell me its interpretation." (Dan 4:8–9)

There is a man [Daniel] in your kingdom who is endowed with a spirit of *the holy gods*. In the days of your father he was found to have enlightenment, understanding, and wisdom like the wisdom of *the gods*. Your father, King Nebuchadnezzar, made him chief of the magicians, enchanters, Chaldeans, and diviners. (Dan 5:11)

"holy ones"

It was also about these that Enoch, in the seventh generation from Adam, prophesied, saying, "See, the Lord is coming with ten thousands of his *holy ones*." (Jude 1:14)

The above references hinting at the plurality of God have been discredited or explained away by scholars past and present; however, their retention in the canon of Scripture still testifies to the mystery of the many Persons in the Godhead. Explanations disparaging the idea of a multiplicity of Persons include one especially propounded by the rabbis—that God spoke in the presence of angels, who were spectators in Genesis 1 and 3, and thus the use of "us" refers to their presence. Also, there is the idea that God spoke as a king and as such refers to himself in the royal plural as "we" or "us." I will leave these matters open-ended as we will never conclusively prove the exact meaning of these texts.

Appearances of a Preincarnate Christ? "the Angel of the Lord," "the Man," and "the Redeeming Angel"[4]

Examining appearances of "the angel of the Lord" in the Older Testament can be likened to amateur detective work: clues are evident to even the casual reader that "the angel of the Lord" is equivalent to "the Lord" or God. In Genesis 16:7, "the angel of the Lord" appears to Hagar. Later in the same incident "the angel of Lord" is replaced with "the Lord" (v. 13). In Genesis 22, "the angel of the Lord" is used in verse 15, then switched with "the Lord" in verse 16. A similar switch of titles occurs in Genesis 31: in verse 11 where "the angel of God" is replaced with "I am the God of Bethel" (v. 13). In Genesis 32:24, Jacob wrestles with "a man" at the place he calls Peniel, and he equates "the man" with "the face of God" (v. 30). In Exodus 3:2, "the angel of the Lord" appears in the burning bush to Moses, and later becomes "the Lord," "God," and "I am" (v. 14). In Judges 6:11–15, "the angel of the Lord" appears to Gideon, only to become "the Lord" a few verses later (14, 16).

Backward-looking Scriptures on these theophanies reinforce the notion that "the angel of the Lord" is equal to "the Lord" or God. Consider Exodus 6:2–3: "God also spoke to Moses and said to him: 'I am the Lord. I appeared to Abraham, Isaac, and Jacob as God Almighty, but by my name 'The Lord' I did not make myself known to them.'"

Exodus 14:19 and Judges 2:1 proclaim that "the angel of God" led Israel out of Egyptian captivity, but a later Scripture describing this deliverance says it was simply "the Lord." Isaiah 63:9 says that it was the "angel of his presence," who was responsible for the Egyptian deliverance. Exodus 15:2–3 reads, "He has become my salvation . . . the Lord is a man of war; the Lord is his name."

In Numbers 22:31 "the angel of the Lord" appears to Balaam with his sword drawn. In Joshua 5:13–14, "a man" or "commander of the army of the Lord" appears with his sword drawn. Joshua falls down and worships this "man." We can assume that if this was not the Lord but an angel, the "man" would have forbad Joshua to worship him. The full understanding of

---

4. Other hidden inferences: "wisdom" (Prov 8:22), "righteous branch" (Jer 23:5–6), "man of sorrows" and "servant" (Isa 53), "stone" and "rock" (Isa 8:14), "son of man" (Dan 7:13), "branch" (Zech 6:12), and "angel of great counsel" (Isa 9:6).

"Prince of the Lord's Army" becomes clear as this "man," the Lord, turns out to be commander-in-chief with Joshua in the conquest of Canaan, destroying all of Israel's enemies (Josh 11) even committing genocide (Josh 6:21).[5] "For the Lord fought for Israel," Joshua 10:14b claims, an act contingent on Israel's obedience as the Lord refrained from fighting for Israel in the face of their disobedience (Judg 2:2–3). If this "man" is, in fact, the preincarnate Yeshua, the image corresponds to "the One on a white horse," "the Word of God," "King of Kings," with blood-splattered robes and sword, who "judges and makes war" in the apocalypse (Rev 19). So too, 1 Chronicles 21:16, 30 shows the connection between "the angel of the Lord" and judgment: "David looked up and saw the angel of the Lord standing between earth and heaven, and in his hand a drawn sword stretched out over Jerusalem. Then David and the elders, clothed in sackcloth, fell on their faces . . . . David . . . was afraid of the sword of the angel of the Lord." Again, in this passage, "the angel of the Lord," "the Lord" are addressed as God. The involvement of "the angel of the Lord" in judgment and destruction is unsettling.

More mysteries abound: Who is the god-man who saves Daniel and his friends in the fiery furnace (Dan 3:25)? "I see four men unbound, walking in the middle of the fire, and they are not hurt; and *the fourth has the appearance of a god.*" And, who is Jacob's redeeming angel? "[Jacob] blessed Joseph, and said, 'The God before whom my ancestors Abraham and Isaac walked, the God who has been my shepherd all my life to this day, *the angel who has redeemed me* from all harm, bless the boys; and in them let my name be perpetuated, and the name of my ancestors Abraham and Isaac; and let them grow into a multitude on the earth'" (Gen 48:15–16).

Israel's Second God

Barker convincingly shows that Judaism at the time of Yeshua was not strictly monotheistic, but acknowledged a Second God in "the angel of the Lord," "the man," and "redeeming angel." This, she posits, is how early Jewish Christians readily accepted Yeshua as Lord. Philo, a Jewish philosopher living in Alexandria at the time of the first Christians, portrayed Judaism as having two deities: God and "the Logos."[6] Philo mentions "the Logos" (*Memra*) in the Targum, supporting the idea that the Jews then were not "monotheistic."[7] Also, the Wisdom of Solomon, written by a Greek-speaking

---

5. "The Lord of hosts" orders a genocide against the Amalekites (1 Sam 15:3).
6. Barker, *The Great Angel*, 114.
7. Ibid., 152.

Jew from Alexandria, Egypt,[8] just before the time of Jesus, records a separate identity from God in heaven, namely, "Wisdom." The author saw the deliverance of the Jewish people from Egypt as by "Wisdom":

> Wisdom delivered a holy people and blameless race from a nation of oppressors. She entered the soul of a servant of the Lord, and withstood dread kings with wonders and signs. She gave to holy people the reward of their labors; she guided them along a marvelous way, and became a shelter to them by day, and a starry flame through the night. (Wisdom 10:15–17)

James Kugel, a Judaic expert on ancient texts, states that in Wisdom of Solomon, "Wisdom as God's intermediary is wonderfully ambiguous."[9] I believe the book's saying that "Wisdom" "holds all things together" (1:7), "fills the world," and is "the spirit of the Lord" could be references to a preincarnate Yeshua.

Early Christians including Eusebius, Justin, Irenaeus, and Clement of Alexandria say that Yeshua's deity is not a Christian innovation but ties into a preincarnate Yeshua found in the Older Testament. *El Elyon* had become for them the Father and "Angel of the Lord," "Angel of Great Counsel," "the Holy One of Israel," and "YHWH" became the Son.[10] Examples from Eusebius:

> Remember how Moses calls the Being, Who appeared to the patriarchs and often delivered to them the oracles written down in Scripture, sometimes God and Lord and sometimes the Angel of the Lord. He clearly implies that this was not the Omnipotent God but a secondary Being, rightly called the God and Lord of holy men, but the Angel of the Most High his Father. (*Proof* 1.5)[11]

> And when, as the Captain of the Angels he leads them he is called: The Angel of Great Counsel, and as Leader of the Armies of heaven: Captain of the Host of the Lord. (*Proof* 4.10)[12]

Similarly, Novatian, the first theologian of the Roman Church, identifies the second God as the agent of creation, the angel who appeared to

---

8. Kugel, *The God of Old*, 21. This book appears in some Christian Bibles as one of the biblical apocrypha, while others include it alongside Proverbs, Ecclesiastes, and other canonical works. It is not considered part of the Jewish Bible.

9. Ibid., 23.

10. Eusebius, *Preparation for the Gospel*, quoted in ibid., 190–212.

11. Ibid., 198.

12. Ibid., 207.

Abraham, spoke to Hagar, destroyed Sodom, and wrestled with Jacob.[13] Further clues to the labyrinth of connections are found in the Newer Testament.

The Newer Testament

The Christian hymn, found in Philippians 2:6–11 establishes Yeshua's identity:

> who, though he was in the form of God,
> did not count equality with God a thing to be grasped,
> but emptied himself, taking the form of a servant,
> being born in the likeness of men.
> And being found in human form he humbled himself
> and became obedient unto death, even death on a cross.
> Therefore God has highly exalted him
> and bestowed on him the name which is above every name,
> that at the name of Jesus every knee should bow,
> in heaven and on earth and under the earth,
> and every tongue confess that Jesus Christ is Lord,
> to the glory of God the Father.

What did it mean when early Christians said that Yeshua was "Lord" or "Son of God"? Barker claims that at the time of Yeshua, Judaism believed in a second God—YHWH—who represented "the angel of the Lord," "the Lord of Hosts," "the man," or "the Lord."[14] *El Elyon* represented "the Most High God," referenced in the Newer Testament, for example, at Gabriel's annunciation to Mary that Yeshua was to be "Son of the Most High God" (Luke 1:32). The same words are used by the demoniac: "What have you to do with me, Jesus, Son of the Most High God?" (Mark 5:7).

Paul applied the "Lord" (YHWH) texts to Yeshua. For example, the statements "Jesus is Lord" (Rom 10:9; 1 Cor 12:3) or "Jesus Christ is Lord" (Phil. 2:11) identify Yeshua as YHWH, the second God of Israel, not as *El Elyon*. Evidence for equating the Newer Testament word "Lord" with YHWH can be found in Luke 10:27: "You shall love the *Lord* your God with all your heart, and with all your soul, and with all your strength, and with all your mind; and your neighbor as yourself." Here "Lord" is translated from the Greek, *Kyrios* in the Newer Testament; but "Lord" is more accurately rendered as YHWH, since the origin that Luke is quoting in Deuteronomy 6:5 also reads YHWH. Further, Barker asserts that when "Lord" (*Kyrios*)

---

13. Ibid., 197.
14. Barker, *The Great Angel*, 1–3.

appears in the Newer Testament, there are many reasons why YHWH is the preferred meaning.[15]

Many copies of the Greek Old Testament did not use the title "the Lord" but preferred the title YHWH. The practice of using "the Lord" in the Older Testament was a Christian innovation.[16] When Christianity became separated from its Jewish roots, the usage of YHWH was dropped. "This removal of the tetragram ... created a confusion in the minds of early Gentile Christians about the relationship between the Lord God and the Lord Christ which is reflected in the MS tradition of the NT itself."[17]

Parallel Scriptures between the Newer Testament and the Older Testament also connect Yeshua to YHWH:

- Romans 10:13: "Everyone who calls on the name of the *Lord* shall be saved."
  Joel 2:32a: "Then everyone who calls on the name of the *Lord* [YHWH] shall be saved."

- Romans 4:8: "Blessed is the one against whom the *Lord* will not reckon sin."
  Psalm 32:2a: "Happy are those to whom the *Lord* [YHWH] imputes no iniquity"

- Ephesians 4:8: "When he [Jesus] ascended on high he made captivity itself a captive; he gave gifts to his people."
  Psalm 68:18 (NRSV): "You ascended the high mount, leading captives in your train and receiving gifts from people, even from those who rebel against the *Lord* [YHWH] God's abiding there."

- 2 Thessalonians 2:8: "And then the lawless one will be revealed, whom the *Lord* Jesus will destroy with the breath of his mouth, annihilating him by the manifestation of his coming."
  Isaiah 11:4: "But with righteousness *he* [YHWH] shall judge the poor, and decide with equity for the meek of the earth; he shall strike the earth with the rod of his mouth, and with the breath of his lips he shall kill the wicked."

- Yeshua is the husband of the Church (Eph 5:21–33) just as YHWH was the husband of Israel (Hos 2:20).

- Revelation 1:17: "Do not be afraid; *I* [Yeshua] *am the first and the last.*"
  Isaiah 44:6: "Thus says the *Lord* [YHWH], the King of Israel, and his Redeemer, the Lord of hosts: *I am the first and I am the last.*"

15. Ibid., 213–31.
16. Howard, "The Tetragram and the New Testament," 63–83.
17. Ibid., 63.

The prophets isolate YHWH as the one who delivers and fights for his chosen, for example, Isaiah 33:22: "For the *Lord* is our judge, the *Lord* is our ruler, the *Lord* is our king; he will save us." YHWH was the Savior's name, as in Isaiah 43:3: "For I am the *Lord* your God, the Holy One of Israel, your *Savior*." Isaiah 43:11 says, "I, I am the *Lord*, and besides me there is no *savior*." Similarly, the Psalms often sound the common cry, "Save me, YHWH." In the Newer Testament, some old versions of Jude 5 say that it was *Yeshua* (not "the Lord") who delivered the Israelites from Egypt, identifying YHWH as the preincarnate Christ.[18] (Numbers 20:16 recalls that the Lord sent an "angel" to deliver the Israelites from Egypt.)

Designed to Confound

When the Lord appeared to Moses, the Lord's name was revealed as "I am who I am." It appears that the Lord deliberately chose this name to *perplex* both Moses and Pharaoh. Similarly, the narratives of theophanies go out of their way to show the confusion of the people who see these "angels" and "men." Joshua, for the longest time, cannot grasp who "the man with sword drawn" is (Josh 5:13-15). The parents of Samson (Manoah and wife) cannot figure out who "the angel of the Lord" with no name is (Judg 13:2-4).[19] James Kugel explains how these narratives have gone out of their way to stress the moment of confusion. Manoah's wife clearly thinks her visitor is a "man of God," "some sort of prophet," and then she refers to the being as "the same man is back who appeared to me last time." Apparently this God-sent-messenger looks very much like an ordinary person. There is a tension in the narrative as Samson's parents are kept in the dark; furthermore, the angel avoids giving his name.[20]

Likewise, the same happens to Abraham when he meets the "three men" (Gen 18:1-14). Kugel says, "the passage begins by asserting that 'the Lord appeared' to Abraham—but this assertion seems to come from the narrator's point of view,"[21] because Abraham is in a fog as he entertains these men and only in the end does it dawn on him that the messenger is the Lord. Kugel adds:

---

18. Some translations of the Bible indicate this in their footnotes (e.g., RSV).

19. Also compare the theophanies of Numbers 22:22-31, Judges 6:11-13, Genesis 32:24-30, and Exodus 3:1-7.

20. Kugel, *The God of Old*, 5-36.

21. Ibid., 12.

> the narrator actually goes out of his way to make sure that the reader understands that these various biblical figures took a while to realize what was going on. . . . the angel is essentially an illusion, a piece of the supernatural that poses as ordinary reality for a time. The angel, in other words, is not some lesser order of divine being; it is God Himself, but God unrecognized, God intruding into ordinary reality. The angel can thus be invisible, as the angel was with Balaam, or contained in a bush, as with Moses but mostly appears to be a fairly ordinary-looking human. . . . [therefore] the spiritual and the material . . . are not neatly segregated but intersect constantly.[22]

The concealed identity of YHWH in the above-mentioned theophanies reminds me of Jesus' behavior after the resurrection (Luke 24:13–31). The story goes that, on the road to Emmaus, Jesus, disguised as "a man," hid his identity from the two disciples who were walking with him. All the while, they talked about this Jesus of Nazareth. Only at the end of the day "were their eyes opened" to recognize the identity of "the man," at which point the revealed Jesus disappeared. Again, typical of the Older Testament theophanies, it seems part of YHWH's personality to both hide and make known his identity. The story of Joseph, who was "killed" by his brothers, is particularly moving. When years later the brothers go to Egypt for food, unbeknownst to them, Joseph is alive. However, Joseph, for the longest time, does not reveal his identity. He is gruff and nasty to them; then, only after "he could not control himself" (45:1) did he finally disclose himself (Gen 45:1–15). Joseph is an archetypal Yeshua. In the present day, Yeshua restrains from revealing his identity to the Jews—his brothers. There's more: Yeshua, speaking in parables, does the same thing—true knowledge is deliberately hidden. Only those seeking will uncover the mysteries of the kingdom of God veiled in the parables (Luke 8:10).

Conclusion

The identification of Yeshua as YHWH and not *El Elyon* is an unfinished study: possibly, in the distant future, when the full inclusion of the Jews occurs (Rom 11:12),[23] Jewish oral tradition will further inform the theoph-

---

22. Ibid., 13, 34, 35.

23. Paul indicates that there will come a time when Jews will finally acknowledge Jesus as the Messiah. With this, possibly, Jewish oral tradition will shed more light on the preincarnate Jesus. Maybe Jews will shed light on 1 Cor 15:28, which refers to God's multiplicity "all in all." See Dickson, *The Gospel according to Moses*, 224.

anies and their implications of "polytheism." Currently Judaism is doggedly against any hint of "polytheism," as Judaism—in its latest incarnation established after the destruction of the temple, at the dawn of Christianity—expressly defines itself in reaction to Christianity. Any concession to the plurality of Persons in the Godhead would concede to Christianity. Philo's work gives a clue that the Jewish oral tradition once spoke of "the Word" or "Wisdom" and perhaps about "the redeeming angel." It can be surmised that the painful and bitter split of Christianity from Judaism (and sometimes even anything Jewish) in the first century affected lost meanings of Yeshua's fuller identity and preincarnate existence. In many respects, twenty-first-century Christians are like tourists in a foreign country, missing the archeological depths of the Older Testament. I myself identify with Manoah's wife—"hey, umm, the same *man* is back who appeared to me last time"—clueless of the full gravity of the theophany in front of them.

"The angel of the Lord" with the drawn sword—the One who wages war on behalf of Israel and "the man" whom Joshua worships—is this Yeshua? Many—to name a few: Justin Martyr, Derek Prince, Dietrich Bonhoeffer, N. T. Wright, Leonard Sweet, and Scot McKnight— believe this is Yeshua preincarnate.[24]

The theophanies examined show a God who has a personality, who is gritty, willful, relational, loving, and engaging. Things don't quite fit about the Jewish God: He is One with three Persons; there is unity and diversity within the Godhead; he is male and female; he is totally other but evidences temporality; we can never see his face,[25] yet we can.[26]

---

24. Leonard Sweet and Frank Viola, *Jesus*, xix, 6n35.

25. Deuteronomy 4:12: "Then the Lord spoke to you out of the fire. You heard the sound of words but saw no form; there was only a voice."

26. Isaiah 6:5 or John 14:9: "Jesus said to him, Have I been with you all this time, Philip, and you still do not know me? Whoever has seen me has seen the Father. How can you say, 'Show us the Father'?"

Appendix B

MORE COMPETING SCRIPTURES IN THE BIBLE

- Humans are worthless dust (Gen 3:19; 18:27; Job 10:9; 42:6; Ps 22:30); yet unique image bearers, made only a little lower than the angels (Gen 1:26; Ps 8:5).
- To obey you sometimes must disobey, for example, Abraham sacrificing Isaac.[1]
- Do not make a graven image—e.g., the golden calf (Exod 32:8); yet make a graven image and behold it—e.g., the bronze serpent on the pole (Num 21:6–9). Later, the bronze serpent became a false idol to the Hebrews (2 Kgs 18:4).
- On the odd occasion, show no pity (Exod 21:24), yet always act with love and mercy (Mic 6:8).
- Do not answer a fool (Prov 26:4), do answer a fool (Prov 26:5).
- The psalmist calls for the destruction of enemies (Ps 118:10–12); Yeshua commands the opposite (Matt 5:43).
- Yeshua brings destruction and sorrow, also salvation and joy (Luke 2:34–38).
- Paul induces sadness to bring joy (2 Cor 7:8–9).
- The Lord will answer your prayer because of works (Acts 10:4); no, faith is needed (Rom 4:13; Heb 11:6).

---

1. YHWH commands Abraham to sacrifice his son, yet had said not to murder (Gen 9:6).

- YHWH is kind and harsh (Rom 11:22 CEB).
- Give your money away and focus on heaven (Luke 12:33); yet wealth can be noble and the Lord can give you the power to get wealth (Deut 8:17-18).
- Paul says to bear one another's burdens, yet each person is to bear their own load (Gal 6:2, 5).
- The Lord affirms Adam's *need* for a human companion (Gen 2:18, the Lord himself was not the solution); but Paul lets on, and recommends, that a person *only* needs Christ, and can do without a helpmate (1 Cor 7:7-8; Phil 4:11-13; Col 2:10).
- The child will not share the guilt of the parent (Ezek 18:20; Deut 24:16); yet God punishes children for the iniquity of the parents (Exod 20:5).
- God is radically transcendent, yet he is radically immanent (Acts 17:24-28).
- Abraham's offspring are to be a blessing to *all the nations*, yet Abraham's offspring utterly destroy the Canaanites, taking their land (not a blessing to the Canaanites).[2]
- The Promised Land is "given" to Abraham, yet Abraham pays gold so Sarah can be buried there, and later the Israelites pay with their lives to gain it (Deut 32:49).
- God's grace cannot be earned (Eph 2:8-9); yet it can be brought on by having the right attitude.[3] We cannot earn eternal life, yet we can become *worthy* of his kingdom (2 Thess 1:5).
- The kingdom of God is *already here* (Matt 12:28); but the kingdom is *not yet* (Mark 14:25).
- Once-saved-always-saved (John 10:29); but if you forsake him, he will cast you off forever (Heb 10:26-29; 2 Pet 2:20; 1 Chron 28:9).
- The order of conversion is thus: believe (Acts 8:12a), be baptized in water (v. 12b), then receive the Holy Spirit (vv. 15-19);[4] and yet, on occasion, the Holy Spirit falls first (Acts 10:44-46), then comes water baptism (v. 47), and the time of believing is murky (vv. 44-48). Or,

---

2. See Genesis 18:18 and Numbers 21:3.

3. Fuller, *Gospel and Law,* 108-9. There is the possibility of missing the blessings of God's grace by having the wrong attitude; examples include Acts 13:43; 2 Cor 6:1; Gal 5:4; Jas 4:6; 1 Pet 5:5.

4. In Acts 19:1-6 the baptism in the Holy Spirit is a definite, subsequent experience after repentance and water baptism.

believe first (Acts 9:5–6, 17), then be filled with the Holy Spirit (v. 17), and then be baptized in water (v. 18).

- Deafness and dumbness is caused by a demon (Mark 9:17–29); yet it is not (Matt 15:30).
- The righteous are blessed with peace, wealth, and health (Deut 8:17–18; Ps 37:25; Isa 48:18; 57:20–21; Eph 2:14; 3 John 1:2); but the wicked have peace, wealth, and health too—sometimes (Ps 73:2–5).
- Work is the key to prosperity (Prov 10:4); yet work can be futile (Eccl 1:3–4).[5]
- The circuit of the sun is glorious and meaningful (Ps 19); yet the sun is a monotonous symbol for life (Eccl 1:5).
- The wind has purpose doing the will of God (Ps 104:3–4); yet it is void and haphazard (Eccl 1:6).
- A river represents vitality (Ps 1:3; 46:4); yet it is a token of dreariness (Eccl 1:7).
- History is pregnant with meaning (Job 42:2); yet history is senseless (Eccl 1:9).
- Yeshua says: Put your sword away (Matt 26:52); and buy a sword (Luke 22:36).
- Yeshua said not to resist evildoers (Matt 5:39); yet he drives the money changers out of the temple (Mark 11:12–19).
- The first will be last (Matt 19:30).
- To save your life, lose it (Mark 8:35).
- To be a slave is to be free (1 Cor 9:19).
- If anybody asks something from you, give it (Matt 5:40). Yet sometimes refrain from giving: the maidens were wise not to give away their extra oil (Matt 25:1–9).
- If you disown Yeshua, he will disown you (Luke 12:9); yet if you speak out against him you will be forgiven (Luke 12:10). Murky.
- Paul claims that we are no longer under the Law, yet he demands we *uphold* the Law (Rom 3:31). Yes and no.

---

5. David Hubbard, in *Beyond Futility*, pits the old wisdom of the Bible (Proverbs) against the new wisdom of Ecclesiastes (anti-proverbs) with regard to work, creation, and history.

- The Lord will forget the sins of the repentant believer (Ps 103:12; Mic 7:19; Heb 8:12); yet he will take into account sins again, though the person will be saved (1 Cor 3:12-15).

- There is no distinction between Jew and Greek, male or female in Christ (Gal 3:28); yet Paul says the gospel is for the Jew *first* then the Greek (Rom 1:16). The Jewish distinction is maintained in Revelation (7:4; 21:12), and anatomically the male remains a male and the female remains a female.

- We must honor our parents (Exod 20:12); yet, in some circumstances, we must be willing to hate them (Luke 14:26).

- We are admonished *not* to be hateful,[6] jealous,[7] or angry,[8] yet, on rare occasions, we should.[9]

- The human heart is deceitfully wicked (Jer 17:9); yet he has given us a new heart and put his law within them (Jer 31:31-33); plus we are a new creation (2 Cor 5:17-21).

- The Lord has plans for good for his people (Jer 29:11); but, once in a while, he "watches over them for evil."[10]

- YHWH is our fortress[11] protecting his temple, city, and people (Ps 46:1-7). But, on unique occasions, YHWH can become our enemy, abandoning his temple, city, and people (Lam 2:1-6).

- If you obey, good things will follow (Deut 30:15-20); nevertheless, oddly, if you obey and are without sin, bad things may happen (Job).

6. Colossians 3:8: "But now you must get rid of all such things—*anger*, wrath, malice, slander, and abusive language from your mouth."

7. Galatians 5:19-21: "Now the works of the flesh are obvious: fornication, impurity, licentiousness, idolatry, sorcery, enmities, strife, *jealousy, anger*, quarrels, dissensions, factions, envy, drunkenness, carousing, and things like these. I am warning you, as I warned you before: those who do such things will not inherit the kingdom of God."

8. Matthew 5:43-44: "You have heard that it was said, 'You shall love your neighbor and *hate* your enemy.' But I say to you, Love your enemies and pray for those who persecute you." John 12:25: "Those who love their life lose it, and those who hate their life in this world will keep it for eternal life."

9. It is okay to be angry but do not sin (Eph 4:26). Jealousy is okay to woo the Jews to Christ (Rom 11:14). In Numbers 5:11-31 the Lord validates the spirit of jealousy between a husband and wife, and we must be willing to hate parents (Luke 14:26).

10. Jeremiah 44:27: "Behold, I will watch over them for evil, and not for good: and all the men of Judah that are in the land of Egypt shall be consumed by the sword and by famine, until there be an end of them." This is done because, ultimately, the Lord wants to bless them and their offspring.

11. Martin Luther based his famous hymn: "A Mighty Fortress Is Our God," on this Psalm.

- Beat your plowshares into swords (Joel 3:10); but then there is a time to do the opposite (Isa 2:4).
- Seek and you will find the Lord;[12] but sometimes, in unique situations, you will seek and *not* find him.[13]
- Pray unceasingly (1 Thess 5:17); but sometimes *do not* pray.[14]
- Strive to serve one another (Gal 5:13); yet there is a time *not* to serve (the story of Mary and Martha, Luke 10:38–40).
- The Lord, at times, repents (Gen 6:6; Exod 32:14); but Samuel says the Lord is not like a man, who needs to repent (1 Sam 15:29).
- Commonly, if you repent, your sins will be forgiven (Acts 3:19); but on rare occasions, if you repent he will not forgive (Heb 10:26–27; Deut 1:45).
- By nature the Lord will not forsake you (Deut 31:8); however, under certain conditions he might (Deut 31:17).
- Some through faith received their loved ones back again from death; but others trusted God and were beaten to death (Heb 11:35).
- The prayer of faith will be answered (James 4:15); better yet, the prayer of the righteous will be answered (James 4:16).
- Show your good works; let your light shine (Matt 5:16; 9:8; 1 Pet 2:12). However, don't show off your righteousness before people (Matt 6:1).
- Israel is mine; Israel is *not* mine (Hos 1:9; 2:1).
- The Lord hates divorce, and the divorcee who remarries is an adulterer (Mal 2:16; Mark 10:10); but because of the hardness of your heart, Moses allows divorce (Matt 19:8).
- Hezekiah is told, you shall die; no, actually you will live (Isa 38:1, 5). Yes and no.
- The Lord says: I have set before you life or death . . . therefore *choose* life (Deut 30:19); but the Lord already knows the Israelites *are destined* to choose death (Deut 31:16). Yes and no.
- The Lord says to Pharaoh, set my people free; but simultaneously he hardens Pharaoh's heart (Exod 4:21; 10:1; 14:17).

12. Deuteronomy 4:29: "From there you will seek the Lord your God, and you will find him if you search after him with all your heart and soul."

13. Hosea 5:6: "With their flocks and herds they shall go to seek the Lord, but they will not find him; he has withdrawn from them."

14. Jeremiah 14:11: "The Lord said to me: Do not pray for the welfare of this people."

- Ask for *anything* you want—not really (Mark 11:24).
- As a rule fast (Matt 6:16); but sometimes don't fast (Luke 5:33–34).
- The Lord brings peace to a community (Prov 16:7); but sometimes he stirs up trouble (Judg 9:22–23).
- Go away; I won't save you anymore (Judg 10:13–14). Yet I will not cast you away (Jer 31:37).
- The Lord, unlike a human, does not lie (Num 23:19); yet, on a rare occasion, he intentionally gave misleading advice about going into battle (Judg 20:18–28).
- Yeshua implies that sickness or mishap is brought on by sin (John 5:14).[15] In John 9:3, he says that blindness is caused neither by the victim's nor the victim's parents' sin.
- The Lord leads me to green pastures (Ps 23); yet, oddly, sometimes he might momentarily bring me into darkness and not light (Lam 3:2).
- The Lord will not fail or forsake you, though in the next paragraph that promise is contradicted because of peoples' sin (compare Deut 31:6, 8, 23 with 31:17).
- Do not warn sinners of their approaching peril (Amos 5:13); yet the watchperson is to warn the people of oncoming danger (Ezek 33:6).
- God's Word is always firm; but sometimes it can be changed.[16]
- The Bible is an exemplary moral book (e.g., the Ten Commandments and the Beatitudes of Yeshua). But on occasion, the Bible seems to be amoral. (For example, in Deuteronomy 31:3–6, YHWH orders the destruction of the Canaanites, and in 1 Samuel 15:1–30, Saul is considered disobedient to YHWH for not tearing Agog, king of the Amalekites, to pieces!)
- The Lord is good and morally pure (Ps 25:8); yet he is perverse to the perverse (Ps 18:26), and even, sometimes, creates "woe and weal" (Isa 45:7).[17]

15. In the healing of the paralytic, Yeshua again connects sickness to sin. He asks, when healing the paralytic, what is the difference, if he says, "rise up and walk" or "go, your sins are forgiven"? (Mark 2:9). Also, Matthew connects healing in general to the forgiveness of sins and the atoning death of Yeshua (Matt 8:17; Isa 53).

16. The story of Jonah and the impending destruction of Nineveh illustrate how God's Word was "unreliable." To the great disappointment of Jonah (who trusted God's Word as *firm*), God did not annihilate Nineveh, and he fell into a great depression (Jonah 4:3). So bad was this incongruence with Jonah's theology that he wanted to die.

17. Cf. 2 Chronicles 21:14–18 (NRSV): "see, the Lord will bring a great plague on

- The gates of hell will not prevail against the Church (Matt 16:18 KJV); yet if salt (church with a small "c") has lost its saltiness, it is good for nothing and will be trampled under foot (Matt 5:13–16).[18]
- The priestly house of Eli will go on forever (1 Sam 2:30); no, it will be terminated because of unrepented sin (1 Sam 2:31–32, 34; 3:12–14).

---

your people, your children, your wives, and all your possessions, and you yourself will have a severe sickness with a disease of your bowels, until your bowels come out, day after day, because of the disease. The Lord aroused against Jehoram the anger of the Philistines and of the Arabs who are near the Ethiopians. They came up against Judah, invaded it, and carried away all the possessions they found that belonged to the king's house, along with his sons and his wives, so that no son was left to him except Jehoahaz, his youngest son. After all this the Lord struck him in his bowels with an incurable disease." Also, 2 Kings 6:33 (NRSV): "While he was still speaking with them, the king came down to him and said, 'This trouble is from the Lord! Why should I hope in the Lord any longer?'" Compare Jeremiah 51:1 (NIV): "This is what the Lord says: 'See, I will stir up the spirit of a destroyer against Babylon and the people of Leb Kamai.'" To all this, Job 5:17–18 shows the purpose of the Lord hurting us: "How happy is the one whom God reproves; therefore do not despise the discipline of the Almighty. For he wounds, but he binds up; he strikes, but his hands heal" (NRSV).

18. For example, the magnificent church of Constantinople was "trampled under foot" and is today Istanbul. Its cathedrals are now mosques or museums.

Appendix C

THE PRACTICAL THEOLOGY OF HASIDISM AND ABRAHAM HESCHEL

HASIDISM,[1] HESCHEL'S CHILDHOOD INFLUENCE, has much in common with Christian devotionalism, incarnational theology, and Pentecostalism in the following ways:

- An orientation of awe and wonder is engendered.
- Hashem is made *accessible* and apprehendable.
- The presence of the Holy Spirit is acknowledged (hearing God's voice, miracles, and sometimes speaking in tongues are evidenced).[2]
- One falls in love with Hashem (considered madness to the outsider).
- Not only good deeds are encouraged, but also correct intention and attitude.

Gershom Scholem, a prolific Jewish historian, tells the history of Hasidism and observes that it adheres to old Kabbalist teaching, but differs in respect to a new spontaneity, inner revival, and experience.[3] Hasidism popularized a mystical life with God, making him accessible to all with good will, and making the individual's relationship to God as practical as possible.

Martin Buber asserts that Hasidism was the "soul-force" of Judaism in the last few centuries.[4] A main tenet of Hasidism that Abraham Heschel

---

1. Ultra-orthodox Judaism.

2. Hasidim (plural; Hasid is singular) have also been known to speak in tongues. Kaplan and Dresner, *Abraham Joshua Heschel*, 5.

3. Hundert, *Essential Papers on Hasidism*, 338–39.

4. Ibid., 500.

demonstrated was engagement with the whole of life with all one's being. Every action and gesture is done to consecrate life, including the mundane routines of eating, working, and resting. Buber favored an illustration of Hasidism that tells of a master who asked his disciples, "What is the most important thing in the world?" One answered, "the Sabbath"; another ,"prayer"; a third, "Yom Kippur." "No," the master explained, "the most important thing is whatever you are doing at the moment!"[5]

Hasidic literature, enigmatic and terse, is difficult to penetrate, especially for outsiders. Like a tourist in a foreign country, the visitor to Hasidic literature is likely to miss its depths. Heschel explains:

> [It] is a tragedy that this great movement is essentially an oral movement, one that cannot be preserved in written form. It is ultimately a living movement. It is not contained fully in any of its books . . . . [In] other words, Hasidism has a very personal dimension . . . . To be Hasid is to be in love with God and with what God created. Once you are in love, you are a different human being . . . . That is the history of Hasidism. Indeed, he who has never been in love will not understand and may consider it madness. That is why there is so much opposition to Hasidism, more than we are willing to admit.[6]

Hasidism would have been pushed to the fringes of Jewish society and relegated as a sect if not for the wise leadership of the movement. The leadership did not declare war on those who were not Hasidic; it emphasized adherence to tradition; it extended unity and mutual responsibility to those in and outside Hasidism; and it avoided radical tendencies.[7] Furthermore, the movement's success and widespread dissemination attests that it satisfied a spiritual need in the people. Simon Dubnow, an authority on Hasidism, suggests that "by an immense psychic influence, Hasidism created a type of believer to whom feeling was more important than external observance."[8] The success of Hasidism can also be ascribed to the way the zaddik (leader)[9] oriented himself to God and flock: he was a mystic trying

---

5. Dresner, *The Circle of the Baal Shem Tov*, xix.

6. Heschel, "Hasidism," 14–16.

7. Bizarre behavior was reported, for example, that Hasidim did somersaults before the Ark of the Covenant or danced like common folk. It has been noted that a Shaker sect in England also did somersaults in their service. Parallels are drawn between the Hasidim and the Quaker and Mennonite sects, as in their giving teachings without preparation. Wilensky, in Hundert, *Essential Papers on Hasidism*, 258.

8. Hundert, *Essential Papers on Hasidism*, 228.

9. *Zaddik* means "leader," but the title is usually reserved for the *master* teacher, the spiritual leader and spiritual visionary to the community at large.

to attain maximum communion with God and simultaneously centered on the needs of his people. As the Baal Shem Tov would say: "[the zaddik] too must go down near the slime and rubbish to raise [the people] up."[10] The more the zaddik stressed his responsibility to help the needs and concerns of his people, the more popular the movement became.

Moshe Rosman, in *Founder of Hasidism*, summarizes the influence of Hasidism:

> In Hasidism the mystical ethos became part of everyday religion; Kaballah was turned into a tool for intensifying communal life, rather than for encouraging isolation; emphasis was placed on the need to relate to God through joy, instead of abnegation; and addressing the individual's needs became a major religious objective. In short, Hasidism created a unique sort of pietism that captured the imagination of the masses of Eastern European Jewry in the nineteenth and early twentieth centuries. After a period of decline, marked especially by the tragic fate of virtually all Hasidic communities during the Holocaust, Hasidism has proven it has the power to flourish in modern democratic societies. Today we are witnessing tremendous growth of Hasidic groups in Israel, America, and Europe.[11]

Gershom Scholem describes a central practice of Hasidism, *devekut* (i.e., communion with God), where people experience the glory of God. This has roots in the old Kabbalists of the thirteenth century. Scholem quotes a source who claims that "Hasidim of old times" took no less than nine hours daily for their study of the Torah:

> [during] *devekut* [they] used to imagine the light of the Shekhinah above their heads, as though it were flowing all around them and they were sitting in the midst of the light, and this is the way I have found it [the meaning of *devekut*] explained in an old manuscript of the ancient ascetics. And while in that [state of meditation], they are all trembling as a natural effect, but [spiritually] rejoicing in trembling.[12]

Laurence J. Silberstein suggests that Heschel was faithful to the Lurianic system in Hasidism by advocating the traditional *mizwot* (doing of good works). The Lurianic myth claims that the primordial divine unity was shattered at the cataclysm of creation. These "divine sparks" fell down

---

10. Shmuel Ettinger, in Hundert, *Essential Papers on Hasidism*, 234.
11. Rosman, *Founder of Hasidism*, 1.
12. Hundert, *Essential Papers on Hasidism*, 279.

to earth and were trapped in shells, causing a cosmic exile where the sparks are separated from their divine source. The individual Jew is assigned to liberate the divine sparks from the shells through a process of redemption (*tiqqun*), which is achieved by doing good deeds (*mitwot*) with the right intention and attitude.[13]

Hasidism had sociological and historical attributes that contributed to its rise; however, its success can be primarily ascribed to the charismatic leadership of the Besht (another name of the Baal Shem Tov). By the way, the movement today is still propelled forward by strong charismatic leaders. The Besht did not merely talk about God; rather, he brought God to the people, generating new inspiration to Judaism, with effects still felt today. Other leaders such as Maimonides, Reb Isaac Luria, and Rebbe Akiva left behind great works, but the Besht left behind a "new people."[14] Tapping people into the inspiration of the *Rauch Kodesh* (Holy Spirit) he made the observance of the Law (which had become petrified) liquid and alive.

The tenets of Hasidism remained embedded with Heschel even after he abandoned their distinctive dress:

> In my childhood and in my youth, I was the recipient of many blessings, I lived in the presence of quite a number of extraordinary persons I could revere. And just as I lived as a child in their presence, their presence continues to live in me as an adult. And yet I am not just a dwelling place for other people, an echo of the past.[15]

Heschel's life work remained on a Hasidic trajectory. Moreover, instead of being a rebbe (rabbi) to his community, he became a rebbe to the world at large. Rabbi Samuel Dresner claims that Heschel approximated the life of a zaddik in his generation—a master scholar, pietist, teacher, leader, and spiritual force.[16] The zaddik lived his life before God in accordance with the psalmist: "I have set the Lord before me at all times" (Ps 16:8). In Hasidic tradition the zaddik was to seek out the sparks of holiness everywhere, even amidst evil. According to classic Hasidic writers, Noah was denounced because he lived in seclusion as an unconcerned leader, causing the flood, even though he "walked *with* God." On the other hand, Abraham was a zaddik as he "walked *before* God in the midst of the city," that is, he was a concerned leader engaged with the goings on of the culture, and would have prevented the flood if he had lived at the time of Noah.

13. Ibid.
14. Heschel, *Moral Grandeur and Spiritual Audacity*, 34.
15. Heschel, "In Search of Exaltation," 29–30, 35.
16. Merkle, *Abraham Joshua Heschel*, 19.

Some of Heschel's grandfather's writings indicate that "the Holy One blessed be He is grieved and participates in the sufferings of Israel, as it is written (Psalm 91:15), 'I will be with them in distress,' and (Isaiah 63:9), 'In all their troubles He was troubled.'"[17] Subsequently, Heschel's father passed on this "religion of sympathy" to him, from which he developed his doctoral dissertation on the "pathos" of God (divine feelings). Also strongly impressed upon the young Heschel was that the Jewish people were not only living in physical exile from the land of Israel but spiritual exile—as the *Shekhinah* (God's indwelling presence) is exiled from the world.[18]

Heschel's father was his first model of piety. Life was considered a sacred drama, especially the high holy days. In Hasidic tradition he learned, from his father, to actualize within himself the spirit of the Bible. "On Passover, he became a *ben horin*, as if 'newly liberated by God' from Egypt; on Shavuot, the holiday commemorating God's revealing the Torah on Mount Sinai, he himself received the Law."[19]

Hasidism was a revolution against traditional Judaism that had become dry and dusty. Talmudic study had become the study of legal problems rather than human problems. Jewish criminal code was complicated (e.g., fifty-five possible explanations could be found to explain why Laban did not treat Jacob well). Students developed tremendous wit and intellectual sharpness in arguing point and counterpoint of the Talmud, but it became more about thoughts than feelings, and more about theory than daily human problems. Heschel experienced this form of education:

> What is left is astuteness, acumen. It is always syllogisms on top of syllogisms, a pyramid on top of three other pyramids. You're always walking from one roof to another. You don't just walk straight, you're always jumping, leaping; there's no straight thinking. The Jews loved this Talmudic study, but the soul was not rested. There was very little for the heart. It was always so dry, so remote from existence, without the slightest awareness that there was also an inner life in human problems. There were no human problems, only legal problems.[20]

During Heschel's university education in Berlin, he once said he could not converse with his professors about his religious experiences because they did not have categories to deal with his inner religious stirrings:

---

17. Kaplan, *Abraham Joshua Heschel*, 16–17.
18. Ibid., 17.
19. Ibid.
20. Heschel, *Moral Grandeur and Spiritual Audacity*, 36.

I became increasingly aware of the gulf that separated my views from those held at the University. I had come with a sense of anxiety: How can I rationally find a way where ultimate meaning lies, a way of living where one would never miss a reference to supreme significance? Why am I here at all, and what is my purpose? I did not even know how to phrase my concern. But to my teachers that was a question unworthy of philosophical analysis.[21]

Also in Berlin, Heschel met weekly with a group of Jewish intellectuals (Koigen's Circle) where he increasingly felt misfit. His concern was not secularism, but reductionism—the corrosive effect of explaining religious phenomena (such as prophetic inspiration) by humanistic means. Kant's influence dominated Berlin at the time, where religion was considered "fiction." To Heschel these "fictions" were no substitute for divine reality. In one of Koigen's meetings, the observation was made that students of Kant usually ended up as atheists.[22] Heschel drew upon Hasidic sources to define his brand of Judaism in which God was a concerned, living being who had *hesed* (lovingkindness) for humanity. He brought a different perspective to these meetings, steering the group's emphasis away from philosophy of culture towards the experience of the individual. This was the direction his dissertation was taking, where the prophet receives God's initiative. He developed his ideas of "radical amazement," "wonder," and "awe," which orient the individual to relate to the holy God of Israel. Typical of Hasidic piety, Heschel's was a theology both integrative and personal where action, piety, prayer, God, and living were inextricably linked.

It became evident that Koigen's method for replenishing Judaism was different from Heschel's. Koigen envisioned a renewal of Judaism through people adopting his all-encompassing cultural theory, where Heschel saw renewal through the individual seeking the face of the living God. Heschel felt that codes, rituals, or dogmas were insufficient to mobilize the Jewish people to undertake God's project on earth. He argued that intuitive knowledge is necessary for the apprehending of God and not so much the pursuing of law or secular nationalism.

This was to be Heschel's pattern in his ensuing life: he did not live a socially cocooned life but readily engaged in the world of ideas around him, he empathized with people by entering their world, learning their categories and world view, and then, after much thought, rebutting their world views in light of biblical theology. In this regard he was a true apologist for Judaism:

---

21. Heschel, *Toward an Understanding of Halacha*, 388.
22. Kaplan, *Abraham Joshua Heschel*, 131.

"he cultivated religious emotions, side-stepping rationalism, attacking ideology and dogma, as he trained minds to receive the living God."[23] Heschel explains how he had great hopes for his humanistic studies in Berlin:

> How can I rationally find a way where ultimate meaning lies . . . ?
>
> Why am I here at all, and what is my purpose?
>
> I did not even know how to phrase my concern. But to my teachers that was a question unworthy of philosophical analysis. . . . My teachers were prisoners of a Greek-German way of thinking. They were fettered in categories which presupposed certain metaphysical assumptions which could be never proved. The questions I was moved by could not even be adequately phrased in categories of their thinking.[24]

Academia predominately used the neo-Kantian theory of knowledge—only that which could be measured, heard, seen, or felt existed. In other words, only what could be derived from sense data, as processed by structures in the mind, existed. In sum, the environment in Berlin tore Heschel apart:

> As an observant believer and a Polish Jew, he benefited from his studies at the University of Berlin, which, nonetheless, neither nurtured his piety nor welcomed him as a Polish Jew. The Hochschule [Jewish Seminary], which deemed sacred texts to be historically derived, did not encompass loyalty to revelation. Nor did the Orthodox Seminary, despite its involvement with philosophy and scientific methods, provide a community. Each institution was, at best, a halfway house.[25]

To neo-Kantians, God was not objectively true, but symbolically true—religion was a fiction, useful to society or humankind's personal well-being. To the professors, God was an Object; to Heschel God was a Subject.[26] Heschel portrays his inner conflict:

> In those months in Berlin I went through moments of profound bitterness. I felt very much alone with my own problems and anxieties. I walked alone in the evenings through the magnificent streets of Berlin. I admired the solidity of its architecture, the overwhelming drive and power of a dynamic civilization . . . .

23. Ibid., 138.
24. Heschel, *Moral Grandeur and Spiritual Audacity*, 127–45.
25. Kaplan, *Abraham Joshua Heschel*, 154.
26. Ibid., 158.

Suddenly I noticed the sun had gone down, evening had arrived. *From what time may one recite the Shema in the evening?* I had forgotten God—I had forgotten Sinai—I had forgotten that sunset is my business—that my task is [quoted in Hebrew] *"to restore the world to the kingship of the Lord."*[27]

On that evening, in the streets of Berlin, I was not in a mood to pray. My heart was heavy, my soul was sad. It was difficult for the lofty words of prayer to break through the dark clouds of my inner life. But how would I dare to *davn* [pray]? How would I dare to miss a *Ma'ariv*? ... "Out of *eimah*, out of fear of God, do we read the *Shema*."[28]

The notions of "awe," "wonder," and "radical amazement" that fill his later writings arose from this personal struggle against the vacuousness of modernity. He believed that the correct orientation of the heart—filled with "awe" and "wonder"—would reinstate people to God and would revitalize Judaism. Religious awe rather than philosophy became Heschel's life concern. "We do not suffer symbolically. We suffer literally, truly, deeply. Symbolic remedies are quackery. The will of God is either real or a delusion."[29]

Buber's concept of "I and Thou" had a wide appeal among many assimilated Jews desiring to rediscover their religion. For Heschel, Buber's theology of the person relating to God was a "vague encounter."[30] Heschel claimed that Buber substituted a "symbol" for the transcendent Subject. To Heschel, God was overwhelmingly real—not to be described in such humanistic and reductionistic terms. He felt that Buber's dialogical religion was reductionistic and merely reflected the existential philosophy of the time.

Heschel also had great respect for Moses Maimonides (1135–1204). Maimonides, or the Ramban (as he is also known), had a yearning from youth to "grasp God, as much as a human being can do so."[31] Although Heschel's ambitions were more modest, he identified with Maimonides' aspiration to conquer science, culture, art, and theology. In Heschel's words: "[The Ramban] didn't simply amass a wealth of heterogeneous facts; rather, he grasped everything intuitively, so that all the elements he acquired arranged themselves naturally into the harmonious framework of his.[32] He

27. Heschel, *Man's Quest for God*, 98.
28. Ibid.
29. Heschel, *Toward an Understanding of Halacha*, 387–88.
30. Kaplan, *Abraham Joshua Heschel*, 223.
31. Ibid., 203.
32. Ibid.

also had intense yearning for prophecy, which resonated with Heschel. Most importantly, Heschel followed Maimonides' example of moving from theory to practice:

> This was Maimonides' last metamorphosis: From metaphysics to medicine, from contemplation to practice, from speculation to the imitation of God . . . . Preoccupation with the concrete man and the effort to aid him in his suffering is now the form of religious devotion.[33]

I agree. This is a good place to end: where the rubber meets the road—*with the concrete and practical*. We are created in his image, and so between us and him are correlations in our personhood, relatedness, emotions, and communication.

---

33. Heschel, *The Insecurity of Freedom*, 290.

BIBLIOGRAPHY

Aaron, David. *Love Is My Religion: Understanding the Spiritual Foundations of Judaism.* Jerusalem: BSD, 2004.
Alexander, John F. *The Secular Squeeze: Reclaiming Christian Depth in a Shallow World.* Downers Grove, IL: InterVarsity Press, 1993.
Althaus, Paul. *The Theology of Martin Luther.* Translated by Robert C. Schultz. Philadelphia: Fortress, 1966.
Ashly, Richard, and R. B. J. Walker. "Speaking the Language of Exile: Dissident Thought in International Studies." *International Studies Quarterly* 34 (1990) 259–68.
Ateek, Naim Stifan. *A Palestinian Christian Cry for Reconciliation.* Maryknoll, NY: Orbis, 2008.
Bacon, Francis. *Essays, Advancement of Learning, New Atlantis, and Other Pieces.* Edited by R. F. Jones. New York: Odyssey, 1937.
Banks, Robert. *God the Worker: Journeys into the Mind, Heart and Imagination of God.* Sutherland, Australia: Albatross, 1992.
Barker, Margaret. *The Great Angel: A Study of Israel's Second God,* Louisville: John Knox, 1992.
Barth, Karl. *Church Dogmatics,* III/1. Edited and translated by Geoffrey W. Bromiley. Edinburgh: T. & T. Clark, 1958.
Basinger, David. "Middle Knowledge and Divine Control: Some Clarifications." *International Journal for Philosophy of Religion* 30 (1991) 129–39.
Bavink, Herman. *The Doctrine of God.* Translated by William Hendriksen. Grand Rapids: Eerdmans, 1951.
Begbie, Jeremy. "The Sense of an Ending." University of California Television. Uploaded on YouTube January 31, 2008. http://www.youtube.com/watch?v=4GfEbzr09q0.
Bell, Rob. *Love Wins: A Book about Heaven, Hell, and the Fate of Every Person Who Ever Lived.* New York: Harper One, 2011.
Bloom, Allen. *The Closing of the American Mind.* New York: Simon & Schuster, 1987.
Blumenthal, David. "Despair and Hope in Post-*Shoah* Jewish Life." *Bridges*, Fall/Winter 1999, 122–23.
———. *Facing the Abusing God: A Theology of Protest.* Louisville: Westminster/John Knox, 1993.
Bond, Allison. "Belief in the Brain: Sacred and Secular Ideas Engage Identical Areas." *Scientific American Mind*, 21, March/April 2010, 13–15.
Boorstin, Daniel J. *The Discoverers.* New York: Random House, 1983.

Brooks, David. "The New Humanism." *The New York Times*, March 7, 2011. http://www.nytimes.com/2011/03/08/opinion/08brooks.html?src=ISMR_HP_LO_MST_FB%20l&_r=0.

Brown, Warren S., Nancey Murphy, and H. Newton Malony. *Whatever Happened to the Soul?* Minneapolis: Fortress, 1998.

Brueggemann, Walter. *Finally Comes the Poet: Daring Speech for Proclamation.* Minneapolis, Fortress, 1989.

———. *From Whom No Secrets Are Hid: Introducing the Psalms.* Louisville: Westminster/John Knox, 2014.

———. *Genesis.* Atlanta: John Knox, 1982.

———. *Great Prayers of the Old Testament.* Louisville: Westminster/John Knox, 2008.

———. *Hopeful Imagination: Prophetic Voices in Exile.* Philadelphia: Fortress, 1985.

———. *The Message of the Psalms.* Minneapolis: Augsburg, 1984.

———. *Old Testament Theology.* Nashville: Abingdon, 2008.

———. *Texts under Negotiation: The Bible and Postmodern Imagination.* Minneapolis: Fortress, 1993.

Buber, Martin. *I and Thou.* Translated by Walter Kaufmann. New York: Touchstone, 1970.

———. "My Way to Hasidism." In *Essential Papers on Hasidism: Origins to Present*, edited by Gershon David Hundert, 499–510. New York: New York Press, 1991.

Bultmann, Rudolph. *Existence and Faith.* Edited by S. M. Ogden. New York: Meridian, 1960.

Campbell, Joseph. *The Inner Reaches of Outer Space: Metaphor as Myth and as Religion.* New York: Harper & Row, 1986.

Carney, Brian M. "Why America Will Stay on Top." *The Wall Street Journal*, online, updated March 5, 2011. http://online.wsj.com/article/SB10001424052748703559604576175881248268272.html?mod=WSJ_Opinion_carousel_1.

Cassidy, Michael. *A Witness For Ever: The Dawning of Democracy in South Africa—Stories Behind the Story.* London: Hodder & Stoughton, 1995.

Charnock, Stephen. *Discourses upon the Existence and Attributes of God.* 2 vols. Grand Rapids: Baker, 1979.

Clapp, Rodney. "What Hollywood Doesn't Know about Romantic Love: Celebrating Valentine's Day in the Spirit of the Song of Solomon." *Christianity Today*, February 3, 1984.

Clarke, W. N. "A New Look at the Immutability of God." In *God Knowable and Unknowable*, edited by R. J. Roth, 43–72. New York: Fordham University Press, 1973.

Clines, David. *On the Way to the Postmodern: Old Testament Essays, 1967–1998.* Vol. 2. Sheffield: Sheffield Academic Press, 1998.

———. "Yahweh and the God of Christian Theology." *Theology* 83 (1980) 323–30.

Cohen, Ariel. "Jesus the Palestinian?" *The Jerusalem Post*, December 29, 2014. http://www.jpost.com/Christian-News/Jesus-the-Palestinian-386057.

Cohn-Sherbok, Dan, ed. *Holocaust Theology: A Reader.* New York: University Press, 2002.

Colson, Lowell. *Judgment in Pastoral Counseling.* Nashville and New York: Abingdon, 1969.

Cone, James H. *A Black Theology of Liberation.* Philadelphia: Lippincott, 1970.

Cooke, Bernard. *The Distancing of God.* Minneapolis: Augsburg/Fortress, 1990.

Cross, F. L., ed. *The Oxford Dictionary of the Christian Church*. London: Oxford University Press, 1957.
Dante Alighieri. *Paradise*. Whitefield, MT: Kessinger, 2004.
Darg, Christine. "It's Complicated." *The Jerusalem Post*, September 9, 2010. http://www.jpost.com/ChristianInIsrael/Features/Article.aspx?id=187278.
Dickson, Anthol. *The Gospel according to Moses: What My Jewish Friends Taught Me about Jesus*. Grand Rapids: Brazos, 2003.
Dooyeveerd, Herman. *A Critique of Theoretical Thought*. 3 Vols. Translated by D. H. Freeman and W. S. Young. Philadelphia: Presbyterian and Reformed, 1969.
———. *In the Twilight of Western Thought*. Nutley, NJ: Craig, 1960.
Dresner, Samuel H., ed. *The Circle of the Baal Shem Tov: Studies in Hasidism*. Chicago: University of Chicago Press, 1985.
Dresner, Samuel H. "Heschel the Man." In *Abraham Joshua Heschel: Exploring His Life and Thought*, edited by John C. Merkle, 3–27. New York: Macmillan, 1985.
Dubnow, Simon. *History of Hasidism* [Hebrew]. Tel Aviv, 1930.
Dyrness, William A. *Invitation to Cross-Cultural Theology: Case Studies in Vernacular Theologies*. Grand Rapids: Zondervan, 1992.
Eldredge, John. *Wild at Heart: A Personal Guide to Discover the Secret of Your Masculine Soul*. Nashville: Thomas Nelson, 2002.
Erickson, Millard J. *Christian Theology*. 3 vols. Grand Rapids: Baker, 1983.
———. *Postmodernizing the Faith: Evangelical Responses to the Challenge of Postmodernism*. Grand Rapids: Baker, 1998.
Fairweather, Eugene R., ed. *A Scholastic Miscellany: Anselm to Ockham*. New York: Macmillan, 1970.
Fretheim, Terence E. *The Suffering of God: An Old Testament Perspective*. Philadelphia: Fortress, 1984.
———. *The Theology of the Old Testament: A Relational Theology of Creation*. New York: Harper & Row, 1958.
Fretheim, Terence E., and Karlfried Froehlich. *The Bible as Word of God: In a Postmodern Age*. Minneapolis: Fortress, 1998.
Fretheim, Terence E., and Curtis L. Thompson, eds. *God, Evil, and Suffering: Essays in Honor of Paul R. Sponheim*. St. Paul, MN: Word and World, 2000.
Fromm, Erich. *You Shall Be Gods*. Greenwich, CT: Fawcett, 1966.
Fuller, Daniel. *Gospel and Law: Contrast or Continuum? The Hermeneutics of Dispensationalism and Covenant Theology*. Grand Rapids: Eerdmans, 1980.
Goldberg, Philip. "Making Space for Sane Spirituality." *Huffington Post*. Updated May 25, 2011. http://www.huffingtonpost.com/philip-goldberg/sane-spirituality-lets-ma_b_786430.html.
Gowan, Donald E. *Theology in Exodus: Biblical Theology in the Form of a Commentary*. Louisville: Westminster/John Knox, 1994.
Green, Arthur, ed. *Jewish Spirituality 2: From the Sixteenth-Century Revival to the Present*. New York: Crossroad, 1987.
Guinness, Os. *The American Hour: A Time of Reckoning and the Once and Future Role of Faith*. New York: Free Press, 1993.
Hallman, Joseph M. *The Descent of God: Divine Suffering in History and Theology*. Minneapolis: Fortress, 1991.
Hanson, Anthony Tyrrell. *The Wrath of the Lamb*. London: SPCK, 1957.

Henry, Carl. *God, Revelation and Authority,* Vol. 5: *God Who Stands and Stays,* Part 1. Waco, TX: Word, 1982.

Heschel, Abraham J. *Between God and Man: An Interpretation of Judaism.* Selected, edited, and introduced by Fritz A. Rothschild. New York: Simon & Schuster, 1959.

———. *God in Search of Man.* New York: Farrar/Strauss & Cudahy, 1955.

———. "Hasidism." *Jewish Heritage* 14, no. 3 (1972) 14–16.

———. "In Search of Exaltation." *Jewish Heritage* 13 (Fall 1971) 29–35.

———. *The Insecurity of Freedom.* New York: Farrar, Straus & Giroux, 1966.

———. *Man Is Not Alone: A Philosophy of Religion.* New York: Farrar, Straus & Giroux, 1951.

———. *Man's Quest for God: Studies in Prayer and Symbolism.* New York: Macmillan, 1981.

———. *Moral Grandeur and Spiritual Audacity: Essays.* Edited by Susannah Heschel. New York: Farrar, Straus & Giroux, 1996.

———. *A Passion for Truth.* New York: Farrar, Straus & Giroux, 1973.

———. *The Prophets: An Introduction, Volume 1.* New York: Harper & Row, 1962.

———. *The Prophets, Volume 2.* New York: Harper & Row, 1962.

———. *The Sabbath.* New York: Farrar, Straus & Giroux, 1951.

Heschel, Susannah. *The Aryan Jesus: Christian Theologians and the Bible in Nazi Germany.* Princeton: Princeton University Press, 2008.

Hiebert, Paul G. *Missiological Implications of Epistemological Shifts: Affirming Truth in a Modern/Postmodern World.* Harrisburg, PA: Trinity Press, 1999.

Hill, W. J. "Does the World Make a Difference to God?" *Thomist* 38 (1974) 146–64.

Howard, G. "The Tetragram and the New Testament." *Journal of Biblical Literature* 96 (1977) 63–83.

Hubbard, David. *Beyond Futility: Messages of Hope from the Book of Ecclesiastes.* Grand Rapids: Eerdmans, 1976.

Huffman, Douglas S., and Eric L. Johnson, eds. *God under Fire: Modern Scholarship Reinvents God.* Grand Rapids: Zondervan, 2002.

Hummel, Charles E. *The Galileo Connection: Resolving Conflicts between Science and the Bible.* Downers Grove, IL: InterVarsity Press, 1986.

Hundert, Gershon David, ed. *Essential Papers on Hasidism: Origins to Present.* New York: New York Press, 1991.

Illingworth, R. J. *Personality—Divine and Human, the Bampton Lectures for 1892.* London: Macmillan, 1894.

Jacob, Edmond. *Theology of the Old Testament.* Translated by Arthur W. Heathcote and Philip J. Allcock. London: Hodder & Stoughton, 1958.

Jacobs, Jill. "Do First, Understand Later." My Jewish Learning website. http://www.myjewishlearning.com/holidays/Jewish_Holidays/Shavuot/Themes_and_Theology/Celebrating_Submission/Accepting_the_Torah.shtml (last accessed October 2015).

Kaplan, E. K., and S. H. Dresner. *Abraham Joshua Heschel: Prophetic Witness.* New Haven: Yale University Press, 1998.

Keillor, Steven J. *God's Judgments: Interpreting History and the Christian Faith.* Downers Grove, IL: IVP Academic, 2007.

Kelsey, Morton. *Encounter with God: A Theology of Christian Experience.* London: Hodder & Stoughton, 1972.

Kierkegaard, Søren. *Either/Or: A Fragment of Life.* Abridged, translated, and with an introduction and notes by Alastair Hannay. New York: Penguin Books, 1992.

Kraft, Charles H. *Christianity in Culture: A Study in Dynamic Biblical Theologizing in Cross-Cultural Perspective.* Maryknoll, NY: Orbis, 1979.

Kugel, James L. *The God of Old: Inside the Lost World of the Bible.* New York: Free Press, 2003.

Laudin, Larry. *Beyond Positivism and Relativism: Theory, Method and Evidence.* Boulder, CO: Westview Press, 1996.

Landy, Francis. "The Name of God and the Image of God and Man: A Response to David Clines." *Theology* 84 (1981) 164–70.

Laytner, Anson. *Arguing with God, A Jewish Tradition.* New Jersey: Jason Aronson, 1998.

Lee, Jung Young. *God Suffers for Us: A Systematic Inquiry into a Concept of Divine Passibility.* The Hague: Martinus Nijhoff, 1974.

Lewis, C. S. *A Grief Observed.* New York: Bantam, 1976.

———. *The Weight of Glory, and Other Addresses.* New York: Harper Collins, 1949, 2001.

Lister, Rob. *God Is Impassible and Impassioned: Toward a Theology of Divine Emotion.* Wheaton, IL: Crossway, 2012.

Luther, Martin. *The Creation: A Commentary on the First Five Chapters of the Book of Genesis.* Translated by H. Cole. Edinburgh: T. & T. Clark, 1858.

———. *On the Jews and Their Lies* [1543]. Translated by Martin H. Bertram. In *Luther's Works,* vol. 47. Philadelphia: Fortress, 1971.

Luzzatto, Moshe Chayim. *The Way of God.* Translated by Aryeh Kaplan. Jerusalem: Feldheim, 1988.

Marty, Martin, and Jerald Brauer. *The Unrelieved Paradox: Studies in the Theology of Franz Bibfeldt.* Grand Rapids: Eerdmans, 1994.

McWilliams, Warren. *The Passion of God: Divine Suffering in Contemporary Protestant Theology.* Macon, GA: Mercer University Press, 1985.

"Medieval and Reformation Christianity: Part Seven." [Podcast] From the series *History and Theology,* www.maxieburch.net (last accessed April 2010).

Merkle, John C., ed. *Abraham J. Heschel: Exploring His Life and Thought.* New York: Macmillan, 1985.

Miles, Jack. *God: A Biography.* New York: Alfred A. Knopf, 1995.

Miskotte, K. H. *When the Gods Are Silent.* London: Collins, 1967.

Moltmann, Jürgen. *The Crucified God.* London: SCM, 1974.

Moore, Robert, and Douglas Gillette. *King, Warrior, Magician, Lover: Rediscovering the Archetypes of the Mature Masculine.* San Francisco: Harper, 1990.

Moreland, J. P., and S. B. Rae. *Body and Soul: Human Nature and the Crisis in Ethics.* Downers Grove, IL: InterVarsity Press, 2000.

Morris, Naomi. "Study Links Willingness to Cheat, Viewpoint on God." *Los Angeles Times,* April 30, 2011. http://www.latimes.com/news/local/la-me-beliefs-morals-20110430,0,4211564.story?track=rss&utm_source=feedburner&utm_medium=feed&utm_campaign=Feed%3A+latimes%2Fmostviewed+%28L.A.+Times+-+Most+Viewed+Stories%29.

Mozley, J. K. *The Impassibility of God: A Survey of Christian Thought.* London: Cambridge University Press, 1926.

Nee, Watchman. *What Shall This Man Do?* London: Victory, 1961.

Neff, David. "Closed to Openness: Scholars Vote: God Knows Future." *Christianity Today*, January 7, 2002. http://www.christianitytoday.com/ct/2002/january7/15.21.html.

Nietzsche, Friedrich. *Thus Spoke Zarathustra*. Translated by Thomas Common. Blacksburg, VA: Thrifty, 2009.

Ohlrich, Charles. *The Suffering God: Hope & Comfort for Those Who Hurt*. Downers Grove, IL: InterVarsity Press, 1982.

Origen: An Exhortation to Martyrdom, Prayer and Selected Works. Translated by Rowan Greer. Mahwah, NJ: Paulist, 1979.

Packer, J. I. *Evangelism and Sovereignty*. Leicester, UK: Inter-Varsity Press, 1961.

———. *Knowing God*. Downers Grove, IL: InterVarsity Press, 1973.

Patai, Raphael. *The Jewish Mind*. New York: Charles Scribner's Sons, 1977.

Peacocke, A. R. *Creation and the World of Science*. Oxford: Clarendon, 1979.

Phillips, J. B. *Your God Is Too Small*. London: Macmillan, 1952.

Phipps, William. "The Sensuousness of Agape." *Theology Today* 29, no. 4 (1973) 370–79.

Pinnock, Clark. *Most Moved Mover: A Theology of God's Openness*. Grand Rapids: Baker, 2001.

Pinnock, Clark, et al. *The Openness of God: A Biblical Challenge to the Traditional Understanding of God*. Downers Grove, IL: InterVarsity Press, 1994.

Piper, John, and Justin Taylor, eds. *Suffering and the Sovereignty of God*. Wheaton, IL: Crossway, 2006.

Plantinga, Alvin. "Advice to Christian Philosophers." *Faith and Philosophy* 1 (July 1984) 253–71.

Polanyi, Michael. *Personal Knowledge: Towards a Post-critical Philosophy*. Chicago: University of Chicago Press, 1974.

———. *Science, Faith and Society*. Chicago: University of Chicago Press, 1964.

Prager, Dennis, and Joseph Telushkin. *Why the Jews? The Reason for Antisemitism*. New York: Simon & Schuster, 1983.

"Prisoners Have Higher Self-esteem than Community Members." *Metro*, January 13, 2014.

Rad, Gerhard von. *Genesis*. Translated by John H. Marks. London: SCM, 1961.

———. *The Message of the Prophets*. New York: Harper & Row, 1972.

Reade, W. H. V. *The Christian Challenge to Philosophy*. London: SPCK, 1951.

Reilly, Robert. *The Closing of the Muslim Mind: How Intellectual Suicide Created the Modern Islamist*. Wilmington, DE: ISI, 2010.

Reus, Edward. *History of the Canon of the Holy Scriptures in the Christian Church*. Translated by D. Hunger. Edinburgh: R. W. Hunter, 1891.

Richardson, Bradford. "Jeremiah Wright: 'Jesus was a Palestinian.'" *The Hill*, October 10, 2015. http://thehill.com/blogs/blog-briefing-room/256592-jeremiah-wright-jesus-was-a-palestinian.

Ricoeur, Paul. *The Philosophy of Paul Ricoeur*. Edited by C. E. Reagen and D. Steward. Boston: Beacon, 1979.

Rorty, Richard. *Philosophy and the Mirror of Nature*. Princeton: Princeton University Press, 1979.

Rosman, Moshe. *Founder of Hasidism: A Quest for the Historical Baal Shem Tov*. Berkeley: University of California Press, 1996.

Rossing, Barbara. *The Rapture Exposed: The Message of Hope in the Book of Revelation*. New York: Basic, 2004.

Sanders, John. *The God Who Risks: A Theology of Providence*. Downers Grove, IL: InterVarsity Press, 1998.
Satinover, Jeffrey. *Homosexuality and the Politics of Truth*. Grand Rapids: Baker, 1996.
Schoonenberg, P. "God as Relating and (Be)coming: A Meta-Thomistic Consideration." *Listening* 14 (1979) 265–78.
Schwöbel, Christoph, and Colin E. Gunton, eds. *Persons, Divine and Human*. Edinburgh: T. & T. Clark, 1991.
Sheesley, Joel C. "Jerome Witkin: A Profile." *Image: A Journal of the Arts & Religion*, Issue 11, Fall 1995.
Showers, James. "Jesus the 'Palestinian.'" On The Friends of Israel website, http://www.foi.org/free-resources/article/jesus-palestinian/.
Smedes, Lewis. *Love within Limits*. Grand Rapids: Eerdmans, 1978.
Smith, George Adam. "The Hebrew Genius as Exhibited in the Old Testament." In *The Legacy of Israel*, edited by Edwyn R. Bevan and Charles Singer, 1–28. Oxford: Clarendon, 1944.
Smith, James K. A. *Desiring the Kingdom: Worship, Worldview, and Cultural Formation*. Grand Rapids: Baker Academic, 2009.
Somashekhar, Sandhya. "Health Survey Gives Government Its First Large-Scale Data on Gay, Bisexual Population." *The Washington Post*, July 15, 2014. https://www.washingtonpost.com/national/health-science/health-survey-gives-government-its-first-large-scale-data-on-gay-bisexual-population/2014/07/14/2db9f4b0–92f-11e4-bbf1-cc51275e7f8f_story.html.
Spurgeon, Charles H. *Morning and Evening*. Grand Rapids: Daybreak, 1980.
Stammer, Larry. "Rabbis Vote to Revive Observance of Traditions." *Los Angeles Times*, May 27 1999, A3.
Stokes, W. "Freedom as Perfection: Whitehead, Thomas, and Augustine." *Proceedings of the American Catholic Philosophical Association* 36 (1962) 134–42.
Stratton, George Malcolm. *Anger: Its Religious and Moral Significance*. London: George Allen & Unwin, 1923.
Sullivan, Laura. "Experts: Bad Economies Don't Cause Crime Waves." NPR, November 20, 2008.
Sweeney, Marvin. *Reading the Hebrew Bible after the Shoah: Engaging Holocaust Theology*. Minneapolis: Fortress, 2008.
Sweet, Leonard, and Frank Viola. *Jesus: A Theography*. Nashville: Thomas Nelson, 2012.
Tiessen, Terrance. *Providence and Prayer: How Does God Work in the World?* Downers Grove, IL: InterVarsity Press, 2000.
Torrance, T. F. *Theological Science*. Oxford: Oxford University Press, 1978.
Toulmin, Stephen. *Cosmopolis: The Hidden Agenda of Modernity*. New York: Free Press, 1990.
Turner, Steve. *Imagine: A Vision for Christians in the Arts*. Downers Grove, IL: InterVarsity Press, 2001.
Van Biema, David. "Mother Teresa's Crisis of Faith." *Time*, August 23, 2007. http://time.com/4126238/mother-teresas-crisis-of-faith/.
Veenker, Jody, "Spirituality without Religion." *Christianity Today*, December 6, 1999, 34–35.
Von Hugel, Baron Friedrich. *Essays and Addresses on the Philosophy of Religion*. Second Series. London: J.M. Dent & Sons, 1926.

Ware, Bruce A. "An Evangelical Reexamination of the Doctrine of the Immutability of God." PhD dissertation, Fuller Theological Seminary, Pasadena, CA, 1984.

———. *God's Lesser Glory: The Diminished God of Open Theism*. Wheaton, IL: Crossway, 2000.

Warfield, B. B. "The Terminology of Love in the New Testament." *The Princeton Theological Review* 16 (1918) 1–45.

Weinandy, Thomas G. *Does God Suffer?* Notre Dame, IN: University of Notre Dame Press, 2000.

Wiesel, Elie. *Night*. New York: Bantam, 1982.

Willard, Dallas. *The Spirit of the Disciplines: Understanding How God Changes Lives*. San Francisco: Harper & Row, 1988.

Williams, Charles. *Outlines of Romantic Theology with which is reprinted Religion and Love in Dante: The Theology of Romantic Love*. Edited by Alice Mary Hadfield. Grand Rapids: Eerdmans, 1990.

Wilson, Marvin R. *Our Father Abraham: Jewish Roots of the Christian Faith*. Grand Rapids: Eerdmans, 1989.

Wright, N. T. *Jesus and the Victory of God: Christian Origins and the Questions of God*. Vol. 2. Minneapolis: Fortress, 1996.

Wright, Robert. *The Evolution of God*. New York: Little Brown, 2009.

Wyschogrod, Michael. *The Body of Faith: Judaism as Corporeal Election*. New York: Seabury, 1983.

Zenger, Erich. *A God of Vengeance: Understanding the Psalms of Divine Wrath*. Translated by Linda M. Mahoney. Louisville: Westminster/John Knox, 1996.

www.ingramcontent.com/pod-product-compliance
Lightning Source LLC
Chambersburg PA
CBHW060606230426
43670CB00011B/1995